IWGIA:
a history

Jens Dahl

Copenhagen 2009 – Document No. 125

IWGIA: a history

Author: Jens Dahl
Proofreading: Elaine Bolton and Business Language Services BLS
Cover and typesetting: Jorge Monrás
Print: Eks-skolens Trykkeri, Copenhagen, Denmark
ISBN: 978-87-91563-52-2
ISSN: 0105-4503
Copyright: The author and IWGIA – 2009 – All Rights Reserved

This book has been prepared with financial support from
the Danish and Norwegian Ministries of Foreign Affairs.

Distribution in North America:
Transaction Publishers
390 Campus Drive / Somerset,
New Jersey 08873
www.transactionpub.com

Title: IWGIA: a history   **HURIDOCS CIP DATA**
Author: Dahl, Jens
Corporate Author: IWGIA
Place of Publication: Copenhagen, Denmark
Publisher: IWGIA
Distributors: Transaction Publisher; Central Books
Date of Publication: October 2009
Pages: 208
Reference to series: IWGIA
Document no. 125
ISSN: 0105-4503
ISBN: 9788791563522
Language: English
Index terms: Indigenous peoples, NGOs
Geographical area: World

**INTERNATIONAL WORK GROUP
FOR INDIGENOUS AFFAIRS**
Classensgade 11 E, DK 2100 - Copenhagen, Denmark
Tel: (45) 35 27 05 00 - Fax: (45) 35 27 05 07
E-mail: iwgia@iwgia.org - Web: www.iwgia.org

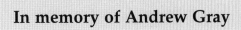

CONTENTS

FOREWORD – IWGIA 40 YEARS 10

INTRODUCTION – IWGIA: A HISTORY 14

PART I
IWGIA AND THE DEVELOPMENT OF THE INDIGENOUS MOVEMENT

Introduction..20

Chapter 1: The early years 24

    Raising awareness 26
    Advocacy: the first experience 27
    Growing up 29
    IWGIA and the anthropologists...30
    Support to human rights defenders 31
    IWGIA and the UN 32

Chapter 2: The emergence of indigenous organisations......................34

    The situation in the early 1970s 34
    The Arctic Peoples' Conference in 1973..37
    The founding of the World Council of Indigenous Peoples 39
    Geneva 1977 40
    Government policies – Geneva 1978 42
    South and Central America 44
    The emerging international indigenous movement 46
    The role of IWGIA..49

Chapter 3: Diversification and globalisation..52

    The organisation's development..52
    Campaigning and lobbying 55
        Yanomami..56
        Chittagong Hill Tracts (CHT)..56

Animal rights..58
"Going global"..60
    Asia..62
    Russia..62
    Africa..65
    New opportunities in the Arctic..68

Chapter 4: Human rights and development projects..........70

The UN Working Group on Indigenous Populations..................71
Other international developments..72
The Human Rights Fund for Indigenous Peoples......................73
Projects 76
Government funding..80
The International Year, the Decade and the Danish policy......82

Chapter 5: The pro-active period...84

The Permanent Forum process 87
Confronting new dilemmas..91
The establishment of the Permanent Forum..............................92
IWGIA and the Draft Declaration process 93
IWGIA and the African Commission on Human and Peoples' Rights.......95

PART II
THE PILLARS OF IWGIA

Introduction 104

Chapter 6: The holistic approach...106

The South-South programme 106

Chapter 7: From documentation to publication to communication...............110

Chapter 8: Human Rights..114

The Human Rights Fund for Indigenous Peoples....................116

International, regional and national initiatives:
the Special Rapporteur and Human Rights Observatories 118

Chapter 9: Projects and partnerships 120

Partnership policy and strategy 120
Project strategy 124
Case studies 129
    Titling of land in Peru and the Philippines 130
    First People of the Kalahari (FPK) 133
    Asian indigenous organisations 139
    Traditional institutions 141
    Russia 142
Summing up 145

PART III
MAJOR ISSUES

Chapter 10: The concept of indigenous peoples 148

The relational approach 149
A global concept 152
The African debate 153
Class versus ethnicity 155

Chapter 11: Advocacy, representation or self-determination 158

The principle of non-interference 161

Chapter 12: Cooperation with non-indigenous NGOs 164

Chapter 13: IWGIA and governments 170

Government responsibility 170
Collaborating with governments 171
Indigenous peoples' participation in national institutions 172

PART IV:
IWGIA: HISTORY AND FUTURE

Chapter 14: An organisation of professionals 176

    The growth of an organisation 176
    Professionalisation 178
    A membership organisation 182
    Development of a corporate spirit 183

Chapter 15: Future Challenges

    From opposition to policy making 188
    IWGIA's impact 189
    Networks and regional focus 190

NOTES 192

ACRONYMS 198

BOARD MEMBERS OF IWGIA 201

CHAIRPERSONS (PRESIDENTS) OF IWGIA' BOARD 203

IWGIA'S DIRECTORS 203

REFERENCES 204

FOREWORD – IWGIA 40 YEARS

As a former Director and Board Member of IWGIA, Jens Dahl has had a privileged vantage point from which to scrutinize 40 years of IWGIA's history. IWGIA was-of indigenous peoples. The idea of forming such an organisation came during the 38th International Congress of Americanists, which took place in Stuttgart, Germany in 1968, and where a number of anthropologists presented alarming reports on atrocities committed against indigenous peoples in Venezuela, Colombia, Peru, Paraguay and Brazil.

In a post-conference meeting on August 22, 1968, at the home of the Norwegian social anthropologist Helge Kleivan, outside Copenhagen, Kleivan, Milton R. Freeman, Lars Persson and Georg Henriksen decided to form the International Work Group for Indigenous Affairs, commonly known under the difficult acronym of IWGIA. Soon thereafter, the newly-formed group embarked on what is still a core part of IWGIA's work: documenting cases and situations relating to indigenous peoples and communicating information to the larger world regarding the gross violations of the human rights of indigenous peoples – information that hardly anyone had thus far felt it necessary to communicate.

Out of these beginnings grew a professional organisation which, while still being involved in documentation, publications and information dissemination, now also undertakes international human rights activities and empowerment projects.

During IWGIA's first years, Jens Dahl came to know Helge Kleivan, first as a teacher while Jens was a student of social anthropology at the University of Copenhagen, Denmark, and, a few years later, as a colleague when Jens joined Helge at the Department of Eskimology, University of Copenhagen.

Jens Dahl is someone who has invested his life and career in working for and with indigenous peoples as they have begun to make themselves felt and present in the modern world.

Jens has thus closely followed the path-breaking 40 years, not only of IWGIA as an organisation but, more importantly, of the indigenous movement itself, experiencing how indigenous peoples rose from desperate situations to found organisations, from local communities and via national and regional associations to establish alliances on the international scene. Everything had to be created more or less from scratch; experiences collected and further reflected steps taken or daring attempts launched – and the counter-forces were many and much more powerful. IWGIA was itself a part of, and a partner in, this extremely complicated and difficult process.

After Jens retired from his job as IWGIA's Director in 2006, and as IWGIA's 40th anniversary was approaching, IWGIA's Board invited him to write a history of the organisation. We soon agreed that we were not looking for a classical chronological outline of what has happened in IWGIA over the last 40 years. We wanted to incorporate the turbulence, strain and difficulties that have also been an ingredient of these years.

By structuring the book into four parts (IWGIA from an historical perspective, the pillars of IWGIA, a close look at some of the issues dominating the 40 years, challenges and trends for the future), Jens has provided what IWGIA wanted: an original and inspiring perspective on IWGIA's 40 intense years of interaction and partnerships with indigenous individuals and organisations, academia, governments and the international human rights scene. The result is a book that not only reflects the complexity of organisational and political developments but also provides a privileged insider's view, with reflections that Jens has developed during his committed and professional career both as an academic and an IWGIA employee, based on an inspiring partnership with the global indigenous world.

The book depicts how, for the past 40 years, IWGIA has taken an analytical as well as an action-oriented approach to working with indigenous issues – always in close partnership with indigenous organisations. This partnership approach has been a fundamental part of all IWGIA's activities, favouring mutual understanding and increasingly enabling a more pro-active approach from IWGIA's side. As Jens makes clear, one effect of this has been an increased emphasis on indigenous peoples' own participation in the decision-making processes at national, regional and international level, along with the development of dialogue with governments. Quite some distance from the time when IWGIA worked mostly on behalf of indigenous communities and individuals.

"IWGIA: a history" is a comprehensive and incisive view that includes Jens' own reflections. He has at the same time been able to incorporate IWGIA's own analysis of the first 40 years of the organisation. It is a book that neither Jens nor IWGIA intended to be a "complete" summing-up of developments in IWGIA and the indigenous world but rather a work that could incite further discussion and reflection. By integrating history with critical reflections on the future, the book may also serve as an inspiration to those facing the new challenges brought about by a world that is constantly changing, and which mean, for example, that working with indigenous issues now also involves focusing on climate change, forms of self-government, indigenous youth and indigenous peoples in urban settings. This book is an invitation to the readers to attempt to come to grips with how a commitment-driven human rights organisation has challenged and responded to advances and transformations in the wider world of indigenous peoples.

Espen Wæhle
October 2009

INTRODUCTION

IWGIA: a history

One often comes across the idea that social scientists must refrain from expressing opinions which can be characterized as political. It is high time we all recognize this dilemma as part of an old doctrine of academic conduct inherent in contemporary social science. Any concern with politically sensitive issues can be branded as 'political', due among other reasons, to the fact that our research draws its data from human reality, which is at the same time the very object of activities and decisions of politicians.

Confronted by a world where genocide, exploitation and deprivation of control over one's own life are constant facts of life for fellow human beings, social science must become the indefatigable eye watching over human inviolability. Only then will the social scientist become anything more than a predator consuming data. And only then will the concept of responsibility mean more that a buttonhole flower worn at academic ceremonies.

Helge Kleivan[1]

When I left my post as director of IWGIA in October 2006, the Board asked me if I would write a history of the organisation for its 40th anniversary in 2008.

I accepted because it was a challenge and because I am one of the few people to have followed the organisation at close hand since its establishment in 1968. If I was a little reluctant to take on the task, it was because of the challenge: how could I, as a person who had for many years been involved in, and responsible for, the day-to-day work of the organisation produce an objective narrative of something so close to me? The answer was very simple: I cannot!

It did not appeal to me to write the equivalent of a 40-year "annual" report. The challenge - and my ambition - became instead to link the history of a human rights organisation with the development of its "object", namely the relationship between IWGIA and the international indigenous movement.

In 1968, when IWGIA was established, one of its founding fathers and for 15 years the spearhead of the organisation, Helge Kleivan, was my teacher at the Department of Ethnology and Anthropology of the University of Copenhagen.

Those who worked as volunteers in the IWGIA office were student friends of mine from the department.

In 1975, I took up a position at the Department of Eskimology and became a colleague of Helge Kleivan, a connection that was to last until he passed away in 1983. At that time, and for many years afterwards, the Department of Eskimology and IWGIA shared premises at Fiolstræde 10 in the centre of Copenhagen, and every day I would meet and discuss indigenous issues with Helge and the other people working in the IWGIA secretariat.

In 1987, I became a Board member of IWGIA, and in 1989 co-director, a position I was to hold until 1994 when I returned to my position at the university. I remained a Board member in the ensuing years and returned as director in 1998 until my retirement in 2006. So be in no doubt: what you have in front of you is an insider's narrative and analysis.

Soon after I started to write, I realised that I was at risk of falling between all the stools available. I did not want to, and indeed could not, write a scientific analysis but I did want to make a proper and sober documentation of the events and viewpoints relevant to the history and development of the organisation. I knew that IWGIA's archives were in a disorganised state and had been for many years. Compiling chronology and establishing the order of many of the activities in which IWGIA has been involved therefore turned out to be more demanding than I would have wished. There were huge gaps in the archives, partly because large numbers of documents, letters etc. were held in Helge Kleivan's personal archive, which is now part of the Danish National Archive. I was fortunately granted access to these.

I did not wish to produce something so voluminous that no one would read it. There were, however, issues and initiatives for which proper documentation would need to be provided to outsiders, so that they could judge the reliability of my text. As a concerned and responsible insider in the organisation, I felt it necessary to consult people who could respond to some of my reflections. Similarly, I wanted to find out the opinion of others concerning important events in the development of the indigenous movement, specifically events that were of significance to the work of IWGIA; this led me to the books and journals.

By and large, I have known all the main actors in IWGIA since 1968. During all these years, I have listened to and discussed the work of the organisation with a large number of people both from within and outside, including the rumours and gossip. Part of IWGIA's strength has been the competency, creativity and dedication of people who often worked in the organisation for many years and this outweighs any of the personal conflicts or conflicts of principle that have also been part of IWGIA's history. When I contacted people connected to IWGIA over the years, I made it clear that my aim was to focus on the history of IWGIA as an organisation rather than its personalities. The importance of personalities in any kind of organisation cannot be ignored, however, so I can only hope that I have managed to represent these people respectfully and in a way that provides meaning to the narrative.

IWGIA's activities should be judged in their own right and not from the perspective of other organisations. Even though I want to, and feel I must, defend IWGIA's policies and strategies, I have endeavoured to produce an open and transparent narrative. Only in a few cases, where IWGIA has been criticised by other organisations on matters of approach or policy, have these differences between IWGIA and other organisations been included.

The first thing I did before I started writing was to take all IWGIA's English publications from 1968 to 2006 and spread them out on the floor in my house. They took up close to 30m2. This was only the English ones and did not include publications in Spanish or other languages! The first publications were rather simple – the more recent glossy and colourful. I flipped through them all, recalling many of the articles and documents. I have to admit I was impressed and I felt that IWGIA had been a success! And I had a share in it! I decided that one of the questions for which I would try to find an answer had to be: why has IWGIA been a success? From this strong position I also felt better equipped to expose some of the failures of the organisation and to take up some controversial and critical discussions.

Working in a human rights organisation such as IWGIA can be stressful; the daily reports on human rights violations and injustices against indigenous partners, and sometimes friends, takes a personal toll. One way of dealing with this is to use any opportunity to look for humorous moments, and to really get to know each other. Memories of the food, beer and wine we have shared with indigenous partners, and with each other, serve to lighten the load. Without all the jokes and laughs we have had together and about the personalities that have entered our world, we would never have been able to realise that we, our indigenous friends included, can sometimes feel marginalised on the edges of mainstream society. I have touched upon this in the text, mostly as parallel stories. We have learned from indigenous peoples that cultural acceptance, respect and knowing each other all start with the sharing of food. True partnerships, solidarity, and mutual understanding develop when they are based on more than a single-stranded business-like relationship.

This book is about IWGIA. It is about the 40 years this organisation has worked to defend the human rights of indigenous peoples. It is not about specific events, specific indigenous groups or other NGOs. When these are referred to, it is illustrate the work of IWGIA. I am not writing about the World Council of Indigenous Peoples or the Permanent Forum on Indigenous Issues but about their significance to IWGIA. If you, the reader, feel that the role of IWGIA is sometimes exaggerated or too much in focus – well, that was my intention.

Information and documentation for this book comes from a wide range of sources: IWGIA publications; IWGIA's archive; internal IWGIA reports; academic journals and books; journals and periodicals of other organisations; Norad's archive; and the personal archive of Helge Kleivan. A number of people have been contacted by mail or interviewed when the opportunity presented itself. These included current and former employees of IWGIA, current and former Board members, indigenous individuals and others with whom IWGIA has worked.

I am responsible for this manuscript, although I have relied on the help of many people who have worked for or with IWGIA. E-mails have been sent to many parts of the world. Not everyone responded but those quoted by name have given their consent. Many people have had an opportunity to comment upon draft sections of the manuscript and, as such, it is also the product of collective effort. I was asked to write IWGIA's history but I felt I had a right to ask people for their help. Without these people, the effort would not have made much sense. Some have given practical assistance, others have guided me to source materials and most have contributed with points of view or advice. As ever, there was a deadline, which restricted the number of people that could be contacted.

Some people have gone to great lengths to support me, provide me with information and guide me in my work. I have relied heavily on the assistance of people in the IWGIA secretariat and the encouragement of the IWGIA Board. Special thanks should go to Lola García-Alix, director of IWGIA, who encouraged me to take on the responsibility of this work and advised me on how to approach the issue. Without this, I would never have been able to undertake this task; to Espen Wæhle, Chair of the IWGIA Board for his suggestions, advice and encouragement; to Kathrin Wessendorf, editor, who worked on the text with a critical and constructive eye that was absolutely necessary; to Joan Carling, Vicky Tauli-Corpuz, Christian Erni, Claus Oreskov, Alejandro Parellada, Frank Sejersen, Joseph Ole Simel and Diana Vinding, who commented on the text and contributed to the text in writing; to Jenneke Arens, Dina Behrenstein, Marianne Jensen, Inge Kleivan, Arthur Krasilnikoff, Mark Münzel, Dan Rosengren, Inger Sjørslev, and Peter Aaby who read drafts or sections of the draft and gave me invaluable advice and information; to Käthe Jepsen, Annette Kjærgaard and Berit Lund who have helped and assisted me in finding a way through IWGIA's archives; to Karen B. Andersen, Ann Fenger Benwell, Joji Cariño, Nilo Cayuqueo, Erica-Irene A. Daes, René Fuerst, Aqqaluk Lynge, Wolfgang Mey, Lucy Mulenkei, Geoff Nettleton, Karsten Soltau and Sharon Venne, whose time I took and who gave me crucial insight into and information about events in IWGIA's history; to Bent Østergaard, who has kept press clippings from IWGIA´s early history; to Turid Arnegaard, Lars Anders Baer, Julian Burger, Ulf Johanson Dahre, Sanjeeb Drong, Leif Dunfjeld, Niels Fock, Miriam Anne Frank, Milton M. R. Freeman, Anette Molbech, Olga Murasjko, Robert Petersen, Aud Talle and Elsebeth Tarp who all, in various ways, assisted me in my work. Alejandro Parellada helped with illustrations and Jorge Monras was responsible for the lay-out. Inge Kleivan and the

Danish National Archive gave me access to Helge Kleivan's archive and Turid Arnegaard helped me access Norad's archive.

What has impressed me most when digging through the archives, reading minutes of Board meetings, talking to people etc., is that so many people have dedicated so much of their life to an organisation like IWGIA. They are not named in this book but we should remember that many people have worked on a voluntary basis and to them we should express our special thanks. Others have had a salary but I know that, without the support of their (our) families, their dedication would not have been possible.

This is a story about IWGIA. It is not the truth but it is one truth. It is my hope that linking IWGIA's history to the international indigenous movement will provide valuable insight into such relationships. It is also an internal narrative on the conditions within an organisation that seeks to do what ought to be done.

The book consists of four parts. The first part takes an historical perspective, describing the main lines of IWGIA's development over 40 years. This chapter also includes consideration of issues, which I consider to have been vital or strategic to the organisation.

In the next part, entitled "The Pillars of IWGIA", I focus on IWGIA's professional base, the structure and the priorities that guide the organisation.

Part 3 deals with a few issues, which have played a prominent role within the organisation. I consider the issues chosen as being of importance not only to IWGIA but to all human rights NGOs and, ultimately, indigenous organisations.

The final part summarises some of the trends, developments and challenges that may arise in the future.

The text is accompanied by boxes which either tell a story, give a human aspect to the text or reproduce a statement of key importance to IWGIA. The footnotes and annexes are documentary sections.

If a specific location is not given, the documents referred to will be found in IWGIA's archives.

PART 1

IWGIA AND THE DEVELOPMENT OF THE INDIGENOUS MOVEMENT

INTRODUCTION

IWGIA was founded as an international organisation by a group of concerned individuals driven by a global perspective to defend the rights of indigenous peoples. Logically, therefore, IWGIA's history mirrors the history of the international indigenous movement. IWGIA was never meant to be a regionally specific solidarity organisation, although there were focal points from the beginning. Over the years, these focal points changed and developed to reflect fundamental changes in the indigenous world and the indigenous movements.

IWGIA was created in response to reports of gross violations of the human rights of Indians in South America. IWGIA was also a child of the protest against colonialism and trends within anthropology that started in 1968 and developed in the years that followed. When the first indigenous organisations grew out of localised or regional ethnic movements, IWGIA changed its focus. A former member of IWGIA's staff recalls that, in the late 1970s and early 1980s, their work had two main directions. Firstly, documentation, including documenting the process of self-organisation itself. Secondly, supporting indigenous peoples' efforts to establish their own organisations.[2]

IWGIA developed close relations with a number of regional indigenous organisations that entered the international political arena in the 1970s. With the adoption of the revised International Labour Organisation "Convention Concerning Indigenous and Tribal Peoples in Independent Countries" (ILO Convention 169) in 1989 and the approval of the Draft Declaration on the Rights of Indigenous Peoples (referred to hereinafter as the Draft Declaration) by the UN Working Group on Indigenous Populations (WGIP or Working Group) in 1994 and by the United Nations' Sub-Commission on Prevention of Discrimination and Protection of Minorities (referred to as the Sub-Commission), the status of indigenous peoples changed from being objects to being subjects of international law.[3] Starting in the 1980s, and with increasing speed in the 1990s, a new world opened up for indigenous peoples as national donor agencies and international efforts began funding programmes and projects aimed directly at benefiting indigenous communities and organisations.[4]

These developments have had an enormous impact on indigenous movements throughout the world, and were seen by IWGIA as an opportunity not only to promote the rights of indigenous peoples but also to take a pro-active role in developing strong links with the Scandinavian governments, which were beginning to expand their aid policies to include, first and foremost, human rights issues. IWGIA also became heavily involved in international processes related to the promotion and recognition of indigenous peoples' rights, such as establishing a permanent forum for indigenous peoples, activities around the drafting of the UN Declaration on the Rights of Indigenous Peoples (the Declaration), promoting the work of the UN Special Rapporteur on the human rights and fundamental freedoms of indigenous people (referred to as the Special Rapporteur) in 2001, and also within the African Commission on Human and Peoples' Rights (referred to as the African Commission) when this body, with the encouragement of IWGIA and others, agreed to take up indigenous issues. The increased importance of international issues to indigenous peoples and to IWGIA was linked to this new global focus on human rights that was increasingly being adopted by states.

Documentation and publishing, human rights and support for indigenous projects became the pillars of IWGIA's work. What made IWGIA unique in this respect – and this remains the case to this day – was that these activities were combined into what the organisation has labelled an holistic perspective.

The participants who decided to establish IWGIA in Stuttgart, 1968: (from the left) Niels Fock, Eva Krener, Helge Kleivan, Cyril Belshaw, Georg Henriksen, unknown, Henning Siverts

PRESS RELEASE

Soon after the meeting in Stuttgart a press release announced the formation of the new organisation:

"At the 38th International Congress of Americanists which took place August 11th to 18th, at Stuttgart, Germany, detailed documentation was presented by a number of participants, on atrocities and forced integration of Indian tribes in various Latin-American countries.

Land-grabbing and wholesale extermination of Indian tribes was documented, not only for Brazil, but also from Colombia and Venezuela. Local police incite settlers and even tourists to shoot unarmed Indians on sight.

Reports from Peru state that Indian villages have been bombed with napalm, and Indians hunted down by colonists and army units During the last ten years the Bari Indians of the Colombia-Venezuela border have been reduced to around 600, from an original population of 2,000. The neighbouring Yuko tribe, which in 1958 numbered around 1,500, now have only 300 survivors, 1,200 having been exterminated by colonists and by introduced diseases, or have been forcibly dispossessed of their land.

Missions of several denominations are active in land-grabbing and destruction of the Indian economy and culture; usually no medical aid is provided by these missions, and following the destruction of Indian society the missions leave the area to proselytize among other tribes. With the abrupt withdrawal of the missions, the Christianized Indians are left to survive in slum conditions with no economic prospects. Because Governmental institutions in the countries concerned have taken no steps to prevent or control exploitation of the Indians, social scientists meeting at the Congress in Stuttgart, passed a resolution protesting and condemning the continuing murder, torture and abuse inflicted upon these Indians.

A committee of social scientists was formed with responsibility for establishing a documentation centre in Paris and for organizing subsequent international meetings. A work group was also constituted to work toward practical solutions of the problems of ethnic minorities throughout the world. The first meeting of the International Work Group for Indigenous Affairs took place in Copenhagen on August 22nd, with participants from Canada, Denmark, Norway and Sweden present."

During the first years, massacres against indigenous peoples played a prominent role in the work of the organisation. This document is from 1978.

CHAPTER 1

THE EARLY YEARS

IWGIA was established at the 38th International Congress of Americanists, which took place in Stuttgart, Germany, in August 1968. At the conference, anthropologists who had come directly from the field documented serious atrocities being carried out against indigenous peoples in Brazil, Colombia, Peru and Venezuela. They told of, for example, a number of Engvera Indians who had been killed and then tied to the walls of their houses to scare the rest of the tribe away from the area. In many places it was documented that not only were the indigenous peoples being driven from their lands but also that some people were making it their business to expel indigenous peoples, hunting them down or spreading fatal diseases by distributing infected blankets. It also emerged that the atrocities in Brazil were being carried out with the consent of that country's government (Henriksen 1998). Further reports documented that missionaries of different denominations were taking an active role in appropriating lands belonging to the Indians and destroying their economies and cultures. At the heart of these revelations was the so-called "Massacre of Parallel 11", which took place in Matto Grosso in 1963 and which had been made public in Brazilian newspapers in 1967 by one of those who had committed the atrocities.[5]

During the Stuttgart conference, ad hoc meetings were called and the participants were profoundly moved by the reported atrocities. And yet there seems to have been no agreement as to what could, or should, be done. Participating anthropologists and the organisers of the meetings were reluctant to call for political action at what was a very academic forum. The anthropologist Cyril Belshaw (later to be Chair of the International Union of Anthropological and Ethnological Societies, IUAES) was instrumental in reconciling viewpoints that included those who were against taking political action, and those who wanted to protect their research objects. Helge Kleivan pressed for the establishment of a special committee under the IUAES, and this was for some time chaired by Cyril Belshaw.[6]

A resolution was adopted in Stuttgart and, later that year in September, at the International Congress of Anthropological and Ethnological Sciences in Japan, another resolution was adopted by the Permanent Council of the IUAES. At this stage it was important for IWGIA's founders to obtain the full support of fellow anthropologists before approaching the general public.

RESOLUTION

Adopted unanimously by the Permanent Council of the International Union of Anthropological and Ethnological Sciences, Tokyo, September 1968

"In view of substantial information received that force and other forms of questionable pressure have recently been, and continue to be used against indigenous peoples in many parts of the world, and furthermore strongly believing that current programs for the acculturation and assimilation of indigenous societies are often harmful, immediately or ultimately, to their physical and mental health, and to their social and economic well-being,

1. we protest and repudiate genocide, and the use of force as an instrument of cultural change, in programs of social, economic and political development, and in the separation of indigenous peoples from their land;
2. we request the governments concerned to institute effective protection under the law for indigenous peoples, and to discipline government officials and others guilty of actions that contravene the International Declaration of Human Rights;
3. we urge governments, anthropologists, and others to re-examine current policies in order to provide ethically just and scientifically enlightened programs of acculturation which allow the peoples concerned a free and informed basis for choice.

We support in principle the International Work Group of Indigenous Affairs now based in Sweden, and other groups working in the same direction".

(IWGIA Newsletter no.2, October 1968)

In Stuttgart, the participants had had the opportunity to sign up in support of establishing IWGIA. After the conference, Helge Kleivan, Milton Freeman, Lars Persson and Georg Henriksen met at Helge's home north of Copenhagen to discuss future strategies. The small group also met with the Rector of the University of Copenhagen, Mogens Fog, who was willing to support the initiative. The first meeting of the International Work Group for Indigenous Affairs was held on August 22, 1968.[7]

One of the founders, Lars Persson, was appointed preliminary Chair, and Helge Kleivan became the Secretary. A secretariat was set up at the home of Lars Persson in Sweden. In addition to Lars Persson and Helge Kleivan, the founders of the organisation included Georg Henriksen, Henning Siverts, Niels Fock and Milton Freeman. They were all anthropologists with an in-depth knowledge of indigenous peoples and issues in the Americas.

The first public announcement of the establishment of the work group came in the form of an article in the Norwegian newspaper *Verdens Gang*, on August 31. A few days later, the first reaction – a defence of missionaries - appeared in the same paper.[8]

Raising awareness

In the early years, IWGIA was preoccupied with documentation and raising the world's awareness of the situation of indigenous peoples, primarily in South and Central American countries such as Colombia, Paraguay and Brazil. As the first IWGIA Newsletter in August 1968 (1 page) stated, "The work group intends to use knowledge collected by social scientists to seek solutions to the problems arising from forced acculturation and integration in various countries throughout the world".

IWGIA's objective was specific in the sense that it only dealt with indigenous peoples. Organisations similar to IWGIA were established in the following years, such as Survival International (1969),[9] the Netherlands Centre for Indigenous Peoples, WIP/NCIV (1969), Cultural Survival (1972) and *Gesellschaft für Bedrohte Völker* (originally established in 1968 in opposition to the genocide in Biafra, this became a broad human rights organisation in 1970). As the first human rights organisation, the Anti-Slavery Society had been formed in the UK as early as 1839 and, under the name of Anti-Slavery International, it also included activities with indigenous peoples and communities. However, these organisations were, and still are, broader in their scope, dealing with minorities, tribal peoples and ethnic groups.

Documentation became the first pillar of IWGIA's work. It relied on the professional contributions of fellow anthropologists and was targeted at a politically aware public. In the early years, IWGIA's publications were written by researchers, and the first indigenous author did not appear until 1978 when Julio Tumiri, an Aymara from Bolivia, edited a volume on the indigenous movement in his country.

Over the years, this documentation became ever more ambitious and professional, and developed into a series of documents and regular newsletters. These early years could be termed the anthropological period, during which great efforts were made to create awareness among fellow anthropologists and to establish the credibility of IWGIA's work.

HELGE KLEIVAN
1924-1983

Helge Kleivan was the driving force behind IWGIA's establishment in 1968. His vision for linking professional academic knowledge with respect for the human rights of indigenous peoples became a guiding light for everyone working in the organisation. In this, equal partnership with indigenous peoples and indigenous organisations was a factor not open to compromise.

Helge Kleivan was Norwegian but he worked and lived in Denmark for many years. It was due to his Norwegian background that IWGIA developed close links with the Norwegian Ministry of Foreign Affairs from the very start, and he had an enormous ability to mobilise his Norwegian network, the Sámi included.

It was his professional attachment to the Inuit, to Greenland and to Canada which naturally linked IWGIA to organisations such as the Inuit Circumpolar Conference and the National Indian Brotherhood.

His academic articles were of scholarly eminence but even more important was the fact that they were used by those he wrote about, the indigenous Inuit and Sámi.

Advocacy: the first experience

One of the first activities undertaken by IWGIA besides documentation was therefore trying to attract the attention of the governments and UN agencies. This proved to be no easy task!

From the very beginning, Persson and Kleivan were active in sending appeals to European and the Canadian Ministries of Foreign Affairs, and trying to raise awareness among academics and in the press. In December 1969, representatives from IWGIA met with three Scandinavian ministries, including the Danish Minister of Foreign Affairs, Poul Hartling (Liberal), and the precarious situation of indigenous peoples was raised in the Danish Parliament.[10] The pressure on the Minister of Foreign Affairs followed a number of articles in Danish newspapers submitted by anthropologists, and the Danish Ethnographical Association's reporting on the killings of Indians in Brazil. Fine words but a complete lack of action from Poul Hartling, who soon became Prime Minister, gave rise to angry newspaper articles by Bent Østergaard, a member of the IWGIA secretariat. Between 1969 and 1974, he wrote a large number of articles and book reviews in newspapers and journals focusing on the genocide of Indians in Brazil, Paraguay and other countries.

It is worth mentioning that, in the early years, the press in the Nordic countries showed an interest in indigenous issues. This was in part motivated by the "spectacular" atrocities against Indians in South America. As a result of all these efforts, in 1973 53% of the members of the Danish Parliament signed a letter to the Minister of Foreign Affairs urging him to make efforts to stop the persecution of and encroachment against the Aché Indians in Paraguay (Newsletter no.8).

One of IWGIA's main aims in the early years was to establish field groups that could conduct surveys and produce documentation on selected regions. Funding and support was needed, and governments were approached. Promises were made but did not always materialise and some frustration is apparent in the first regular Newsletter dating from August 1971: "Despite the promise made in December 1969 by the Danish Minister of Foreign Affairs, both Danish and Swedish Government spokesmen now maintain that there could be no question of granting any money for such field groups, unless direct requests had been received from the governments of the countries in question." This response was probably more the result of a lack of information about the conditions of indigenous peoples than outright cynicism. In a discussion in February 1972 on the Norwegian radio, the Norwegian Deputy Minister of Foreign Affairs (*Statssekretær*) Thorvald Stoltenberg (later to become Minister of Foreign Affairs, in a Labour government) expressed his support for IWGIA's work but also stressed that, "as a government we cannot support projects and activities in any other country unless this takes place in the form of government to government cooperation, and we do not enter any project unless there has been a request from, and in cooperation with, that government".[11] As we shall see later, Stoltenberg was the same person who, five years later, presented a complete turnaround in Norwegian policy on indigenous issues. The Norwegian government was also the first to provide financial support for IWGIA's work.

The idea of establishing field groups never materialised for IWGIA, but the idea can be compared to the concept of the UN Special Rapporteur, whose mandate includes compiling information and communications from all relevant sources on violations of the human rights and fundamental freedoms of indigenous peoples. In the late 1980s, IWGIA introduced networking in order to enhance knowledge and information about selected regions.

Growing up

In these early years, the lack of response from governments and the large number of unproductive meetings with politicians that Helge Kleivan, Lars Persson and others experienced could have put an end to the initiative. IWGIA, however, responded by making an important change of strategy in late 1970 and early 1971, taking the first steps towards becoming a fully-fledged organisation with a clear vision for the coming years.

A few years after its foundation, the focus of IWGIA's activities was still placing the indigenous peoples in the position of fairly passive partners. In August 1971, IWGIA stated its goals as follows: a) to establish field groups, b) to obtain consultative status under ECOSOC (the UN's Economic and Social Council), c) to help establish channels of communication for indigenous groups, d) to produce documentation, e) to encourage anthropologists to become concerned, and f) to get more supporters.[12] Another ambition was also to publish a Yearbook on indigenous issues but this did not come to fruition for another 15 years. Peter Aaby, a student of anthropology, joined the organisation and the production of documents and reports was now used to attract members, establish a network and create continuity. At this time, IWGIA managed to obtain a small office at the University of Copenhagen.[13]

The structure of the organisation now consisted of 1) members, 2) a secretariat, 3) a documentation centre, 4) local groups, and 5) an international scientific board. The documentation centre had acquired a permanent location in Copenhagen. The secretariat was made up of seven people: Helge Kleivan, Lars Persson, Peter Aaby, Klaus Ferdinand, Karl Eric Knutsson, Axel Sommerfelt and Bent Østergaard. This structure proved impractical as these people were split between Norway, Sweden and Denmark. The documentation centre in Copenhagen became permanent, as did the secretariat with Helge Kleivan, Peter Aaby and Bent Østergaard as the leading figures. At this stage there was also consideration given to the position of local groups within the organisation, i.e. how independently they could act within IWGIA.[14] I will address the issue of local groups later.

In the early years, there was little funding for IWGIA's activities other than membership fees and subscriptions to IWGIA's publications.[15] All people worked on a voluntary basis. However, in 1971 the Norwegian Ministry of Foreign Affairs[16] gave a small grant, and, in 1972, IWGIA received three grants from the Norwegian Agency for Development Cooperation (Norad), each of 25,000 Norwegian kroner.[17] These, along with other small donations, were used to publish documents. A small grant from the Swedish International Development Cooperation Agency (Sida) was used to support the preparation of the first meeting of the World Conference of Indigenous Peoples in 1975. The only steady income remained that coming from the members, of whom there were about 1,000 in 1973. A few small grants given to IWGIA were used to support imprisoned indigenous activists, indigenous meetings in the Americas, etc (Newsletter 16, Dec. 1976).

In 1973, the IWGIA Newsletter reported that support had been given to three indigenous projects to produce a film, buy land and organise a congress. It must be stressed that IWGIA was a human rights organisation, in contrast to the many development NGOs (including missionary organisations) that arose when the concept of development aid became mainstream. It was not until the 1990s that projects in support of indigenous empowerment and self-development became a real pillar of IWGIA's work.

IWGIA and the anthropologists

In the early years of IWGIA, one of the founders' major goals was to mobilize fellow anthropologists who were working with and among indigenous communities to become active. They were not very successful, although a few active groups were established.[18] Often, the IWGIA founders perceived a lack of anthropological engagement and this created both frustration and anger, as evidenced in an article in IWGIA's December 1973 Newsletter referring to the decision by IUAES to establish a Commission on Ethnocide and Genocide:

> *That the above mandate was passed with an overwhelming majority in a plenary session of the congress should not, however, disguise the fact that many well-known anthropologists, and even a majority of the members of the Permanent Council of the IUAES, did all they could to avoid any commitment by anthropologists to co-operate with the peoples from whom they for so long have drawn all their data.*

Anthropologists of note, such as Margaret Mead, were implacably opposed to what was regarded as a mixing of the political and scientific fields and, potentially, involvement in the internal disputes of indigenous peoples themselves,[19] whilst Edmund Leach found the initiatives as suggested by IWGIA to be counter-productive. These anthropologists were also opposed to having the Indian leader Vine Deloria speak to the General Assembly. Only after pressure and with the support of the Chair, Sol Tax, was he allowed to speak.[20]

Mark Münzel, former Board member of IWGIA, gives the following explanation:

The lack of response from fellow scientists was primarily because the anthropological ideal of science was non-political and engagement against regimes that persecuted or discriminated indigenous peoples was political. A scientist could write a polite letter asking a government to be nice, but not proceed to public action, which might have political consequences.[21]

Another reason was fear among anthropologists that engaging with an organisation such as IWGIA could endanger their access for conducting fieldwork in indigenous territories. This attitude was prevalent although the Barbados Declaration of 1971[22] made some anthropologists, and specifically those working in the Amazon region, "look seriously at their commitment to the peoples they studied" (Wright 1988:371).

This lack of response and understanding for the relevance of his work among his colleagues at the Department of Anthropology and Ethnology drove Helge Kleivan to leave his position in September 1972. From 1973 on, he held a full-time position within the Department of Eskimology.

The same frustration was experienced by other support organisations as well. The director of Survival International is similarly quoted as stating, "that the 1970s were dominated by the rather fruitless attempt to establish academic credibility" (Houtman 1985). One consequence of this lack of academic response was that Survival International focused primarily on the media and the public in order to reach as many people as possible and raise public awareness.

Although IWGIA chose a different path, the reaction of both organisations was to support the increased organisational capacity of the indigenous peoples themselves. Both organisations worked to support the self-development of indigenous peoples but where Survival did this by supporting projects and an action-oriented approach, IWGIA emphasised documentation and human rights. While Survival increased its focus on the grassroots level, IWGIA became increasingly involved with international indigenous organisations and international human rights processes.

The move to support the seeds of the first international indigenous organisations was a significant change in IWGIA's work at that time.

Support to human rights defenders

From the very beginning, and throughout the 1970s, IWGIA made great efforts to support human rights defenders who were jailed by the authorities, forced into exile or in other ways intimidated. One of these was Chase Sardí, an anthropologist who was arrested by the military government in Paraguay in late 1975. He was IWGIA's key contact person in that country and an advisor to IWGIA's campaign for the defence of the rights of the Aché Indians, which was running at the time. On behalf of IWGIA, a member of the Danish Parliament (later Minister of Justice) for the Social Democrats (Labour) and professor of law at the University of Copenhagen, Ole Espersen, travelled to Paraguay to seek the release of Chase Sardí and to provide support for his family. In this and in other cases, letters were sent and contact made with the Nordic Ministries of Foreign Affairs to request their intervention.

Another case was that of the Bolivian Aymara leaders, Julio Tumiri and Constantino Lima, who visited Copenhagen and Oslo where meetings were organised. Julio Tumiri spent some months in Copenhagen writing. Some time after having returned to Bolivia following the 1975 founding meeting of the World Council of Indigenous Peoples (WCIP), Constantino was arrested and IWGIA made great efforts to obtain his release and get asylum granted in Canada. In this and other cases that involved indigenous peoples under pressure from military regimes, the Nordic embassies and representations in countries such as Peru, Paraguay, Chile and Argentina were very supportive.

Nilo Cayuqueo, a Mapuche from Argentina, was active in organising a South American indigenous meeting in Paraguay in 1972 during the Stroessner regime. In the 1970s, he was a key person in organising indigenous peoples in the region, including establishing branches of the WCIP. He was in close touch with IWGIA from 1977 on, following the WCIP Congress in Kiruna and the NGO meeting in Geneva. He had to flee from Argentina in 1979; 29 years later he recalls the event:

> *When I came back to Argentina from Geneva the military was looking for me, so I went into hiding and had to move around from place to place. One day I phoned Helge Kleivan in Copenhagen from a payphone in Buenos Aires. He called me back later and promised to arrange a ticket for me to Peru. The military used to kidnap people when they tried to leave the country, but a tall European from the Danish embassy or consulate helped me into the airport, and I managed to get to Peru where I stayed with the support of IWGIA.*[23]

IWGIA and the UN

From the start, IWGIA had taken a human rights approach in its dealings with indigenous peoples. One of its main ambitions was therefore to have the United Nations take up the violations of the human rights of indigenous peoples. In its very first circular, called Newsletter, dated August 1968, IWGIA said that, "The Work Group intends to establish itself under the U.N. in co-operation with the Office of Legal Affairs and the Commission on Human Rights". This idea was expressed in early letters to Scandinavian Ministries of Foreign Affairs, in which IWGIA urges them and their governments to assist in establishing "a non-national body of social scientists that can act as an advisory board for governments in countries who face serious and critical situations resulting from internal ethnic conflicts."[24] For many years, this ambition remained unachieved, and it was only in the early 1980s, when the United Nations' Working Group on Indigenous Populations was established (1982) and the process of revising the ILO Convention 107 began, that IWGIA began focussing on the United Nations, and the UN Human Rights work became the second pillar of its work.[25] This was, however, at a later stage and, as Helge Kleivan stated in 1981, "our preoccupation with UN initiatives faded away in favour of trying to help indigenous peoples more directly in their own struggle to set up a world organization".[26]

CHAPTER 2

THE EMERGENCE OF INDIGENOUS ORGANISATIONS

During its early years, IWGIA focussed on South and Central America. The first significant change came when indigenous peoples themselves started to organise on a regional, national and international level. Most significant was the fact that these organisations were focused on the idea of being indigenous and not just on representing an ethnic group. IWGIA policy was to support indigenous organisations as the *a priori* legitimate representatives of indigenous peoples. In the 1970s, when the mainstream anthropological tradition was still that of indigenous peoples being primitive peoples whose knowledge had to be collected before their cultures vanished, the open – and perhaps at times uncritical - attitude taken by IWGIA marked an important break with that tradition.

It became apparent that significant changes were underway in indigenous peoples' own ability to speak for themselves, and this had a major impact on IWGIA's work and the direction of its activities. The speed with which indigenous organisations developed was surprising and, with their limited experience of self-organising, an NGO such as IWGIA came to take on a new role.

The situation in the early 1970s

Although organisations with an indigenous profile had earlier been established, such as the Sámi Council (1956), the Shuar Federation, Ecuador (1964), the Alaska Federation of Natives (1966) etc, the 1970s offered new opportunities for linking local, national and international efforts.

A number of indigenous organisations had been established in Canada and the U.S. in the late 1960s and early 1970s: the National Indian Brotherhood in Canada was formed in 1968 to represent the Status and Treaty Indians; the *Inuit Tapirissat of Canada* was founded in 1971; the American Indian Movement (AIM) in the U.S. emerged around the same time; the International Indian Treaty Council was established in the U.S. in 1974. In the first half of the 1970s, indigenous peoples also came together on a regional basis and started regional organisations, centred around the concept of being indigenous. A number of local and regional indigenous organisations were founded in Colombia, Peru, Ecuador and Bolivia,[27] initially in the Andes region. This potential was met with the founding of a number of international indigenous NGOs in the mid-1970s and

Alcatraz during takeover by Indians - Photo: Michelle Vignes

At AIM convention and treaty conference in Modbridge South Dakota, 1974 - Photo: Michelle Vignes

in the early 1980s, such as the South American regional organisations *Consejo Indio de Sud America* CISA (1980) and the *Coordinadora de las Organizaciones Indígenas de la Cuenca Amazónica*, COICA (1984).

IWGIA associated itself very strongly with some of these organisations, such as the *Inuit Tapirissat of Canada*, the Inuit Circumpolar Conference, the National Indian Brotherhood, the World Council of Indigenous Peoples, the Sámi Council and CISA. Besides focussing on Latin America, IWGIA created strong links with indigenous organisations in the rich Euro-American countries.

Developments in northern Canada in the 1970s had a great impact on IWGIA. One reason for this may be that Helge Kleivan had carried out fieldwork there and had a significant network of researchers as well as contacts among the indigenous peoples. The establishment of large-scale development projects in the North encouraged IWGIA to work more directly with indigenous organisations. These projects included the proposed building of a gigantic hydro-electric scheme at James Bay in Arctic Quebec, which led to a court case in 1971 and eventually— in 1973— to the first court victory by Indians and Inuit in that province, plus the settlement of major land claims in Alaska (1971). IWGIA became involved over the next few years as the Inuit made land claims, and large development projects were launched in the North such as the Mackenzie Valley Pipeline project (Berger 1977). Although the situation in Canada, the USA and Greenland could not be directly compared with the genocide and ethnocide that was taking place in South America, the Indians and Inuit had experienced all the negative effects of integration and assimilation (Kleivan, H. 1973). It was not least in Canada that major conflicts between the state and indigenous Indians and Inuit emerged, the same old conflict between the elephant and the mouse, as Helge Kleivan wrote (1976). Even in a democratic country such as Canada, all appeals for respect for the unique indigenous cultures were in vain. Faced with this situation, the indigenous peoples looked outside their communities and countries for support.

A similar organisational process was taking place in Latin America and several local and regional indigenous organisations were founded in Colombia, Peru, Ecuador and Bolivia,[28] initially in the Andes region. As was noted by the group of committed Latin American anthropologists who authored the Barbados Declaration of 1971:

> ... *it is important to emphasise, in all its historical significance, the growing ethnic consciousness observable at present among Indian societies throughout the continent. More peoples are assuming direct control over their defence against the ethnocidal and genocidal policies of the national society.*

It was also during the 1970s that indigenous peoples came into a number of serious and spectacular conflicts with their respective states. To name but a few: the American Indian occupation of Alcatraz Island (1969-71) in the U.S.; the organising of an Aboriginals Embassy in front of the Australian parliament in Canberra in 1972; the Canadian Inuit and Indian involvement in the James Bay conflict of 1971-1973; the confrontations between the American Indian Movement (AIM) and the federal government at Wounded Knee, South Dakota (USA) in 1973 and again in 1975; the 1974 march to the Canadian parliament; the Maori 1975 march to the parliament in Wellington (New Zealand) to claim their land rights; the Alta conflict in Norway from 1979-81 involving the Sámi people protesting against the building of a hydropower plant.

All these events had an enormous impact on the rise of the international indigenous movement, and indigenous peoples were later to bring the experiences they gained in the 1970s with them to the United Nations in the early 1980s. What the Sámi historian Henry Minde wrote about the significance of the Alta conflict to the Sámi people could be said to characterise the situation of indigenous peoples in a number of Euro-American democracies: "The Alta case went through several stages: from a hydro-electric power proposal, to a local community matter, to an environmental concern, to Sámi rights, before ending up as an Indigenous peoples' issue" (Minde 2005:19).

The Arctic Peoples' Conference in 1973

IWGIA's first involvement with the international indigenous movement came about while working with the indigenous peoples in the North. The Arctic Peoples' Conference marked a turning point for the indigenous movement, but also for IWGIA.

In 1973, two members of IWGIA, Helge Kleivan and Peter Aaby, together with the Greenlandic professor Robert Petersen, were instrumental in supporting the organisation of the first Arctic Peoples' Conference. The initiative had come from James Wah-Shee, president of the Federation of Natives North of 60, Canada.[29] He and others had come to Copenhagen after a meeting in France to discuss the idea of holding a conference organised by Arctic peoples. Convened by Greenlanders in Denmark, the meeting took place in Copenhagen in November of that year.

For the Arctic peoples (with the exception of those living in the USSR), the conference was of tremendous importance for their subsequent active involvement in international affairs. The fact that the conference was convened in the Danish Parliament and thus accepted by the authorities was of great significance to the indigenous participants – and to IWGIA. IWGIA's role, however, was not an easy one because it had to avoid any implication that its base in Denmark would affect its impartiality in relation to conflicts between the Greenlanders and most other Arctic indigenous peoples. In addition, there were internal conflicts between the Greenlanders that came out into the open. The background to

TO BE INDIGENOUS

In October 2008, Aqqaluk Lynge, president of Inuit Circumpolar Council (ICC), Greenland, former president of ICC International and former member of the Greenlandic Parliament for Inuit Ataqatigiit, recalled the significance of IWGIA and Helge Kleivan to the early indigenous movement in the Arctic:

"In the early 1970s I was chair of the 'Young Greenlander's Council' in Copenhagen. We had close relationships with other Greenlanders in Copenhagen and some of us came regularly to the Department of Eskimology at the University of Copenhagen. There we met with the Greenlandic professor Robert Petersen and Helge Kleivan, and thus we also came to know about IWGIA.

In May 1973 we came back from a meeting on Arctic oil and gas development in Le Havre, France. In Le Havre we had met the National Indian Brotherhood including James Wah-Shee from the Northwest Territories who joined us back in Copenhagen where we discussed the possibilities of organising an Arctic Peoples' Conference. We also introduced him to IWGIA.

It was at this time that we came to know about the concept of 'indigenous peoples' and the work of Helge Kleivan and IWGIA. We did not even know about the ILO Convention 107.

The Arctic Peoples' Conference was a turning point for us. We were first of all thinking of ourselves as 'Inuit' but Helge Kleivan urged us to include the Sámi in our organising efforts and he inspired us to consider ourselves as part of a broader indigenous movement.

The Arctic Peoples' Conference was instrumental for the process leading to the founding of the World Council of Indigenous Peoples, and the work of Helge Kleivan and IWGIA was of significant inspiration to us when we a few years later, having returned home to Greenland founded the political movement *Inuit Ataqatigiit*."

this was that the Greenlanders had at that time initiated a process that was to lead to Home Rule in 1979, and some of the participants were obviously more concerned with this process than with joining any activity that could jeopardize it in the eyes of the Danish authorities, something that could be anticipated as a consequence of the creation of new bonds of solidarity across borders.[30]

The Arctic Peoples' Conference marked the beginning of IWGIA's active involvement with the international indigenous movement. Together with the establishment of the World Council of Indigenous Peoples (WCIP), it was also the start of a long-term partnership between IWGIA and the indigenous peoples of the Americas.

The founding of the World Council of Indigenous Peoples

The idea of bringing the world's indigenous peoples together may have originated with the president of the National Indian Brotherhood (NIB) in Canada, Chief George Manuel, during visits to New Zealand, Australia and Scandinavia in 1971 and 1972.[31] George Manuel participated in the Stockholm Conference on the Human Environment in 1972 and, in connection with this, he visited IWGIA in June 1972 where he mentioned the idea of an international conference.[32] The possibility of IWGIA playing a role in the preparations for this conference was discussed during this visit.[33] A relationship of trust had developed between Helge Kleivan and George Manuel, and Kleivan promised Manuel that he would support the preparation of an international conference of indigenous peoples (Kleivan, H. 1973: 173; Kleivan, I. 1992:228). During and following the summer of 1972, IWGIA raised the idea through its network, including the an-

World Council of Indigenous Peoples, 1987 - Photo: IWGIA archive

thropologist Chase Sardi who spread it across South America. NIB had few contacts outside North America, so IWGIA also supported NIB with a small amount of money with which to plan the meeting. The idea was discussed in 1972 at the NIB General Assembly where George Manuel was given a mandate to explore the possibility of holding such an international conference.[34]

In a letter from NIB dated July 18, 1973, IWGIA was directly asked to host a first preparatory meeting. This meeting, however, took place in Georgetown, Guyana[35] and it was not until June 1975 that IWGIA hosted a meeting, this time a Policy Board Meeting.[36] The meeting in Copenhagen dealt with the preparations for the international conference, considering, among other things, the funding and accreditation of delegates to the international conference. Contacts had already been established with approximately twenty-four countries but Asia and Africa had to be omitted for practical organizational reasons, although attempts had been made to contact groups in the U.S.S.R., China and other parts of Asia (Sanders 1977:13). The meeting was facilitated and organised by the Greenlandic Committee for International Relations[37] and IWGIA. It was politically supported by the two Greenlandic members of the Danish Parliament and (somewhat) reluctantly by the Greenland Provincial Council.[38] The Danish Prime Minister, Anker Jørgensen (Labour), addressed the meeting, which was politically significant. The organisations present at the Policy Board meeting were the National Congress of American Indians (USA), the Greenlanders Association (Denmark), the Nordic Sámi Council (Scandinavia), the Maori Council (New Zealand), Mink'a (Bolivia) and *Unidad Indígena* (Colombia). The outcome of the meeting was the establishment of a provisional World Council of Indigenous Peoples and a draft charter.[39]

At the International Conference of Indigenous Peoples, which was subsequently convened at Port Alberny, British Colombia, from October 27-31, 1975, indigenous peoples from 18 countries[40] decided to finally establish the World Council for Indigenous Peoples. George Manuel became the first President with Sam Deloria, USA, as Secretary-General. Five members were appointed to the executive, representing the five regions of North America, Central America, South America, Australia/New Zealand and the Arctic (Inuit and Sámi).[41]

Geneva 1977

In 1977, indigenous peoples met in Geneva at an International NGO Conference on Discrimination against Indigenous Populations in the Americas, organised by the Special NGO Committee on Human Rights under the Sub-Committee on Racism, Racial Discrimination, Apartheid and Decolonisation.[42] The NGO conference took place in support of the UN Decade for Action to Combat Racism and Racial Discrimination and enjoyed significant indigenous participation. IW-

Helge Kleivan, René Fuerst and Julio Tumiri in Geneva, 1977 - Photo: IWGIA archive

GIA also participated and supported the participation of WCIP representatives, among them Nilo Cayuqeo who, at that time, was occupied with setting up the indigenous *Consejo Indio de Sud America* (CISA) and supported the production of a documentary ("Indian Summer in Geneva"), which was subsequently widely distributed.[43] The International Indian Treaty Council (IITC), which had been founded by the American Indian Movement (AIM) in 1974, had appointed and invited most of the participants and directed the meeting (Dunbar-Ortiz 2006). Although the IITC tried to keep the WCIP out of the Geneva conference[44] and although this organisation played a minor role in the 1977 conference, through its Sámí members it played a key role in changing Norwegian policy prior to the 1978 conference (below) (Minde 2008).

At the conference, substantial conflicts developed between, on the one hand, George Manuel and other members of the WCIP and, on the other, representatives of the North American Indians, who were organised in the IITC. At that time, the IITC had a Marxist and class-based approach to indigenous issues,[45] as opposed to the indigenous rights-based approach of the majority of the WCIP delegates.

There were different opinions as to what took place in Geneva, however. *The Akwesasne Notes* —an influential American Native magazine—thus wrote,

> *At the same time, native forces that are loyal to Canada or the U.S. were at work trying to disrupt the conference. The World Council of Indigenous Peoples' executive officers were among these. They seemed to continuously try to find ways to discredit the conference and its organizers. People who are viewed by the Canadian or U.S. governments as native leaders found ways to discourage the organization of the conference.*[46]

Roxanne Dunbar-Ortiz, an IITC member and one of the organisers of the 1977 meeting, writes that while the IITC sought allies within the non-aligned movement, "the other international indigenous NGOs eschewed the NAM [Non-aligned countries movement] linkage and rather sought allies in the North Atlantic states" (Dunbar-Ortiz 2006:69).

IWGIA was in somewhat of a dilemma in this fight but continued to provide strong support to the WCIP and its membership organisations such as CISA. IWGIA supported the indigenous position in the sense of stressing the ethnic, philosophical and cultural platform and was, in general, of the opinion that the North American Indians saw everything only from the North American perspective. This also included members of the WCIP, and only the efforts of the South American members were able to prevent a new organisation from being created in competition with the WCIP.[47]

Government policies – Geneva 1978

Thus far, IWGIA's efforts to change policies towards indigenous peoples and to influence government action seemed to have failed. In the early 1970s, IWGIA continued to have problems in attracting the concerned interest of governments. Most efforts were directed at the Nordic governments.[48] The Danish government had all kinds of bureaucratic reasons for not providing support, prompting a leading Danish newspaper to write an article about IWGIA under the heading "World famous – but not among us".[49] When indigenous peoples started organising themselves, changes came gradually in the policy of the Nordic governments. IWGIA was one of the non-indigenous organisations that established a close working relationship with the Norwegian Ministry of Foreign Affairs and Norad.[50]

Looking back over the first 10 years of IWGIA's history, the organisation concluded thus:

After ten years of hard work, we have come to the sad conclusion that no government seems inclined to act on this situation [oppression of indigenous peoples] on its own initiative. Therefore our strategy must increasingly be one of direct appeal to the public. We will also demand clear statements from any government expressing opinions on human rights, as to how it will implement its human rights principles (IWGIA Newsletter 19, June 1978).

However, as this was being written in IWGIA's Newsletter, a few countries were becoming aware of the need to direct efforts towards indigenous peoples. Spearheading this was the Norwegian government. This seems to have started at a conference in Geneva in August 1978 (one year after the NGO conference) marking the first five years of the UN Decade to Combat Racism and Racial Discrimination. The Norwegian government took the initiative to draw up some positions of principle on indigenous peoples (Sverre 1985). The speech given by the Norwegian Deputy Minister of Foreign Affairs, Thorvald Stoltenberg, can be seen as a major breakthrough for indigenous peoples, and definitely for IWGIA's efforts. In specific terms, he urged the UN to support the establishment of representative ethnic organisations. In general terms, he attacked the principle of non-interference in matters of minority rights:

[The]… concept of sovereignty is an obstacle to international action for minority rights. International action which seeks to eliminate racial discrimination should therefore not be seen as a violation of the sovereignty of the state concerned, or as an intervention in its internal affairs – it should rather be seen as a contribution to the strengthening of sovereignty.[51]

The statement was a complete turn around compared with the Norwegian government's position referred to by Stoltenberg six years earlier. It opened up a new perspective on indigenous rights and led to new possibilities of governments supporting indigenous peoples financially. Norway had taken the lead and IWGIA received the message with enormous enthusiasm.[52]

In 1977 and 1978, IWGIA brought indigenous peoples from Bolivia and representatives of the WCIP to Oslo to discuss development support. Norad and the Ministry of Foreign Affairs obviously had legal and political problems in giving direct support to indigenous organisations outside Norway, and to organisations that were often in opposition to their governments. The minutes from these meetings between IWGIA and the WCIP (the Nordic Sámi Council was a member) were instrumental in changing official Norwegian policy. And no less important was the active support of interested persons within the administration.

The Norwegian government took the Geneva initiative further when a Nordic meeting of foreign affairs ministers in the autumn of 1979 decided "to consider the possibilities of a closer Nordic co-operation for the purpose of promoting the interest of indigenous populations" (Sverre: 190), and a permanent Nordic working group of senior officials was established to coordinate the endeavours of the Nordic countries in terms of promoting the interests of indigenous populations.

From then on, the Norwegian government began to support indigenous organisations directly through Norad, or indirectly through organisations such as IWGIA and WCIP. The first organisations to be supported were the Nordic Sámi Council, WCIP and *Consejo Indio de Sud America* (CISA) in South America. It was also at this time that IWGIA received its first regular financial support from the Norwegian government.[53]

This represented a significant change in policy as well as in practice. Until then, support for indigenous peoples had primarily been given to Norwegian church organisations working in health, education and agriculture. Now indigenous organisations could be supported directly and without the involvement or endorsement of the government of the country in which the indigenous groups lived.

Norway played a key role in establishing the United Nations' Working Group on Indigenous Populations (Sanders 1989:408) and it was perhaps not without reason that the first chair of the WGIP, when it was established in 1982, was the Norwegian member of the Sub-Commission, Asbjørn Eide.

South and Central America

The people in IWGIA worked hard to help set up CISA, and Helge Kleivan retained a strong personal commitment to the organisation and its publication *Pueblo Indio*. It may be that the establishment of CISA was seen by IWGIA as a major breakthrough in IWGIA's support for the founding of indigenous organisations.

During the 1977 conference in Geneva, the indigenous peoples of South America decided to hold a regional meeting, coordinated from Argentina and with support from IWGIA.[54] IWGIA spent much time fundraising for the first CISA conference, which was finally convened in Cuzco, Peru in early 1980 with the participation of Helge Kleivan and Jørgen Brøchner Jørgensen from IWGIA.

IWGIA continued its working relationship with the WCIP until this organisation ceased to function in the 1990s. One of the last coordinated efforts between IWGIA and the WCIP was the attempt to establish a Nicaragua committee in the early 1980s.

IWGIA's stated aim to remain neutral in internal conflicts between indigenous peoples was challenged in the early 1980s during the civil war in Nicaragua. Most indigenous peoples (Miskitu, Suma, Rama) on the Atlantic Coast had been supportive of the Sandinistas in the overthrow of the Somoza regime, but conflicts soon developed. The Atlantic Coast has a history quite different from the rest of Nicaragua, and government policies violated the rights of the indigenous peoples. This situation was exacerbated during the Contra war, when the government forced some of the indigenous peoples to relocate away from their traditional lands on the border with Honduras, now a war zone. Some indigenous peoples fled to neighbouring countries and some joined the "Contras" to fight against the Sandinistas. The "Contras" were supported by the US and the indigenous peoples thus became victims of a wider conflict in which they themselves ended up fighting their own indigenous relatives inside Nicaragua. After a visit by Helge Kleivan to Nicaragua (with a significant military escort) in late 1981, IWGIA took a very critical position of US policy in the region (Kleivan, H. 1982). Given the Reagan administration's policy, which combined economic sanctions with the use of terror, IWGIA saw no future for the indigenous peoples if the Sandinistas were defeated.[55] In this, IWGIA shared the point of view of some of the indigenous leaders, although others like Brooklyn Rivera had at that time given up and left the country (Frühling et al:53ff). Some of the indigenous leaders brought the issue to the WCIP meeting in Australia in 1981.

The complicated, serious and tragic situation of the Atlantic Coast was discussed at an IWGIA Board meeting in January 1982, and contact was made with the WCIP suggesting that a commission be established.[56] The WCIP, the regional organisation CORPI, CISA and IWGIA subsequently established a Nicaragua Commission to investigate the conflict.[57] IWGIA was frustrated that the only clear point of view coming out of Nicaragua on the conflict, was that of the "counter revolutionary Miskitu leader, S. Fagoth and a few other Nicaraguan Miskitu Indians living abroad" (ibid.).

IWGIA started to raise funds for the Commission, but with very little success. The Danish Minister of Foreign Affairs, Kjeld Olesen (Labour), dismissed the application due to its political nature and because the government had already provided support for the relocation of 10,000 Miskitu Indians.[58]

IWGIA always defended the rights of the indigenous peoples of the Atlantic Coast but was reluctant to support the "Contras", who were seen more as a weapon of US interest than actual freedom fighters. In a press release from 1984, IWGIA states: "IWGIA asks the international community to seek to improve conditions of refugees in Honduras and Costa Rica and allow the freedom *not* to fight against their brothers in Nicaragua."[59]

Others accused the Sandinistas of genocide and the "Contras" were supported not only by the US government but also by influential Indian organisations from the US.[60] Inside and outside Nicaragua, old indigenous friends became new enemies following the overthrow of the Somoza regime (Sanders 1985), and it was in this murky situation that IWGIA urged WCIP to take a role. The commission never convened in its original form, although the WCIP tried to intervene.[61] The complicated situation of the Atlantic Coast made it impossible to create the necessary unity within IWGIA on the strategy to be followed.[62] Even within the WCIP, there were different opinions on the strategy to be adopted, which led to internal conflicts some years later.[63]

The emerging international indigenous movement

The capacity built up by indigenous organisations during the 1970s was undoubtedly a precondition for their access to the UN. From the late 1970s on, IWGIA's history became closely linked to the international indigenous organisations' involvement with the UN.

A number of events can be regarded as turning points for indigenous peoples worldwide – and for IWGIA. Amongst the most important were the 1977 NGO Conference; the UN Conference on Racism in 1978; the Fourth Russell Tribunal held in Rotterdam in November 1980 (The Rights of the Indians in the Americas) and the 1981 conference on Indigenous Peoples and the Land. From events like these came demands that indigenous peoples have their own focal point within the UN human rights system. This resulted in the UN Working Group on Indigenous Populations (WGIP) being established in 1982. The international indigenous process was spearheaded by the North American Indians and Aboriginals from Australia, and soon joined by Sámi and Inuit. The International Indian Treaty Council played a key role in the 1977 conference (Minde 2008) and came up with the first drafts of a Declaration on the Rights of Indigenous Peoples.[64]

The 1977 NGO conference had adopted a "Declaration of Principles", and "Principles for Guiding the Deliberations of the Working Group" were presented to the WGIP in 1982.[65] These principles were drafted by a small group of American lawyers and activists.[66] As advisor to WCIP Chair George Manuel, Douglas Sanders produced a first draft declaration ("International Covenant on the Rights of Indigenous Peoples"), which was produced in preparation for the WCIP General Assembly in Canberra in 1981 (Minde 2008). A revised version of this was presented by the Nordic Sámi Council at the WCIP General Assembly held in Panama in 1984. Based on this, a 17-point Declaration of Principles was adopted and presented to the WGIP in Geneva in 1985 (ibid.).

This begs the question as to why the first initiative to create regional and international indigenous organisations came from the rich countries despite the fact that indigenous peoples in Latin America were those who were suffering the most? Douglas Sanders provides an explanation when referring to the founding conference of the WCIP:

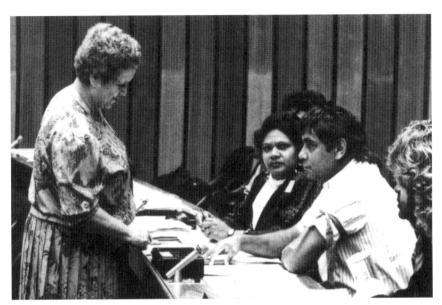
Chairwoman of the Working Group on Indigenous Populations, Mdm. Erica-Irene A. Daes with Aboriginal representatives, Geneva 1990 – Photo: Espen Røysamb

The cumulative effect of funding programs, in a number of countries, made the international conference possible. They were a necessary precondition, but not in themselves sufficient. Leadership had to come from some quarter. It came from Canada and George Manuel, a political figure who developed out of the strong Indian political tradition of British Columbia. The international conference brought together delegates from countries with policies which supported indigenous organizations with public or semi-public funding and delegates from countries where indigenous people might be recognized by governments as peasants or workers, but not as politically distinct groups within the nation....

These factors seem to explain why the initiative for the World Council came from North America and Europe, although the crisis area for indigenous people is clearly in the hinterland of Latin America. There have been long struggles by Indian people in Latin America to gain political power and protect their peoples. But the resources were not available to them to internationalise the struggle through the formation of an international body (Sanders 1977:23-4).

For the North American Indians in the USA, "the conclusion is certain that no remedy is available and no legal relief is possible under United States law with respect to all of the fundamental issues of Indian rights and Indian relations with the United States" (Coulter 1977). The Indians had to turn to the international community.

IWGIA AND WCIP

In "A tribute to Helge Kleivan" the World Council of Indigenous Peoples wrote:

"The World Council of Indigenous Peoples is deeply indebted to Helge Kleivan for its establishment. In 1972, when George Manuel was exploring the feasibility of an international conference of Indigenous peoples, the only non-Indigenous international organization to give enthusiastic and unconditional support to the idea was IWGIA under the leadership of Helge Kleivan. When a financial shortfall threatened to prevent this first conference, it was he who personally assisted WCIP to obtain the necessary funds for this event. In 1978 when our fledgling organization was faced with bankruptcy, it was IWGIA and Helge Kleivan' support that led to receipt of necessary financial support from Norway.

Most important is the fact that well before the voice of Indigenous people was heard internationally, Helge Kleivan had foreseen the need for positive academic assistance to Indigenous communities and public education about the situations and treatment of Indigenous peoples. As a founding member of IWGIA and through its publications, Helge Kleivan created empathy and international action for the protection of the rights of Indigenous peoples".

(World Council of Indigenous Peoples Newsletter no.4, February 1984)

The organisational efforts in the Euro-American countries were driven by increased encroachment by national governments and multinational companies onto indigenous lands and territories. IWGIA was in full support of the indigenous peoples concerned, such as during the Alta case in Norway, the James Bay development in Quebec, and the Mackenzie Valley Pipeline project, and also documented their situation in its publications.

The planned construction of a hydro-electric dam at Alta in Finnmark, Norway, was met with fierce opposition from, among others, Sámi, due to its damaging effect on their reindeer herding. The Alta case had tremendous significance for IWGIA and its strong support for the protesting Sámi did not go unnoticed. Robert Paine wrote, "NSR [*Norske Samers Riksforbund*] has issued a statement of unqualified support, and NRL [*Norske Reindriftsholderes Landsforbund*], clearly impressed by the joint statement from WCIP and IWGIA, recognizes the hunger strike ..." (Paine 1985:198). In the long-term, the Alta case caused the Norwegian government to change their policy towards the Sámi, in particular, and towards indigenous peoples in general.

> **WORLD COUNCIL OF INDIGENOUS PEOPLES (WCIP)**
>
> **1975** October. Founding meeting in Port Alberny, Canada
> Chair: George Manuel.
> **1977** August 2. General Assembly in Kiruna, Sweden
> Chair: George Manuel
> **1981** April-May 3. General Assembly in Canberra, Australia
> Chair: José Carlos Morales
> **1984** September 4. General Assembly, Panama
> Chair: Clem Cartier
> **1987** July 5. General Assembly in Lima, Peru
> Chair: Donald Rojas
> **1990**, August 6. General Assembly in Tromsø, Norway
> Chair: Jorge Valiente
> **1993** December 7. General Assembly in Guatemala City, Guatemala
> Chair: Jorge Valiente
> **1996** app. The organisation is no longer active

The role of IWGIA

One might ask why IWGIA came to play a key facilitating role in establishing international indigenous organisations such as the WCIP and CISA? It should be remembered that IWGIA was the first non-indigenous organisation established specifically to support indigenous peoples. The enthusiasm and seriousness of its founders and the relentless efforts of Peter Aaby and Helge Kleivan, with support from, among others, Kleivan's colleague Professor Robert Petersen, gave IWGIA an unparalleled reputation among indigenous peoples. Also, the fact that Helge Kleivan, a Norwegian citizen, had good connections with key people in the Norwegian Ministry of Foreign Affairs enabled him to mount support in Oslo as few others could.

The Documents published by IWGIA in the early years were all very similar. They focused on a group of people among whom the authors had conducted fieldwork. They briefly described a case of conflict, followed by a short description of the group's history and culture before giving a broad description of the situation of that group of people in the country, and ended with a short summary and suggestions of what could be done. The Documents were still dominated by reports from South America until 1976. It is interesting to note that when the first documents focusing on Canada appeared, these were markedly differ-

THE NOBEL PEACE PRIZE 1977

In January 1977, two members of the Norwegian Parliament, Ottar Brox and Einar Førde, nominated IWGIA and WCIP as candidates for the Nobel Peace Prize. The nomination highlighted IWGIA's efforts to raise the issue of human rights violations in, among other countries, Paraguay. Specifically mentioned was IWGIA's intimate cooperation with indigenous organisations.

The nomination ended by stressing that, by giving the Peace Prize to WCIP and IWGIA, the Nobel Committee would emphasise the fact that work for vulnerable indigenous peoples is an important part of the efforts to create peace in the world.

At first, the two members of the Norwegian parliament had only considered nominating IWGIA for the prize but, when informed about the suggestion, Helge Kleivan intervened because he found it wrong not to include the indigenous peoples themselves and, specifically, the first world-wide indigenous organisation. In order to promote this viewpoint, he travelled to Oslo to meet with people there and he communicated with George Manuel about it (notes and letters in Helge Kleivan's archive).

The proposal was well referred to in the Norwegian and Danish media but, in the end, the Peace Prize went to Amnesty International.

ent. These Documents had a thematic focus or dealt with organisational matters. Obviously, indigenous peoples in the North were not faced with the same kind of gross violations of human rights as those in South and Central America. However, as indigenous awareness grew, there was a need for different expressions and methods and, in turn, ambitions changed. At a meeting in August 1979, Helge Kleivan stated that the focus on Latin America was easy to explain but that it did not reflect an overall priority.

Along with the Documents, Newsletters were produced a number of times each year. These still had a very simple format, hardly distinguishable from the Documents. They were based upon clippings from other journals and newspapers. A few people provided IWGIA with source material, including whole packages of information (much of it handwritten) from Australia[67] and other places. From 1976 on, regular information began to appear from Central and North America, Asia and the Pacific. In retrospect, the reproduction of news in the Newsletter was fairly uncritical, amateurish and focused heavily on massacres.

To judge from IWGIA's Newsletters, the organisation's interest in the international indigenous movements that were established during the 1970s was increasing. The Newsletter and Documents from this period are more varied than in the first few years, with broader themes and regional coverage.

It is worth pointing out the difference in approach to indigenous issues between IWGIA and other support organisations. Firstly, from the 1970s on, IWGIA allied itself closely with indigenous movements. Secondly, IWGIA concentrated its focus entirely on indigenous peoples and indigenous issues, thus limiting its target group. Other major support organisations established at that time had a broader focus and, although they worked with indigenous peoples and communities, they did not consistently work on *indigenous* issues before the establishment of the UN Permanent Forum on Indigenous Issues (Permanent Forum) and the adoption of the UN Declaration on the Rights of Indigenous Peoples. IWGIA's rather narrow focus came to be very significant later on when IWGIA was able to support indigenous peoples in the United Nations like no other organisation, and indeed made this a priority.

IWGIA's and concerned scholars' persistent commitment to combating ethnocide, combined with a relational approach to cultural diversity and to ethnicity in the years following its establishment opened up a new alliance between anthropological perspectives and the emerging indigenous organisations (Wright 1988:366). I will return to this point in depth later.

IWGIA's development in the second part of the 1970s was thus closely linked to the growth of indigenous organisations. Its history cannot be understood without considering this.

International NGO Conference on Indigenous Peoples and the Land, Palais de Nations, Geneva 1981 - Photo: Espen Wæhle

CHAPTER 3

DIVERSIFICATION AND GLOBALISATION

It was the realities of social marginalisation, the lack of political recognition and cultural obliteration experienced by peoples on all continents that shaped IWGIA's approach to indigenous issues. Indigenous peoples' self-representation and IWGIA's relational approach focused the work on peoples barely included in the global discussion on the rights of indigenous peoples.

The developments described in the last chapter greatly influenced IWGIA's work with the indigenous movement in the coming years. In the 1980s, the movement was characterized by three important developments: one was the proliferation of indigenous organisations in new continents, first Asia, then the Pacific, and later also Russia and Africa; another was the incipient inclusion of indigenous peoples into global development aid; the third was that the United Nations became a focus of indigenous peoples' international efforts.

Besides Russia and Africa, IWGIA took the initiative to discuss indigenous issues in parts of the Pacific that were, and still remain in this respect, marginal. In 1998, IWGIA therefore organised a seminar on "Indigenous Peoples and Nations in the Pacific" at which an open dialogue on the concept of indigenousness in Melanesia, Micronesia and Polynesia took place. IWGIA was a leading player in terms of globalising the discussion on indigenousness, which was an important gain for indigenous peoples in the context of a globalisation that otherwise seemed to be a serious threat to them. The inclusion of new groups from Russia, Africa and the Pacific in work on human rights, publications and project assistance now became possible, due to - among other things – the financial support of the Nordic governments.

The organisation's development

If we take a look at IWGIA's publications, there were obviously significant changes in the early 1980s, and even more so in the latter part of the decade. The Newsletter became more substantial and was published regularly. The publications reflected the changes in the indigenous world, and indigenous peoples became the agents of their own destiny, firstly through the creation of a wide range of organisations, local, national and international. Indigenous peoples became contributors to the publications, which downscaled the documentary aspect and fo-

NØRREBRO RADIO

A member of the local group in Copenhagen tells:

Apart from doing political lobby work, the local group pursued a number of communicative activities in order to inform the public about indigenous issues. The writing of newspaper articles, organisation of demonstrations, presentations at schools, high schools and universities as well as participation at larger festivals with posters, presentations and flyers were some of the chosen strategies. Furthermore, the local group developed a programme on indigenous issues at a local radio station in Copenhagen. The programme was aired one hour once a week and was broadcasted for more than 10 years. The local group members used this programme not only to present information on indigenous issues but also to start discussions with radio-listeners who were often encouraged to call in. The enthusiasm of the listeners was fluctuating depending on the time of year or the issue in question. However, as the programme was often hosted by at least two persons one host could always act as a listener calling in. Ten minutes later the roles could be reversed. By changing the tone of your voice it was even possible to get dozens of listeners to call in. The quality of the programme was however never jeopardized.

cused more on activities in which indigenous peoples played an active part. This should be seen in the light of the fact that indigenous peoples, through their increased organisational capacity, had become more pro-active and, to an increasing extent, were able to present their own cases to the world. This also meant that indigenous peoples' own experiences of defending their rights were reported for other indigenous peoples to learn from.

A great deal of effort was made each year to publish statements made by indigenous peoples to the WGIP. This was a clear change when compared to the earlier period, when the arena was completely dominated by researchers. It was a way of letting indigenous peoples present their own cases publicly and in IWGIA's publications. This is now also accompanied by IWGIA's strategy of giving indigenous organisations IWGIA's credentials to speak at the United Nations.

It was also in the 1980s that IWGIA took important steps to evolve from an organisation based primarily upon voluntary work to a professional organisation with paid staff in the secretariat in Copenhagen. The step was taken in 1978 when an administrator and a student of anthropology were employed. Newsletters were published in Spanish from 1981 on[68] (*Boletín*) and Documents from 1982. The Yearbook (later The Indigenous World) was published in English from 1986 and in Spanish (*Anuario*) from 1989. A Russian edition was published in 1992. This new professionalism was symbolically confirmed when IWGIA, in 1987,[69] was able to reveal its new logo, which was soon seen everywhere.

While South and Central America was the focus in the 1970s, IWGIA now began to develop a number of regional focal points, including the Chittagong Hill Tracts, Bangladesh, Nagaland, India and East Timor. This involved IWGIA working in close cooperation with other European organisations and local NGOs. In the case of the Chittagong Hill Tracts campaign, an enduring co-operation was established with organisations and individuals in the Netherlands, Belgium, UK and Germany, and with the indigenous resistance movement and refugees in India.

A number of IWGIA local groups had also been established. After the Lund group (1971 – see annex) came local groups in Denmark and Norway. Some of them had a strong thematic focus. The local group in Oslo, which was very active in the early 1980s, was highly involved in the Alta case and also had a regional focus on North and South America. In the latter part of the decade, the Copenhagen group was specifically active in the Arctic and North America and on issues such as the campaign in defence of indigenous peoples' hunting rights. For a number of years, the local groups in Basel and Lund organised annual film festivals. Most local groups were active in giving lectures at schools and universities, as exemplified by the local group in Lund which established a formal relationship with Østerlen Public High School.

IWGIA is an international organisation and although a few local groups have been established over the years in Scandinavia, Switzerland, Russia, Spain and France, it has never been an aim of the organisation to establish national branches. On the contrary, initiatives for new local and national branches have always been met with some scepticism from IWGIA's Board. Although local groups have been responsible for key IWGIA initiatives, the cyclical and often volatile nature of their membership base is a problem for an international organisation. It must be added that there exists an inherent competition between international leadership and the goals of local organisation.

On a more academic level, IWGIA organised a number of conferences, some of which turned out to be very important. One was a seminar in Copenhagen in November 1984 on the rights of indigenous peoples, with special focus on the Sámi and Inuit areas (IWGIA 1987d). Organised by the IWGIA groups in Oslo and Copenhagen, this conference strengthened IWGIA as an organisation and confirmed IWGIA's interest in Sámi and Inuit matters. In Copenhagen, other conferences were organised in cooperation with other NGOs and the University of Copenhagen.

At a July 1988 meeting of the International Congress of Americanists in Amsterdam, IWGIA organised a symposium entitled "Ethno-development and Development Aid: Indigenous Perspectives" which included only indigenous presentations. The preface to the report of the meeting (IWGIA 1989a) said:

> *Symposia consisting entirely of indigenous peoples are rare. Either indigenous peoples cannot afford to attend or the congress organisers are not interested in encouraging indigenous attendance. IWGIA decided to combat both difficulties by seeking external support to bring a number of indigenous delegates from different parts of the Americas, and define a broad issue – development – as a point of departure for the discussion* (ibid:5).

The 1988 Amsterdam symposium can be seen as a symbol of IWGIA's policy of letting indigenous peoples speak for themselves. This was further emphasised by the South-South Programme (see p.104), which focused on exchanges between indigenous peoples, and resulted in the mailing of IWGIA's Newsletter (later renamed *Indigenous Affairs*) to all interested indigenous organisations free of charge. It also resulted in a policy of letting indigenous peoples use IWGIA's consultative status at the UN to speak for themselves, and in renewed efforts to raise funds for indigenous peoples to attend UN meetings.

Campaigning and lobbying

IWGIA has never had a strong focus on public campaigning and, when it has taken place, it has usually been as a follow-up to IWGIA documents or activities supported or initiated by IWGIA, for example in the UN. However, in the secretariat and local group reports to the Board in the 1970s and 1980s, campaigning was always mentioned as a key activity.

This said, there were a few cases of campaigns that lasted for a number of years, such as support for the rights of the Sámi protesting against the construction of the Alta Dam, support for the indigenous peoples in the Chittagong Hill Tracts, and the Copenhagen IWGIA group's support for the imprisoned Leonard Peltier. One of the first and most long-lasting campaigns was for a vaccination programme among the Yanomami in Brazil.

There is a remarkable difference between the early campaigns of the 1970s and those of the 1980s, and this reflects a change in IWGIA's cooperation with indigenous peoples. One example is the campaign for the defence of the human rights of the Aché in the 1970s. This took place without the direct involvement of Aché indigenous organisations, and the dissemination of information and publications was in English rather than Spanish. This is a logical reflection of the realities of that time and also an indicator of the lack of organisational capacity of the indigenous peoples.

In one case, IWGIA tried to use the annual national collection day in Denmark as a means for large-scale campaigning but with very little success. This may have been because the themes were of little public interest, although an evaluation of IWGIA's annual collection pointed out that campaigning can only be done by organisations that are already known to the general public (and this is far from the case with IWGIA in Denmark). Indigenous themes are, furthermore, not generally known. Even during the massacres in Rwanda, which hit the numerically small Batwa (Pygmies) particularly hard, the press was more concerned with the future of the endangered gorillas. Another possible reason why campaigning had melted into the background by the end of the century was that some of the most active IWGIA local groups had disbanded. Campaigning had, by and large, disappeared by the mid-1990s.

Yanomami

The Yanomami vaccination programme against measles was the first major IWGIA initiative to combine a campaign with fundraising for a project. The efforts were coordinated with Survival International in London, the Anthropology Resource Center in the US and the Yanomami Park Group (CCPY) in Brazil. For IWGIA, it raised new challenges. Judging by the material in the archives, this campaign involved huge efforts throughout most of 1979 and 1980. The Norwegian and Danish governments supported the planning phase, and Norway was very positive with regard to funding the project implementation. Meetings, phone calls and letters between IWGIA, the embassy in Brasilia, the Ministry of Development Cooperation and the Ministry of Foreign Affairs in Copenhagen reveal the enormous problems IWGIA had at that time in getting the Danish authorities to commit to supporting indigenous peoples.

The background to the vaccination programme was the construction of the *Perimetral Norte* highway across Yanomami territory in Roraima. The situation of the approximately 8,600 Yanomami was critical as the area was known to be rich in mineral resources, and the opening of the highway would attract large number of miners and other poor people. If brought into the area, measles would wipe out the Yanomami, which explained the urgency of the vaccination campaign.

Problems with the Brazilian authorities postponed the start of the vaccination programme and the establishment of a Yanomami Indian Park met with resistance.

Chittagong Hill Tracts (CHT)

The peoples of Chittagong Hill Tracts are culturally linked with the people living in the mountain areas of North-east India and Eastern Burma but became part of East Pakistan (later to become Bangladesh) at independence. The relationship between the lowlands and the mountains, which had always been characterized by conflicts, deteriorated dramatically some ten years later when thousands of indigenous peoples lost their lands following the construction of the Kaptai dam. In addition, after Bangladesh obtained independence from Pakistan, the government started to relocate Bengali settlers on indigenous lands from which the hill peoples were evicted. In the act, the Bangladesh army killed thousands of indigenous peoples, thereby giving rise to a guerrilla movement that retaliated from bases in India and Burma.

The human rights violations were vast, and the first report published by IWGIA in 1984 was written by Wolfgang Mey (Mey 1984) who had conducted research and fieldwork in CHT. He had approached IWGIA the previous year, during an anthropological conference in Quebec, offering to compile a document. Anti-Slavery, Amnesty International and the ILO had already published reports on the situation (OCCHTC 1986) but with limited or no effect on the Bangladesh government. Wolfgang Mey put IWGIA in touch with the Organising Committee Chittagong Hill Tracts Campaign (OCCHTC) in the Netherlands and with researchers familiar with the situation.

The issue of a commission was raised by Ramendu S. Dewan, a Chakma and the foreign spokesperson of the *Jumma* peoples, when - during a visit to the Danish Parliament in 1985 - the Bangladesh Minister of Finance expressed support for a fact-finding mission to visit CHT (CHT Commission 1991:1-2). IW-

Ramendu Dewan (left) at the UNWGIP, 1990, and demonstration in Dhaka on 12 June 2000 to mark the 4th anniversary of the abduction of Kalpana Chakma an indigenous from the Chittagong Hill Tracts.
Photos: Espen Røysamb and IWGIA archive

GIA, represented by Andrew Gray, Teresa Aparicio and Espen Wæhle, brought this suggestion to the first international CHT conference, organised by the OCCHTC in Amsterdam 10 months later (October 1986). The European NGOs and indigenous peoples from the region supported the suggestion. This developed into a creative working relationship that was legitimised by close contacts with the partners in CHT: primarily the *Jana Samhati Samiti* (JSS) or the People's United Party and its armed wing, the *Shanti Bahini*, which was outlawed in Bangladesh and the CHT refugees living in India. It took three years and several meetings in Amsterdam, Copenhagen and London to establish the Chittagong Hill Tracts Commission but at the end of 1989 a number of political obstacles had at last been dealt with and financial support ensured.

The Commission, including experts and advisors from IWGIA and OCCHTC, travelled to the CHT and to refugee camps in Tripura (India) in late 1990 and early 1991 and was very successful. The resulting report: "Life is not ours. Land and Human Rights in the Chittagong Hill Tracts, Bangladesh" became the most important lobbying tool for years on the CHT. The report of the Commission's findings was launched in the House of Lords, London on May 23, 1991 and updates were produced in 1992, 1994, 1997 and 2000, along with translations into Bengali.

The Commission's report put the CHT back on the agenda, and made it possible for IWGIA to raise the issue with donors who, at the outset, were often far from being in agreement with IWGIA. Some may even have considered IWGIA as inconvenient and troublesome, incessantly raising an issue concerning 600,000 people in a country of more than 100 million inhabitants. However, there were also donors such as Danida and others that took the issue seriously, raised concerns and allocated resources earmarked for the CHT. In the UN, IWGIA made sure that the *Jummas* came to the meetings and presented their case before the Working Group on Indigenous Populations.

In the years ahead, IWGIA followed the situation fairly closely and, after the peace agreement in 1997, tried to influence government and donor agencies to find ways of putting pressure on the Bangladesh government to implement the agreement. IWGIA and its partners undoubtedly played a key role in defending the human rights of the indigenous peoples of the CHT against all odds.[70]

Animal rights

One of the most important and successful campaigns took place in defence of the Arctic indigenous peoples' hunting rights. During the late 1970s, European and North American animal rights movements (such as Greenpeace, the Humane Society and WSPA) launched campaign after campaign against seal hunting, whale hunting and trapping. In response to these, IWGIA and indigenous partners such as Indigenous Survival International (an international alliance of indigenous nations and organizations from Canada, Alaska and Greenland, formed in 1984), the Inuit Circumpolar Conference and Inuit Tapirissat of Canada reacted with counter campaigns in defence of indigenous peoples' hunting rights and rights to their natural resources. One of the most important aims was to prevent a general European Union ban on the import of hunting and trapping products. These efforts lasted for years and, although the animal rights movement had broad support among the general public and among a large number of European politicians, the rights of indigenous peoples were upheld and a general EU import ban did not come about.

The success of the campaign was, above all, due to the unrelenting efforts of the Greenlandic Member of the European Parliament, Finn Lynge,[71] who cooperated with the Greenlandic Home Rule, the Greenlandic Hunters' and Fishermen's Organisation and lobbying groups such as IWGIA. IWGIA had long had close relations with these and with another key actor, Hans Pavia Rosing, Greenlandic mem-

ANIMAL RIGHTS – HUMAN RIGHTS

In the 1980s, groups in the animal rights movements such as Greenpeace started campaigns against the commercial and systematic hunting (killing) of baby seals. Although this hunt only took place in Newfoundland, Canada, it soon became a campaign against any form of seal hunting. The Inuit hunters of Greenland and northern Canada, who relied on seal hunting, had nothing to do with the killing of baby seals. Later, campaigns were directed against the steel jawed leg-hold trap, mainly used by Indians and Inuit in Canada. It was important to give the hunters who relied on trapping time to change to hunting methods other than the leg-hold trap.

The European Parliament worked on the adoption of a resolution to ban the import of all fur products from countries that allowed the steel jawed leg-hold trap. Because of the campaigns against the killing of baby seals, members of the European Parliament and members of national parliaments worked on a general ban of seal products. One of IWGIA's strategies was to lobby the parliamentarians to consider the real issues and to recognise the rights of Arctic indigenous peoples. A parallel strategy was to inform the general public about the living conditions in the Arctic. Speeches were given in schools, conferences were organised, and papers were written.

Frank Sejersen

ber of the Danish Parliament. The work undertaken by these individuals and organisations was an uphill struggle. The animal rights movement was very popular at that time and had a huge amount of support (no least financial) while it was often very difficult for IWGIA to obtain support from other NGOs.

In October 1982, a dispute broke out in public between IWGIA (Helge Kleivan) and a member of the Danish Parliament.[72] It was the classic example of a campaign group (in this case from the animal rights movement) wanting to achieve public attention and support. It does this by targeting a general issue without considering the implications for specific groups. A journalist had reacted with a general attack on the movement responsible for the campaign. The politician, who saw herself as a defender of the environment, launched a counterattack. IWGIA felt it necessary to point out that her blanket defence of the campaign meant that she was guilty of exactly the type of action that she had opposed.

"Going global"

We have to remember that, even in the 1980s, the most important international arena for indigenous peoples - the United Nations - was dominated by indigenous organisations from North America and Australia, with some participation from Latin America. In 1981, at the NGO Conference on Indigenous Peoples and Land in Geneva, for example, the vast majority of the participants came from the USA and Canada, representing more than 25 indigenous organisations, while less than 10 organisations from Latin America and one Maori organisation participated. The six indigenous NGOs with ECOSOC consultative status (WCIP, IITC, ICC, CISA, ILRC and Australian National Conference of Aborigines) were invited to the 1981 conference to submit statements[73] (Dunbar-Ortiz:67). In 1985 there were 50 indigenous organizations present at the WGIP although "to date there have been no participants from India, Burma, Thailand, China, the USSR anywhere in Africa, Pakistan or the Pacific" (Burger 1987:268).

With the entry of indigenous organisations onto the international scene, these became IWGIA's main partners. They were not grassroots organisations but international NGOs and regional or national umbrella organisations such as the Cordillera Peoples' Alliance, the Inuit Circumpolar Conference, the World Council of Indigenous Peoples, and so on.

When IWGIA was founded in 1968, this was because of reports of the human rights situation in South America. The increased focus on Central and North America, the Arctic and other Western countries with indigenous peoples followed logically because they identified with the struggle of the South American Indians. The American Indians, the Maori, the Aboriginals, the Sámi, the Inuit and the Pacific Islanders were all well-established and recognised as the aboriginal peoples of their countries or regions. But besides being aboriginals they also

GEORG HENRIKSEN
1940 -2007

Photo: Kathrin Wessendorf

Georg Henriksen was one of the founding fathers of IWGIA and he played a key role in shaping the development of the organisation.

Georg Henriksen had a long career in social anthropology, including as a Research Fellow at the Memorial University of Newfoundland, and as Professor of Social Anthropology at the University of Bergen. Georg served on numerous boards and commissions at the University of Bergen (including as Dean of the Faculty of Social Sciences) and at the Norwegian Research Council.

Since his first stay in Canada, he repeatedly carried out fieldwork among different indigenous peoples, first of all the Naskapi Indians (now Mushuau Innu) in Labrador, Canada, but also the Cree Indians of James Bay, the Mic Mac Indians of Nova Scotia and Prince Edward Island, the Turkana pastoral nomads of Kenya and the Sámi people of Helgeland, Norway.

Georg was a Board member from 1981 to 2005 and he chaired the Board for 15 years. Under Georg's wise leadership the organisation developed from a small NGO run by volunteers and a small staff into a professional organisation with a substantial publications programme and projects supporting a large number of indigenous projects. Georg's personal integrity and his insistence on combining anthropological knowledge, political advocacy and solidarity with indigenous peoples has been a guide to everyone in the organisation.

Georg remembered the early visions of engaging with indigenous peoples globally, and it was for him a dream come true that indigenous peoples from Asia, Africa and Russia should gain opportunities that had earlier been denied them. He encouraged everyone in IWGIA to continue the efforts to promote indigenous rights in these regions, even when the outside world was opposed, sceptical or obstructive.

came to consider themselves as indigenous, thus linking their marginal position in modern states not only with their aboriginality ("we were here first") but also with their marginal and discriminated position in those modern states. Connections to peoples in Asia with similar structural positions within states came logically as an extension of the Pacific linkage and this seems by and large to have taken place without serious problems, discussion or consideration among indigenous peoples. As we shall see, Russia and Africa were, however, in some respects different. IWGIA's involvement with indigenous peoples in these regions reflected internal developments as well as conscious moves on the part of IWGIA.

In the latter part of the 1980s, granting financial support to indigenous organisations to implement their own projects started to become an important activity, and this was covered in the publications. This was a deliberate move later to be labelled IWGIA's "holistic approach".

Asia

One of the first new regions to come more into focus was Asia. IWGIA's main efforts were aimed at promoting human rights, supporting indigenous peoples from the region to participate in UN meetings and, later, providing project support. Its first long-term partner in Asia was the Cordillera Peoples' Alliance (CPA). CPA was founded in June 1984 in Bontoc, Mountain Province, by 150 delegates from 27 organizations attending the Cordillera People's Congress. The founders of CPA were mainly indigenous leaders and activists who spearheaded the successful opposition to the World Bank-funded Chico Dam project and the commercial logging operations of the Cellophil Resources Corporation.[74]

IWGIA's first contact with the indigenous peoples of the Cordilleras was in 1981 when Joji Cariño and Geoff Nettleton presented the Chico Dam issue at the NGO Conference on Indigenous Peoples and Land in Geneva. They met with Jørgen Brøchner Jørgensen and Espen Wæhle and were invited to visit IWGIA's office in Copenhagen early the following year.[75] This soon developed into a lasting relationship and, in 1987, Teresa Aparicio, co-director of IWGIA, went to the Cordilleras to conduct an evaluation of another indigenous organisation that had applied to Norad for project funding (IWGIA 1987a).

Russia

The Sámi of the Nordic countries, organised in the Nordic Sámi Council, and the Inuit of Greenland and North America, organised in the Inuit Circumpolar Conference, had always wanted to include their relatives in the Kola Peninsula (Sámi) and in Chukotka (Inuit) within their organisations. They were prevented from hav-

The first national meeting of indigenous peoples in Russia. The Kremlin, Moscow, March 1990 – Photo: Jens Dahl

ing these connections during the Soviet period although the Soviet authorities had recognised the unique nature of a number of small ethnic minorities since the early years of communist rule, and had given them special status. The new open policy established during the Gorbachev era suddenly gave the indigenous peoples of Russia the opportunity to be aligned with the global indigenous movement.

Concerned about the development in the North, including the cultural and environmental effect on indigenous peoples, a group of Arctic scholars came together in 1987 and established a group that they called "Uneasy North" (*Trevozhnyi Sever*).[76] When two of the members, Alexander Pika and Boris Prokhorov wrote an article in the journal *Kommunist* in 1988 (printed by IWGIA in English in 1989), they were contacted by the indigenous leaders Vladimir Sanghi, Yevdokiya Gayer and Yeremey Aipin to assist in organising a congress of Russian indigenous peoples.[77] Alexander Pika became an IWGIA Board member but was lost in an accident at sea outside Chukotka in September 1995. Olga Murashko, also an anthropologist replaced him as a Board member. IWGIA was one of the first support organisations outside the Soviet Union to publish (in 1989) on issues relating to the indigenous peoples there, and to include the work of Russian scholars.[78]

Following Michael Gorbachev's 1987 Murmansk speech, and the announcement of *glasnost* and *perestrojka,* signalling an end to the Cold War in the Arctic, it was still problematic to criticise government policy. The focus in early articles was on pressing environmental issues. Some personal contacts had been established with Russian scholars during the Inuit Studies Conference that took place in Copenhagen in the autumn of 1988, and again in 1989 when Georg Henriksen participated in a conference in Leningrad. Other contacts were established when Jens Dahl, on behalf of IWGIA, joined the "Next Stop Soviet" initiative in Moscow and Western Siberia.

In February 1990, two indigenous representatives from Russia, Chuner Taksami and Yuri Rytkheu, who were participating in a UNESCO meeting in Copenhagen, visited the IWGIA secretariat and invited IWGIA to participate in the forthcoming meeting with ICC and the Nordic Sámi Institute.[79] This first meeting of indigenous peoples in Russia took place in March 1990 in Moscow and IWGIA was invited, along with a few Western indigenous NGOs. It gave IWGIA the opportunity to invite Vladimir Sanghi - the elected Chair of an organisation called "Small Indigenous Peoples of the Soviet North, Siberia and the Far East" - to participate in the forthcoming meeting of the Working Group on Indigenous Populations in Geneva, in July of that year.

The 1990 meeting of the WGIP marked the entrance of Russian indigenous peoples onto the international human rights scene. Since then, IWGIA has invited (usually through the Human Rights Fund for Indigenous Peoples – see below) representatives of the Russian indigenous peoples to participate in all UN human rights meetings dealing with indigenous issues. The Russian indigenous peoples played a key role during the negotiations for the establishment of a Permanent Forum for indigenous peoples and in the Commission on Human Rights' Working Group dealing with the Draft Declaration on the Rights of Indigenous Peoples. They were often the ones who knew that a compromise had to be found. IWGIA's role as a key facilitator of Russian indigenous participation was often quite difficult and, to some extent, controversial. This produced its share of criticism. The historical relations that developed between IWGIA and the Organisation of Small Peoples of the Russian North, Siberia and Far East (RAIPON) illustrate not only a close working relationship but one founded on trust. It is not surprising that there were people who, being critical of the Russian organisation, were also critical of IWGIA's supportive role.

Following the Moscow conference in 1990, Russian indigenous organisations, first and foremost RAIPON, were established and cooperation with IWGIA was extended to include legal issues and project-related activities. This was facilitated by the establishment of an IWGIA local group in Moscow, which followed an IWGIA visit to indigenous communities in 1992. The members of the IWGIA group were researchers from the group "Uneasy North" who had a close working relationship with RAIPON.

Africa

IWGIA's entry onto the African scene was quite different. While the concept of being indigenous in the post-Soviet era was fairly uncontroversial, it was not the case for those peoples in Africa who came to identify themselves as indigenous. It was no less controversial for IWGIA to take a leading role among anthropologists and non-indigenous support organisations in favour of extending its activities to peoples in Africa. And in this respect IWGIA *did* take a more pro-active role than had been the case in Asia, South or Central America. One simple reason for this was that very few people in Africa at that time were even organised on the basis of ethnicity, never mind indigenousness. It was well into the 1990s before IWGIA became actively and permanently involved with indigenous peoples in Africa.

The reasons seem obvious: the idea of distinguishing some peoples (ethnic groups) from others in Africa was extremely controversial amongst those in power in the independent African states, and anthropologists and researchers working in Africa have always accepted that "Africa is different" from the rest of the world, thus indirectly accepting the worldview of those politicians who were desperately trying to legitimise an often dubious power base that relied on negating the significance of anything ethnic. Since the professional base of IWGIA was to be found among anthropologists, we can assume that there was very little external pressure or incitement for IWGIA to take up issues of marginal peoples on that continent.

The fact that one of the first IWGIA Documents (No.2, 1971) dealt with indigenous peoples in Eritrea indicates that the founders of the organisation considered the concept of indigenousness as being globally applicable. For the next two decades, however, there were only scattered references to the situation in Africa in the Newsletters, and it was to take 14 years for the next document to be published. This document was on the pastoral Maasai in Tanzania and was published in 1985 by the anthropologist and later IWGIA Board member, Kaj Århem.

The first direct contact between IWGIA and an indigenous representative from Africa occurred when the Maasai anthropologist and member of the Tanzanian Parliament, Lazaro Moringe Parkipuny, took part in the meeting of the International Union of Anthropological and Ethnological Sciences in Quebec and Vancouver in 1983. Lazaro Parkipuny - who was a speaker at a session on human rights - viewed the position of his Maasai people in relation to the Tanzanian state in terms of indigenousness. Because of his firm defence of Maasai rights, he was a controversial person and his appearance at the conference was not without problems. His invitation to participate in the Congress was delivered in person to the parliamentary office in Dar Es Salaam where the desk officer at first denied that there was any member of parliament by that name. After some insistence he acknowledged that, "ah yes, that is the cow-man". The letter never reached Parkipuny and no-one knew if he would turn up in Canada. It took another six years for Parkipuny to become the first African indigenous person to address the UN Working Group on Indigenous Populations. This was in 1989 and he had been invited by IWGIA, together with Richard Bellow, a Hadza, also from Tanzania. Claiming indigenousness in Tanzania, as in most other African countries, could be dangerous. This may explain why, in the following years, neither of them responded to the invitations from the Human Rights Fund to participate in the WGIP meeting.

Another impetus for IWGIA to work on indigenous issues in Africa arose after Board member Espen Wæhle completed his anthropological fieldwork in the Congo among the Efe (Mbuti Pygmies) of the Ituri Forest in 1983. He linked the Congo material to the growing concern about the future of rainforests and rainforest peoples. Wæhle was encouraged to examine the situation of the Efe and other Pygmy groups as indigenous peoples by IWGIA members Harald Eidheim and Knut Odner. Both had worked among the Sámi of Norway and both had done fieldwork in Kenya: Eidheim with the Samburu and Odner with Maasai pastoralists. A similar desire to intensify IWGIA's engagement with Africa came from Board member Aud Talle who, for many years, had worked with Maasai and Barabaig people in East Africa.

Over the next years, IWGIA continued to invite indigenous people from Africa to the WGIP in Geneva although there was no clearly defined policy or strategy as to how to proceed in Africa. In the early 1990s, however, two paths were pursued. The first was to provide support to indigenous organisations in Africa. Funding was provided for a new organisation of Bushmen in Botswana, the First Peoples of the Kalahari. Initial contact had been established by a Danish writer, Arthur Krasilnikoff, and a Norwegian anthropologist, Sidsel Saugestad, both associated with IWGIA. IWGIA had recently received the "Nairobi award" from the Danish Press and, in October 1993, at the founding meeting of the First Peoples of the Kalahari, IWGIA gave the money from the award to the new organisation. This marked a long period of close cooperation between IWGIA and the First Peoples of the Kalahari (see section on projects).

The second path was to raise and discuss the issue of indigenous peoples in Africa at seminars and conferences, with the participation of African indigenous people, researchers and African government representatives. There was a thorough discussion of the issue by the Board in the spring of 1985, and again in 1989. A year later, the Board decided to investigate how a seminar could be organised on the issue. In 1993 and 1994, IWGIA visited Kenya, Tanzania, Botswana and Namibia, where contacts were made, and the first meeting discussing indigenous issues in Africa took place outside Copenhagen, in Tune, in June 1993.[80] The indigenous par-

The Parakuyu of Usangu Plains is one of the many indigenous pastoralist people of Tanzania. Photo: Jens Dahl

First People of Kalahari workshop, Ghanzi, Botswana, 1998 – Photo: Sidsel Saugestad

ticipants came from Botswana, Namibia, Ethiopia, Mali, Rwanda and Tanzania, and there were government representatives from Botswana and Namibia.

It was the presentations by the African participants and the insistence of the international human rights lawyer, Howard Berman, that eventually inspired IWGIA to intensify its dealings with indigenous peoples in Africa and apply for observer status with the African Commission on Human and Peoples' Rights. This marked the beginning of a pro-active IWGIA policy which, over the years, has included a number of activities in different regions.

The first path - financial support for indigenous peoples' projects - expanded from Botswana to other parts of Africa, first and foremost Kenya and Tanzania. The second was not developed until 1999, when the opportunity came to take up the issue of indigenous peoples in Africa with the African Commission on Human and Peoples' Rights. IWGIA had acquired NGO observer status with the Commission in 1994, and was waiting for an opportunity to use this status in a strategic and meaningful sense.

New opportunities in the Arctic

In recent years, IWGIA's Arctic activities have been greatly affected by the new opportunities for indigenous peoples in Russia resulting from the disintegration of the Soviet Union and the establishment of the Arctic Council in 1996. Arctic indigenous organisations obtained status as "Permanent Participants" in the Arctic Council, meaning that they have a defined and integrated role in the Council's negotiations and deliberations. By including indigenous organisations in the structure, the Arctic Council is a unique model of an international organisation. With the increased awareness of, and concern about, the impact of climate change, it has improved indigenous peoples' access to research communities. The Arctic Council offers limited opportunities for observers, and IWGIA's first application was turned down. After one year as an ad-hoc observer, however, regular observer status was achieved in 2002. IWGIA saw its role in the Arctic Council as very different to its role in the UN, the Permanent Forum included, where all organisations, indigenous as well as non-indigenous, have obtained *de facto* equal access. IWGIA's response to this has been to disseminate information about the Arctic to indigenous peoples in other parts of the world, including specific issues such as models of self-government and climate change.

Arctic Council Permanent Participants at the meeting in Guovdageaidnu / Kautokeino, November 2008 – Photo: Svein Mathiesen / International Centre for Reindeer Husbandry

Mayor Klemet Erland Haetta welcoming the visitors to Guovdageaidnu / Kautokeino (Norway). Arctic Council meeting, November 2008 – Photo: Johan Mathis Gaup / International Centre for Reindeer Husbandry

CHAPTER 4

HUMAN RIGHTS AND DEVELOPMENT PROJECTS

The hiring of Andrew Gray, an anthropologist with extensive experience of working with indigenous peoples in Peru, as co-director of the IWGIA secretariat in 1983 signalled new times ahead. As an outsider to the organisation he brought new experiences, ideas and viewpoints into the organisation and opened up a new dialogue between the Board and the international secretariat. First, he and the other co-directors, Teresa Aparicio and Jørgen Brøchner Jørgensen, made IWGIA an active partner of indigenous organisations with regard to matters of human rights and self-development projects.

The process that led to the adoption of ILO Convention 169 On Indigenous and Tribal Peoples in Independent Countries in 1989 was especially important as it can be seen as a turning point for IWGIA, as it was a turning point for indigenous peoples. It started a process in which IWGIA's involvement in UN activities came to supersede all other human rights initiatives, and it coincided with increased involvement in facilitating indigenous development projects.

IWGIA had wanted to obtain consultative status with ECOSOC since 1971 but it was not until June 1988 that an application was actually made. Before the UN Committee on Non-Governmental Organisations was due to convene in January 1989, IWGIA discussed the application with the Ministry of Foreign Affairs in Stockholm, as Sweden was a committee member, and copies of the application were also sent to the other Nordic countries. At the meeting of the Committee in New York, IWGIA's activities were scrutinized by a number of governments and Andrew Gray, representing IWGIA, was certain that the application would pass - until the Kenyan member intervened. She "demanded to see the article on Kenya in the Tourism Document [Doc. 61, edited by P. Rossel] before she approved our application. She said that there were no indigenous people in Kenya, and if we were trying to say so she would be against the work" (IWGIA 1989b). The document had to be brought across from the other side of New York but, when it was presented later that day, Kenya did agree to let the application pass, probably due to lobbying from Nicaragua.

The revision of the old ILO Convention 107 took place with the participation of governments, employers and employees but without any formal participation on the part of those at whom the Convention was aimed, the indigenous peoples. A few indigenous NGOs had ILO accreditation and each was allowed to address the committee for 10 minutes although they were not involved in the debates and deliberations (Berman 1989). "Each day there would be a caucus of Indigenous delegates to determine who would speak for the 10 allocated minutes" (Venne 1998:104). Those few who took part as observers in the process felt that this was completely unsatisfactory; they were warned when the parties preferred the terms "participation" and "consultation" instead of "self-determination" and "consent" as demanded by indigenous peoples. Years later, the experience of the ILO process had a tremendous impact on the strong positions taken by indigenous peoples in relation to "self-determination" during the long process of drafting a UN declaration.

Indigenous peoples learned the lesson from the ILO process and intensified their involvement in the drafting of a declaration on the rights of indigenous peoples. IWGIA took up the challenge and was instrumental in developing the framework for development agency policies, playing an active role in contacting and facilitating the participation of indigenous peoples from the "new" continents, including Russia, in the UN processes. The Human Rights Fund for Indigenous Peoples (see later section) became a key instrument in IWGIA's approach to lending support to indigenous peoples' participation in UN processes.

The UN Working Group on Indigenous Populations

The annual meeting of the Working Group on Indigenous Populations (WGIP), established in 1982, became *the* meeting point for indigenous peoples from around the world. A combination of factors may explain this (Niezen 2003). One was an increased awareness of the opportunities of the human rights system; another was the establishment of indigenous organisations around the world at local, national, regional and international levels; yet another was the opportunity to give presentations: "Under Eide's chairmanship, the working group decided on rules of procedure which allowed any indigenous person or indigenous representative to speak" (Sanders 1989:408). The open access that had been established for participation in the WGIP was important and so were the new opportunities that were given to indigenous organisations in developing countries to obtain support from Euro-American NGOs and development agencies. Lastly, it is worth mentioning that the revolution in the communications system, above all with the birth of the Internet, made it possible for indigenous peoples the world over to link up with each other and other relevant organisations such as NGOs. The meetings of the WGIP were also, for many years, the main focus of IWGIA's human rights efforts.

For IWGIA, the annual meetings of the WGIP became a basis for what was to become IWGIA's key strategic effort for many years to come, namely that which later, in the 1990s, was termed the holistic approach. This approach was aimed at combining work with indigenous organisations in relation to a) human rights,

b) publications, c) projects, d) networking and e) lobbying efforts (see later section). In Geneva, contacts were created with indigenous organisations that had been funded by the Human Rights Fund. These were often asked to contribute to IWGIA's publications. Every year, IWGIA representatives would visit one or more regions of the world to make new contacts, find out about local and regional developments and reaffirm already existing relationships with indigenous organisations. These networking trips and visits to IWGIA-supported projects made it possible to urge indigenous organisations to make the most of the opportunities available through the UN system.

Other international developments

The WGIP had been the focal point for indigenous peoples' international efforts since 1982, as it had been for IWGIA. Three other international developments came increasingly to draw indigenous peoples' attention, and they were able to transfer the experiences gained in Geneva - as well as the funding, the participatory structure and the establishment of an indigenous caucus[81] - to these international settings.

Among the most important was the biodiversity process initiated by the United Nation's Conference on Environment and Development in Rio de Janeiro in 1992 and the parallel indigenous Kari-Oca Conference. From the indigenous conference came the Indigenous Peoples' Earth Charter, and from the official meeting the Convention on Biological Diversity. From this moment on, indigenous peoples became involved in a range of international meetings on biodiversity, sustainable development, access and benefit sharing, intellectual property, protected areas and, last but not least, climate change. IWGIA followed some of these processes and took part in some meetings, including the World Summit on Sustainable Development in Johannesburg in 2002. Articles were published on related issues but the environmental process did not become a main objective of IWGIA's international efforts. This was often debated within IWGIA and the choice not to give it priority was primarily dictated by the limited resources available, although IWGIA recognised that environmental issues were often a less controversial road into indigenous rights than the human rights approach. Another reason for giving priority to human rights processes was the diversification of the agenda to include new issues (the Draft Declaration, the Permanent Forum) and because these processes came to include new bodies in addition to the WGIP, such as the Commission on Human Rights itself, the working groups directly under the Commission and, eventually, the mechanism of the Special Rapporteur on the situation of human rights and fundamental freedoms of indigenous people. This proliferation was resource demanding and IWGIA had to concentrate its limited resources elsewhere. Notwithstanding, it must also be stressed that environmental processes have been, and will be, of the utmost significance, including on a practical level, to indigenous peoples and to IWGIA.

The second international development was the number of world conferences dealing with human rights issues. There was the Vienna Conference on Human Rights in 1993, the World Summit for Social Development in Copenhagen in 1995 and the World Conference Against Racism in Durban in 2001.

The third international development was the focus on the rights and problems of indigenous women. IWGIA took part in the World Conference on Women for the first time in Nairobi in 1985 but it was not until the conference in Beijing in 1995 that indigenous women were able to establish their own platform. Prior to Beijing, indigenous women had organised their own international conferences and meetings such as the International Conference of Indigenous Women in Karajsok, Norway in 1990, and in Aotearoa (New Zealand) in 1993. Regional networks had also been established, such as the Indigenous Women's Network (US), the Asia Indigenous Women's Network, and similar initiatives in Africa and Latin America. IWGIA supported these meetings and networks, published on them, and took up specific issues such as the position of indigenous women during armed conflicts.

Like all other NGOs, IWGIA has to deal with the constantly changing policies of donor agencies who one year want everyone to focus on democracy, the next year on participatory development, the next on poverty reduction, and so forth. However, the focus on women has been a constant for many years. IWGIA has often been criticised by donors, particularly Norad and Danida, for having too few activities relating to indigenous women, specifically indigenous women's *projects*. The disturbing fact is that women *have* been a focal point for IWGIA but that indigenous women face what are often insurmountable problems when organising at the local level in contrast to the international scene. IWGIA has focused on indigenous women in documents and in its journal *Indigenous Affairs*, and it was once decided to devote a special section of the annual *The Indigenous World* to women although this only lasted for two consecutive years, probably due to lack of response. All authors are urged to include women's issues in their writing. IWGIA continually supports indigenous women's participation in conferences in general, and in meetings organised by indigenous women in particular. The general strategy is to support indigenous women's self-organising. This is framed within the context of IWGIA's gender strategy, which includes a requirement that all IWGIA-supported projects address women's issues.

The Human Rights Fund for Indigenous Peoples

The involvement of indigenous peoples in all these international activities would not have been possible without the Human Rights Fund for Indigenous Peoples.

This is a consortium of NGOs that was created in 1984 in order to promote and facilitate the participation of indigenous representatives in the newly created UN Working Group on Indigenous Populations. Julian Burger from the Anti-Slavery Society (later Anti-Slavery International) had participated in the WGIP meetings in 1982 and 1983 and realised that only a limited number of indigenous individuals could attend. He obtained the support of the Board of the Anti-Slavery Society to establish a fund. With the institutional capacity of Anti-Slavery, and funding available in Holland, he contacted the WIP (Work Group for Indigenous Peoples) (later NCIV) in Amsterdam and, together, they were able to raise further funding. IWGIA became involved shortly after.[82] While the focus of the Fund was initially only on the WGIP, this changed when indigenous issues began to proliferate in other UN bodies, such as the Commission on Human Rights, the Working Group on the Draft Declaration, the Permanent Forum on Indigenous Issues etc. Besides the importance of the Fund's activities to indigenous peoples, it has been a key component of IWGIA's human rights activities and thus a significant part of IWGIA's holistic strategy. The Human Rights Fund is one of the most successful human rights instruments in which IWGIA has been involved. It is also a good example of successful cooperation between non-indigenous NGOs.

The goal of the Fund was to give "indigenous peoples an opportunity to attend the meetings" and to support "the indigenous peoples in their endeavours to put forward their own statements and thoughts on the declaration" (Cohen 1993:49). From the beginning, the practical aim of the Human Rights Fund was simple and limited: to cover travelling expenses, accommodation and living costs for indigenous peoples participating in the UN meetings. With this restricted and streamlined aim, the Fund has, over the years, funded more than 800 indigenous people's travel to Geneva and New York in order to attend UN meetings.[83] To this should be added the fact that the Fund often provides important logistical support in the form of interpretation at meetings and the renting of meeting rooms for the indigenous caucus, as well as technical and administrative support when requested.

The founders of the Fund and IWGIA have since been joined by KWIA (Belgium), for some years by the Society for Threatened Peoples (*Gesellschaft für Bedrohte Völker*) (Germany) and, more recently, by *Almaciga* (Spain). The narrow aim of the Fund and the limited number of beneficiaries improve the chances of funding and of reaching agreement on policies and decisions, and make it possible to run the activities in an efficient manner with very little administration. The secretariat has always been hosted by IWGIA and, when the Fund increased its activities in the 1990s, a part-time secretary was employed to assist indigenous peoples before, during and after the UN meetings. The members of the Fund meet at least once a year, usually linked to a UN meeting, and the beneficiaries and persons involved have gained an in-depth knowledge of each other, which further explains the long-standing existence of the Fund.

ANDREW GRAY
1955 – 1999

Photo: IWGIA Archive

The death of Andrew Gray, in a Pacific air crash in 1999 was a huge loss to IWGIA but also to the movement for the rights of indigenous peoples. Andrew Gray was in the middle of a networking trip for IWGIA in the South Pacific linking up with indigenous peoples and their organizations in the region as a part of IWGIA's expanding programme in support of the rights of indigenous peoples.

In 1977 Andrew Gray graduated with honours in social anthropology from Edinburgh University and in 1983 he completed his doctorate at Oxford University.

His research took him to the Peruvian Amazon, where he spent 18 months with the Harakmbut people. There, Andrew witnessed at first-hand the threat to his indigenous friends from invading gold miners. The experience turned him from an academic researcher into an indigenous human rights activist and campaigner.

From 1983 to 1989 Andrew was co-director of IWGIA's international secretariat in Copenhagen. From the very first day of his employment, Andrew Gray mobilized his outstanding intellectual resources, enormous capacity and personal commitment to work in promoting the recognition of indigenous peoples' rights.

His contribution to the understanding and promotion of indigenous issues spans the whole spectrum of topics, ranging from indigenous rights, self-determination and self-government to biodiversity and other environmental concerns. He was a hard working and prolific writer who managed to put into print his own thoughts, as well as those of the many indigenous people who put their trust in him.

With Andrew Gray IWGIA strengthened its position as the leading centre for documenting indigenous peoples' rights. Andrew Gray left IWGIA's staff in 1988 but maintained a close working relationship and became the organisation's vice-chairman in 1998.

With his death IWGIA lost a dear friend with a great sense of humour and a vigorous colleague in its work to promote indigenous peoples' rights.

It is the responsibility of each organisation to seek funding for the Fund's activities. The main donors have been the Danish, Norwegian and Dutch governments but important contributions have also been made by churches and a few private foundations.

The Human Rights Fund was the first of its kind, and people within the United Nations took note of and recognised the key role played by the Fund in ensuring that indigenous peoples were able to play an active role in the WGIP. When the UN established its own fund a few years later, the UN Voluntary Fund for Indigenous Peoples, the Human Rights Fund established an excellent working relationship with this body and with the World Council of Churches, which also ran a small participation fund, in order to coordinate funding.

Projects

Given the strategic and financial significance of projects to IWGIA's work, this process within the organisation must be dealt with in some detail, while leaving a discussion on its more fundamental aspects to a later chapter.

IWGIA's active involvement in empowerment projects began in the mid-1980s and signified an important change in policy as well as in strategy. Right from the early years of IWGIA's existence, funds had been raised for small-scale projects and activities initiated and implemented by indigenous peoples such as meetings, publications, campaigning, legal aid etc. Some activities were supported with IWGIA donations but, from 1972 on, when IWGIA received its first financial contribution from Norad, part of this funding was earmarked for project activities.

At a very early stage, IWGIA emphasised the priority of indigenous self-organisation and self-development. This was most often in opposition to government policy, and indigenous peoples still lacked the experience to take on the task.

In the 1980s, however, more and more indigenous peoples started to become aware of the options available to them in the form of so-called "development projects" funded by European and North American development agencies and NGOs. One of the first development agencies to establish a programme that specifically focused on indigenous peoples was Norad. The issue of support to indigenous organisations in South and Central America was discussed by IWGIA and Norad in 1977 and subsequently. Besides the initial political problems, it was obvious that Norad had administrative difficulties with handling direct project support to indigenous organisations. Most of these projects were small and administratively burdensome, and Norad often lacked knowledge of the organisations in question. Given this situation, Norad asked IWGIA to find a model by which projects could be channelled through IWGIA to Norad. One of IWGIA's concerns was to enter "into a situation of paternalistic relations [with] those Indian organisations that we want to support in their efforts for self-organisation

Land Titling, Peru - Photo: Alejandro Parellada

and self-determination".[84] Following some problems with Norad's funding of CISA, a new system was therefore established whereby IWGIA would become a consulting agency for Norad, screening the projects before they were approved for funding by Norad. The agreement with Norad was negotiated in co-operation with the Nordic Sámi Council, which did not at that time have the personnel to do it.[85] Within Norad, a desk officer was employed to handle the Indigenous Latin American programme.

Prior to 1987, projects received by IWGIA had simply been forwarded to Norad but the new situation meant that indigenous organisations could send their proposals directly to Norad. "Yet, in order to be able to process the applications in a defensible way, NORAD still requested the assistance of IWGIA."[86]

The contract (1987-90) between Norad and IWGIA therefore stipulated that IWGIA would use its expertise on South and Central America to review and advise on development projects sent to Norad by indigenous groups either directly or through IWGIA.[87] In the event that Norad lacked specific information, the projects sent to Norad would be forwarded to IWGIA. This ensured the smooth running of the project and IWGIA helped the projects and indigenous organisations by providing constructive suggestions as to how the project could work. IWGIA's role was that of a consultant and, sometimes, an intermediary but the organisation did not have any responsibility for the final approval, which remained solely with Norad.[88]

INITIAL APPROACH TO GOVERNMENTS

In early 1982, Joji Cariño and Geoff Nettleton (an activist and an anthropologist from the Philippines) were invited to visit IWGIA and talk about the opposition of the Cordillera peoples (Philippines) to the Chico Dam Project.

IWGIA organised a number of meetings for them in Copenhagen, including a visit to the Ministry of Foreign Affairs. Twenty-five years on, they still recall the meeting that made the most impression on them, to the extent that they still remember "the attitude on the faces of the people from the Ministry":

"This type of meeting was something completely new for us. We gave them a briefing on the Chico Dam issue. They wrote down and were interested to know what happened in the Philippines. They quickly raised the issue of what sort of support or funding they might be able to provide. Their attitude was that we had to come to terms with the realities and that maybe there was some way that they could use aid to lessen the problem.

We expected the briefing, but we were completely unprepared for the issue of funding and to be honest it was also a sign of our naivety. We were used to informing politicians about the issue but were completely unprepared for the next step: what do you want us to do? Something completely unthinkable in the Philippines. From the meeting in Copenhagen we learned that we needed to have a longer agenda. We told the people in the Ministry that we wanted the World Bank to stop funding the project. They responded by saying that if the dam and the resettlement project could not be stopped how could they address the issue? They asked if they could support the resettlement. But we said no and made it clear that the affected communities did not accept the dams and did not want resettlement at all.

After the meeting we realised that we did not have the organisational capacity to optimise on the possibilities given to us. But the meeting was a very important start for us and it gave us an insight into the social-democratic atmosphere in Scandinavia."

> It should be noted that the resistance was successful and the dams were never built, as announced in 1987 by the new government following the fall of the Marcos regime.
>
> (from interview with Joji Cariño and Geoff Nettleton)
>
>> Note: In June 1982, IWGIA approached the Minister of Foreign Affairs, Keld Olesen, for support for the establishment of a Nicaragua Commission. The application was turned down because of its political nature and because the government had already supported Danish Church Aid in the resettlement of 10,000 Miskitu (Helge Kleivan's archive).

Alongside this, the secretariat had taken another initiative that was to have a long-lasting impact on IWGIA's activities: for the first time, the secretariat had managed to obtain funding from Danida for a large land titling project in Peru. The initiative to involve IWGIA in land titling in Ucayali, in the Peruvian Amazon, had been taken by Søren Hvalkof, a Danish anthropologist with previous experience of this kind of activity in another part of the Amazon, Gran Pajonal. With slavery still common in Ucayali and a very active Shining Path guerrilla movement in the region, the situation was critical but it had, nevertheless, proved possible to establish a working relationship with the Peruvian authorities, i.e. the Ministry of Agriculture.

Land titling and demarcation of communal lands was different from "traditional" development projects and was seen as a precondition for maintaining or achieving land rights and human rights. Discussions had already started with the Peruvian organisation AIDESEP (*Asociación Interétnica de Desarollo de la Selva Peruana*) in 1988 and were followed by discussions between Søren Hvalkof, IWGIA and Danida. Danida's final approval came in August 1989: for the first time, DANDIA agreed to support indigenous peoples directly.

IWGIA's Board had, in general, been reluctant to let the organisation take responsibility for direct support to indigenous projects but also accepted that this might have to become necessary.[89] The Board, however, was divided on the issue. Some members feared that the focus of IWGIA's work would change from information and documentation to project work and that this would affect the relationship with indigenous peoples. Others, including the secretariat, felt that the initiative was coming from indigenous peoples themselves, who were asking IWGIA to raise funds for projects that might help them gain control over their own future. In retrospect, both viewpoints contained elements of truth. Since the late 1980s and early 1990s, it has always been easier to obtain funding for development projects than for publications, advocacy or human rights initiatives. Later experiences have also shown that the fear of creating conflict with indigenous organisations was exaggerated: only very rarely has it been a matter of choosing directly between competing indigenous organisations. On the contrary, project support has actually strengthened IWGIA's relationship with indigenous organisations.

However, it was the precise combination of these two seemingly opposing viewpoints that was to revolutionise IWGIA's strategy on indigenous issues, probably resulting in the most important development in IWGIA's work throughout the whole 1990s to this day - increased project support actually led to increased publication and documentation activities. This situation was epitomised by the "South-South Strategy" proposed to Norad in 1988 as the "South-South Communication Programme". Funding was first received in 1989. A few years later, in 1993, a similar programme was funded by Danida.

Government funding

IWGIA's earliest government funding came from the Norwegian and Danish Ministries of Foreign Affairs. Throughout the 1980s, this was supplemented by support from the two development agencies, Norad and Danida. Support from the Ministries of Foreign Affairs was core funding, while the development agencies gave earmarked funding to projects. In order to be able to determine its own priorities and continue to work on human rights, documentation and publications, IWGIA had a firm policy that core funding was a pre-condition for any commitment to earmarked project support.

For most of the 1980s, IWGIA applied to the Nordic development agencies for support for individual projects but the first discussion for a framework agreement with Norad took place at the end of the decade. The South-South Programme was part of this discussion. A few years later, a similar discussion took place with Danida although when the agency offered IWGIA an annual project programme, IWGIA refused to accept this without core funding. This created some annoyance amongst the Danida negotiators at first but, eventually, it paved the way for a partnership based on mutual understanding and cooperation. When framework agreements were entered into with Denmark and Norway in the 1990s, these included core funding, project funding and support for human rights activities, publications and networking.

In the 1990s, Sweden became an important and steady donor of IWGIA's human rights programme. Like the framework agreements with Norway and Denmark, 2-3 year programmes were funded, increasing IWGIA's possibility of long-term planning. The annual grants from Sweden (Sida) for IWGIA's human rights activities were non-earmarked core funding. The Finnish government has also been a constant donor since the 1990s for various kinds of earmarked activities and IWGIA has received funding for relatively large projects from the European Union.

These agreements improved IWGIA's possibility of making an impact on government policies concerning indigenous issues, and also of adopting a pro-active policy in relation to indigenous peoples and indigenous issues. The increased human rights and project activities were linked and they played a dominant role in IWGIA's policies around the turn of the century.

A few remarks should be made regarding the European Commission's policy on indigenous peoples, which became more focused towards the end of the century. The issue was taken up within the EU in close cooperation with the Danish Ministry of Foreign Affairs, other member states such as the Netherlands, Spain and Germany (Feiring 1997/98:379), a few key individuals within the Commission and IWGIA, along with a few other European NGOs, including the Sámi Council. The result was the adoption of a Ministerial Council resolution in June 1997 inviting the Commission to present a policy paper on cooperation with, and support for, indigenous peoples. The working document[90] became a focal point for the Commission (funded by Denmark) and this has been key in focusing attention on indigenous peoples within the Commission. Increased momentum was gained during the Danish presidency in the second half of 2002.

In 1994, IWGIA adopted a strategy paper entitled "IWGIA and indigenous peoples" (IWGIA 1994). This strategy paper had the clear purpose of making a direct impact on development agencies and establishing IWGIA as an involved partner. When the strategy was adopted, we knew that Danida was in the process of establishing a policy on its future support to indigenous peoples and we hoped to make an impact on this process. Although we were aware of the mood in Danida in favour of giving direct support to indigenous peoples, and to human rights initiatives supporting indigenous peoples, none of us at that time expected that we would have the impact that we did. The "Strategy for Danish Support to Indigenous Peoples" contained most of the important issues, viewpoints and ambitions contained in IWGIA's strategy paper, adopted just a few months earlier. One interpretation is that IWGIA's project activities were instrumental in creating interest within Danida for indigenous issues in general.

Whatever the explanation, the result was the start of a synergetic period of effort between IWGIA and Danida and also, to some extent, Norad and the European Commission, where IWGIA had initiated a working relationship with other European organisations.

But even more important than this was that the new government policy was a product of, and linked to, a Greenlandic political initiative.

The International Year, the Decade and the Danish policy

A new breakthrough in IWGIA's policy came in 1993-4. 1992 had been the year of the global environment meeting in Rio de Janeiro and Rigoberta Menchú Tum had received the Nobel Peace Prize. 1993 was the International Year of the World's Indigenous Peoples and there were expectations that a Decade would be established and indigenous peoples and issues would come to the fore. In Greenland, the Home Rule Parliament had initiated a new era whereby foreign policy would become part of its dealings. One of the Greenlandic members of the Danish Parliament, Hans Pavia Rosing (former president of the Inuit Circumpolar Conference), decided to take up the issue of Danish support for indigenous peoples. In the parliament, he was affiliated to the Danish Social Democratic Party that headed the minority government. As a supporter of the government, he deemed that the time was ripe for him to garner support for active Danish support of indigenous peoples. He gathered around him a small group, including IWGIA, to discuss the issue and the strategy to be adopted. The method chosen was to raise a question in Parliament and follow this up with the adoption of a motion. This took place on November 23, 1993.

Hans Pavia Rosing had done his homework, and the result was a rare unanimous motion in support of the establishment of a permanent forum for indigenous peoples, the adoption of a UN declaration, the ratification of ILO Convention No. 169, the proclamation of a Decade and the presentation of a general strategy for increased, effective Danish assistance to the world's indigenous peoples.[91] With the unanimous decision from the parliament floor, the government not only had to act but also had a unique mandate for taking a radical approach.

It was against this backdrop that IWGIA established a small internal working group to draft a strategy that could have an impact on the policy to be adopted by the Ministry of Foreign Affairs. There were no desk officers in the Ministry with indigenous peoples as part of their portfolio but there were obviously people in the Ministry that were interested in taking up the issue, which had now become topical given the parliament's unanimous vote.

The working relationship between the Ministry, Greenland Home Rule, the Inuit Circumpolar Conference and IWGIA was further developed during the 1990s and into the new century, and consultative meetings were arranged in preparation for major international events.

Ole Henrik Magga, Sámi from Norway and first Chairperson of the UNPFII together with Kofi Annan
Photo: Magne Ove Varsi, Gáldu www.galdu.org

Victoria Tauli-Corpuz, Igorot from the Philippines and second chairperson of the UNPFII, and Ole Henrik Magga
Photo: Magne Ove Varsi, Gáldu www.galdu.org

CHAPTER 5

THE PRO-ACTIVE PERIOD

The late 1980s and early 1990s marked the end of the Cold War. The Soviet Union and Yugoslavia broke up, followed by the outbreak of a number of ethnic and regional conflicts. At the same time, new democracies were established in Latin America and processes towards democratisation were taking place in Asia and in Eastern Europe. From a world perspective, the number of violent conflicts dropped after 1994, although the establishment of new democracies precipitated an increase in the number of non-violent ethnic protests (Gurr 2000:34ff). Indigenous peoples were also able to use the new opportunities to claim their rights under the new democratic regimes: in Latin America, in Russia and in Asia, in countries such as the Philippines and Indonesia.

These developments had an impact on the international indigenous movement and, in an indirect sense, changed the pattern of cooperation between indigenous organisations and NGOs such as IWGIA.

In Geneva, the WGIP and the Commission on Human Rights (CHR) passed the Draft Declaration on the Rights of Indigenous Peoples. The first UN Decade on the World's Indigenous People (1995-2004) was established and the early initiatives for establishing a permanent forum were underway. Indigenous peoples globally were no longer merely in a situation whereby they constantly had to accuse or appeal to governments: they had now established their own positions on the international human rights agenda. In order to take advantage of the political changes, indigenous peoples in many countries had to find new ways of dealing with states. To some extent, indigenous peoples had become partners - in spite of the fact that serious violations of human rights were still taking place in many parts of the world. In Europe and North America, the aim of indigenous peoples was no longer to remain separate from the national society (Stern 2006) but to develop land claims agreements and self-government arrangements by which they could develop new relationships with the mainstream society, albeit on new terms and conditions.

This new context demanded that indigenous peoples revise their human rights strategies, including adopting new positions regarding cooperation and alliances in order to utilize the new opportunities. Not all indigenous peoples and organisations were ready for this and, to this day, this has remained the foremost point of controversy between indigenous peoples in international settings. Some indigenous organisations entered into new partnerships with non-indigenous organisations, including state and non-state development agencies, in order to take full advantage of new democratic and human rights agendas. Others had so little trust in governments that platforms for negotiations could not be established. These differences gave rise to conflicts – and continue to do so - at regular intervals in international settings between hard-line viewpoints and those who seek compromises and agreements with governments.

For non-indigenous organisations such as IWGIA, these changes first became apparent when we were confronted by an increased need for project support on the part of indigenous peoples that often presupposed some kind of governmental support. This new situation demanded, in turn, that IWGIA re-examine its approach regarding a pro-active strategy on indigenous issues. This had often been discussed within the organisation and with other NGOs but it would appear that the circumstances for a change in strategy were not in place until the mid-1990s.

The most important steps taken in the 1990s were to promote dialogue with governments wherever possible and to put pressure on donor governments to support indigenous empowerment initiatives and promote confidence building. The titles of IWGIA's Documents reveal the change: Documents 49-60 (1983-87) all carry the name of a country such as "Australia", "Peru", "Venezuela", etc. and the content deals with human rights violations taking place with government connivance. In the 1990s, Documents appear on "Indigenous Peoples' Experiences with Self-Government", "Saami – Parliamentary Cooperation", etc.

IWGIA supports indigenous peoples' right of self-determination as a matter of policy. IWGIA does not focus on specific regions or groups and has always tried to maintain a balance of non-interference in indigenous matters. IWGIA has always stressed that the points of view expressed in its publications are those of the author and not necessarily shared by IWGIA. Only in a very few cases has IWGIA's editor had to make an author aware that IWGIA would not print an article containing an attack by one indigenous organisation on another. Only in one case did the editor feel it necessary to include an editorial comment at the end of the article distancing IWGIA from part of the content.[92]

From this policy of non-interference, the practice developed of never taking the floor in international settings such as the United Nations but instead giving credentials and speaking time to indigenous peoples to speak for themselves. When this developed into a clear policy, it gained much respect among indigenous peoples as it did not take speaking time in the UN away from them. It also distinguished IWGIA from most other non-indigenous NGOs. This position of non-interference also helped IWGIA not to become involved in internal indigenous matters when indigenous peoples disagreed on strategies and principles in relation to, for example, the drafting of ILO Convention No. 169 or the Dec-

INDIGENOUS PLATFORMS FOR NEGOTIATION

During the last day of the Permanent Forum meeting in 2008 a group of mainly Latin American indigenous peoples seized the microphone and addressed the meeting by force. Reflecting on this episode the Permanent Forum Chair, Victoria Tauli-Corpuz wrote:

"Reflecting on this, I thought maybe it was a good thing it happened so it gave us an opportunity to discuss about the REDD [Reducing Emissions from Deforestation and ecosystem Degradation] issue and to show that within the Forum we did go through an extensive discussion on it. At least it gave a picture of how the Forum is dealing with issues brought before their attention. It also showed how some campaigners are almost at the verge of fundamentalism, refusing to see and understand other views and what the Forum has reached in terms of been done and just sticking with their own line of "no to the market and no to carbon trading as this is carbon colonialism". I agree with their point that emissions trading is one way of passing on the burden of decreasing greenhouse gas emissions to the developing countries, to the indigenous peoples and to the poor. And of course, the best way to cut back greenhouse gas emissions is by changing lifestyles and production and consumption patterns of the rich world. But having said this, we cannot also just say, therefore, emissions trading should be stopped. The rich countries have to meet their targets to cut back on their emissions they cannot change overnight the system which has brought this about. I think what needs to be said and I said this in the paper we prepared for the Forum, is that rich countries should not just rely on emissions trading to cut back their GHG emissions. This should be just one way and the other more sustainable ways such as changing their production and consumption patterns should be their focus.

There needs to be more discussions among indigenous peoples about the market. It is not as if we are against the market per se, because we do market our products in our own communities and some indigenous peoples are also exporting some of their products in the global market, like the exports of sealskin by the Inuit for example. This is why the Inuit are so upset with the environmentalists who stopped their marketing of sealskin. We are against a market which is dominated by a few giant corporations and which are basi-

> cally promoting monopoly capitalism. But we are for a market which promotes exchange of our products and services and which gives premium to small-scale producers and artisans. Sometimes this is called petty capitalism."
>
> (May 2008)

laration. IWGIA, at that time, took the decision always to support the most radical position.

This policy or position appeared to be well-founded and fairly unproblematic until the adoption of the Draft Declaration by the Working Group on Indigenous Populations, and support from development agencies to indigenous peoples became a prime resource for indigenous organisations in Africa, Asia, Russia and the Americas. At this point, in the 1990s, IWGIA made a *de facto* policy change as significant as the one it had made in the mid-1970s when it entered into direct working relationships with indigenous organisations.

It was a gradual process. One of the first people to challenge IWGIA's policy of non-interference was the human rights lawyer, Howard Berman, and, in 1993, IWGIA's Board seriously deliberated on whether the time had finally come to make statements at the UN during the discussions on the Draft Declaration.

The Permanent Forum process

The first serious challenge to IWGIA's policy of non-interference came with the discussion on the possible establishment of a forum for indigenous peoples. Although the idea came from indigenous peoples themselves, there were other indigenous peoples who raised concerns that such a forum might compete with, and endanger the future of, the Working Group on Indigenous Populations, which at that time was still *the* meeting place for indigenous peoples.

The idea of establishing a permanent forum was first suggested during the 1993 World Conference on Human Rights, held in Vienna. This meeting recommended that the UN General Assembly consider establishing such a forum, and this recommendation was supported by the Commission on Human Rights and the WGIP in 1994. In 1998, the Commission on Human Rights established its own working group to deal with the permanent forum issue–the so-called "Open-ended Inter-Sessional Ad-Hoc Working Group to Elaborate and Consider Further Proposals for the Possible Establishment of a Permanent Forum", which held its first meeting that same year.

THE PROCESS FOR THE ESTABLISHMENT OF THE PERMANENT FORUM

1995, June	The first expert meeting on the possible establishment of a permanent forum, Copenhagen.
1977, May	The First International Indigenous Conference for the establishment of a permanent forum, Temuco, Chile.
1977, June-July	Second expert meeting on the possible establishment of a permanent forum, Santiago, Chile (which one)
1998, March	The Second International Indigenous Conference for the establishment of a permanent forum, Kuna Yala, Panama.
1998, Sept.	First Asian Indigenous workshop on the establishment of a permanent forum, Indore, India.
1999, Jan.	African Indigenous workshop on the establishment of a permanent forum, Arusha, Tanzania.
1999, Feb.	The first UN meeting of the Ad Hoc Working Group on the establishment of the Permanent Forum, Geneva.
2000, Jan. 7-8	The indigenous Copenhagen meeting on the Permanent Forum. 'The Copenhagen paper'
2000, Jan.	Asian indigenous regional workshop on the establishment of a permanent forum, Chiang Mai, Thailand.
2000, Feb.	Second meeting of the UN Ad Hoc Working Group on the establishment of the Permanent Forum, Geneva.
2000, April	The Commission on Human Rights vote for the establishment of the Permanent Forum on Indigenous Issues.
2000, July	Ecosoc decide to establish the Permanent Forum on Indigenous Issues.
2000, Oct.	Second Indigenous Copenhagen meeting on the Permanent Forum.
2002, May	First meeting of the Permanent Forum on Indigenous Issues, New York.

The UN Permanent Forum on Indigenous Issues, 2009 – Photo: Miguel Ibanez Sanchez

The first practical step towards the process of establishing such a forum had, however, already been taken in June 1995 when the Danish government hosted a workshop in Copenhagen. The next step was to review existing UN mechanisms dealing with indigenous issues. This was followed by a second meeting of experts held in Santiago (Chile) in June-July 1997(García-Alix 1999b) and indigenous regional meetings in Temuco (Chile), Kuna Yala (Panama), Indore (India), Arusha (Tanzania) (García-Alix 2003:60) and Chiang Mai (Thailand) shortly before the second meeting of the Permanent Forum working group as established by the Commission on Human Rights. For IWGIA, the idea of organising a series of regional indigenous meetings on the establishment of a permanent forum emerged from conversations held with indigenous representatives during the 1996 WGIP meeting in Geneva. The subject was also discussed at a meeting between Danida, IWGIA and indigenous representatives.[93] The first meetings were organised by local or regional indigenous organisations and, to a large extent, funded by IWGIA. The purpose of these meetings was to provide information on the UN process, to give indigenous organisations a chance to discuss the process, and to allow local and regional organisations to provide input on such issues as the structure of the forum, the appointment of delegates etc., thereby giving legitimacy to the process.[94]

These indigenous regional meetings initiated a totally novel approach to UN processes. Indeed, they brought the international human rights processes from Geneva to the regions, and they became the first opportunity for indigenous peoples to prepare for the Geneva meetings. Before this, the WGIP had had its own history, only linked to indigenous communities by the annual statements made by the indigenous participants. Great efforts were now made by some indigenous peoples to establish a forum in which indigenous peoples would be represented by their own delegates. The most important result of these meetings was possibly the creation of indigenous regional networks, and a process that could be used by indigenous peoples in future endeavours.

When meeting in Geneva, there were indigenous peoples - as well as non-indigenous people - who were very sceptical of the idea of a permanent forum, not least some of the indigenous Americans. Some of the most critical voices came from Alfonso Martínez, a member of the WGIP, and Treaty Indians who were very close to IWGIA. This put IWGIA in a dilemma and, for some time, it chose to endorse the idea of a forum but in a cautious way that allowed for reassessment. On the other hand there were indigenous organisations close to IWGIA too that worked hard to have a permanent forum established. The idea received the whole-hearted support of the Danish government, which also endorsed having a separate item on indigenous peoples on the agenda of the Commission on Human Rights. This may have made an impression on IWGIA (and indigenous organisations) and, in some ways, these developments contributed to IWGIA changing its position on a permanent forum from one of lukewarm support to being a prime mover behind its creation.

The first meeting of the Permanent Forum ad-hoc working group under the Commission on Human Rights was held in 1999 and the second and final meeting in February 2000. Shortly before the second meeting of the Permanent Forum Ad-Hoc Working Group, and in co-operation with the Inuit Circumpolar Conference, IWGIA hosted a seminar in Copenhagen, from January 7-8, to prepare indigenous representatives for the working group meeting.[95] The idea for convening such a seminar followed a discussion between IWGIA and the Sámi Council during a meeting in Geneva in 1999. The lesson learned from the process of drafting the Declaration was that indigenous peoples would have increased opportunities for making a constructive impact on the process if the pros and cons of key issues were analysed prior to the meeting. It was clear that it was absolutely necessary for indigenous peoples to be prepared before the second meeting of the ad-hoc working group, and for them to have considered options and strategies. This formed the background to the meeting in Copenhagen, which was a completely new way of working for IWGIA.

A study prepared by the Asian Indigenous and Tribal Peoples Network entitled "The possible positions of the indigenous peoples" (AITPN 1999) was prepared for the Copenhagen meeting. The meeting resulted in concrete recommendations for establishing the Permanent Forum. In February, the "Copenhagen paper" was presented to the indigenous caucus as a discussion paper and came to form the basis for recommendations presented by the caucus to the ad hoc working group.[96] If we look at the suggestions in the Copenhagen caucus paper and compare them with the final result, it is clear that the process was successful. The paper made the options available for discussion for the caucus, thus facilitating a process whereby consensus could be reached. To raise awareness and increase knowledge of the process of creating a permanent body within the UN system, IWGIA published a handbook in English and Spanish (García-Alix 1999a) that was distributed widely among indigenous organisations and persons. It was entitled "The Permanent Forum on Indigenous *Peoples*".[97]

Confronting new dilemmas

The establishment of the Ad-Hoc Working Group by the Commission on Human Rights was to have a lasting – and positive – impact on the whole process and IWGIA came to play a key role in trying to mobilise indigenous peoples around the idea, ensuring their participation in the meetings. During this process, IWGIA entered into a close working relationship with some indigenous organisations – while other links became weaker. Enduring relationships developed with the Sámi Council, the Inuit Circumpolar Conference, Cordillera Peoples' Alliance and Tebtebba Foundation (both from the Philippines), PACOS from Malaysia, RAIPON (Russia) and a number of indigenous individuals from local indigenous organisations in Africa, Asia and Latin America. These closer links became extremely important during the process of drafting a Declaration in the working group on the Draft Declaration under the Commission on Human Rights. At the same time, IWGIA also maintained close links with the Danish government, which was the main mover among governments in the process. However, it also created a number of new dilemmas for IWGIA.

IWGIA had supported indigenous participation in UN meetings through the Human Rights Fund for Indigenous Peoples since 1984. The criteria for supporting indigenous participants included ensuring a regional balance, priority for indigenous women, and for people with links to indigenous organisations etc (see later chapter). People were not supported for representing specific viewpoints. However, the Fund was now being used to bring indigenous peoples to the inter-sessional meetings on the Permanent Forum, and it was mainly being used for people who were positive towards the idea. Indigenous peoples took note when IWGIA (in addition to the Human Rights Fund) also started to directly support indigenous persons that it deemed could make a positive impact on the process. IWGIA had taken sides – and become an active player! Indigenous peoples, however, were fully aware of the dangers of becoming dependent on funding from NGOs such as IWGIA, and when Asian indigenous peoples discussed the issue of appointing members of the Forum, they opposed the idea that this should take place within the indigenous caucus because the composition of the caucus depended on funding from Northern donors.[98]

Another dilemma was caused by IWGIA's close working relationship with the Danish government. It began with the Danish Policy in Support of Indigenous Peoples, published in 1994, which was followed by an active Danish policy in the same vein within the EU and, subsequently, Denmark's active policy within the UN. IWGIA's close relationship with the Danish government was viewed with scepticism by some indigenous peoples who were still distrustful of governments. IWGIA *had* established a permanent dialogue with, among others, the Danish government and the results were visible when the Permanent Forum was established. In the same period, the Danish government had markedly expanded its support for indigenous projects through its development agency, Danida. In cooperation with indigenous organisations, IWGIA had a significant impact on these developments, which only brought about a third dilemma when IWGIA's policy of non-interference was challenged.

IWGIA's policy of non-intervention in conflicts between indigenous peoples had initially been well-founded. But at a time when the United Nations and other international bodies and institutions were drafting instruments with a tendency towards regulating the rights and relationships between indigenous peoples, governments and multinational agencies, this policy, although still to this date preferred by many indigenous peoples, was no longer in harmony with the reality. As clearly expressed by two indigenous leaders, the United Nations is *not* the indigenous peoples' arena and it is not a place for indigenous politics but for negotiations with and among governments. In this context, for IWGIA to take a stance on an issue was not to intervene in internal indigenous matters although some indigenous peoples might try to present it in this way. When IWGIA has been criticized in such matters it is because it has made a difference![99]

The establishment of the Permanent Forum

In April 2000, the Commission on Human Rights voted in favour of a "Permanent Forum on Indigenous Issues" and ECOSOC endorsed the proposal at its July meeting. There still remained a number of unanswered questions, such as the location of the secretariat, the establishment of electoral regions and the process of appointing indigenous representatives. In order to ensure an indigenous consensus in the final process prior to adopting a resolution in the General Assembly, ICC and IWGIA again convened a meeting in Copenhagen in October of that year. This meeting took place in the Greenland Home Rule office.[100]

The significance of these meetings, in general, and for IWGIA in particular, should not be underestimated and nor should the problems associated with such a process. Not everyone can be represented at such a meeting although the ICC and the Sámi Council, in cooperation with IWGIA and others, were careful to try to invite as wide a range of people as possible, both geographically and from indigenous peoples with different backgrounds. But, naturally, those opposed to the establishment of the Permanent Forum were not invited. In actual fact, this did not give rise to very many problems when the recommendations from the Copenhagen meeting in January were presented to the caucus in February 2000.

Once indigenous peoples had agreed on a regional division for the nomination of indigenous experts to the Permanent Forum, regional consultation processes took place in Asia, Central America, South America, Russia, the Pacific and the Arctic, with active support from IWGIA. These consultations were often arduous and, in some cases, a source of controversy, but it was nevertheless the start of a process that focussed on uniting indigenous peoples within regions. It gave new life to the global indigenous caucus, which came to have a tremendous impact on the process of drafting the Declaration.

Given IWGIA's active involvement in the preparatory process for establishing the Permanent Forum, it was logical that – for the first time - the organisation should make a presentation at the opening of the first meeting in New York in May 2002. IWGIA thus made both a general statement and a statement on the African Commission on Human and Peoples' Rights under the Human Rights agenda.

IWGIA and the Draft Declaration process

During the 2002 meeting of the Working Group on the Draft Declaration (WGDD), the gap between indigenous peoples who insisted on a "no change" position and those that considered this position to be no longer realistic became wider (Åhrén 2007). The "no change" people did not see that they could compromise on the text adopted by the WGIP and the Sub-Commission and, by and large, they refused to negotiate any amendments to the text. In 2000, the Sámi Council and the Inuit Circumpolar Conference (ICC) had declared that they would be open to certain amendments (ibid.). An increasing number of indigenous organisations, led by the Sámi Council, Tebtebba and the ICC, were now of the view that the "no change" position was no longer tenable. This led to serious splits in the indigenous caucus that met during the drafting meetings. It was at this point that IWGIA made one of the most significant turnarounds in the recent history of the organisation, supporting those who were in favour of negotiating the text.

This decision was based on the experience of the Permanent Forum process, which in IWGIA's analysis clearly revealed that some kind of preparatory work had to be done by smaller groups of people between meetings in Geneva in order to create a consensus and reach a conclusion. Together with indigenous partners, IWGIA therefore decided to support an indigenous-initiated process that would lead to agreement between like-minded indigenous organisations and create a new momentum in Geneva. It was IWGIA's opinion that the process had come to a point where it was no longer possible to uncompromisingly reject any changes to the text as adopted by the WGIP. With this in mind, IWGIA convened a meeting in Copenhagen in May 2003 together with the ICC, the American Indian Law Alliance from the U.S., the Sámi Council, the Tebtebba Foundation and *Consejo de Todos de las Tierras*, a Mapuche organisation from Chile.

The indigenous conveners invited around 15 indigenous people from all continents. Most were funded through IWGIA's human rights programme. The meeting was open to those who agreed to the agenda and, in all, approximately 25 indigenous and non-indigenous participants attended.[101] The concluding document from the meeting[102] was widely circulated afterwards, and it was earmarked for discussion during the Permanent Forum meeting later that same month. In New York, however, the Chair of the indigenous caucus was a firm "no-change" supporter and he took the unprecedented step of refusing to discuss the Copenhagen paper.[103]

IWGIA was not openly attacked in the indigenous caucus although severely criticized by "no-change" supporters for having excluded them from the meeting in Copenhagen. During the remainder of the process for the final adoption of the Declaration, IWGIA (and the Human Rights Fund) became a firm supporter of the informal core group (usually called the "Copenhagen Initiative") that met several times over the ensuing years. After a meeting in Montreal in August 2006, the loose group now became known as the "Montreal Group" while the process was generally known as the "Copenhagen process". Ultimately, this group of likeminded indigenous organisations was able to give the process the momentum that was needed to achieve a result.

During the whole process, indigenous peoples unanimously agreed on a no-change position to the Draft Declaration with regard to a few key points such as self-determination, rights to land and free, prior and informed consent relating to development issues. To make sure that these key articles remained intact, compromises had to be made on other paragraphs. The innovation of the indigenous organisations within the informal group that initiated the Copenhagen process was that they realised that the indigenous caucus needed to break up into regional caucuses and meet between the Geneva meetings. Without this, it would have been difficult for the indigenous caucus to establish itself in New York in early 2007 with a permanent representation until the adoption of the Declaration.[104]

SELECTED DATES FROM THE DECLARATION PROCESS

2002, Dec.	8th Session of the UN Working Group on the Draft Declaration.
2003, May	Copenhagen meeting on the Draft Declaration.
2003, May	The indigenous caucus refuse to discuss the Copenhagen paper.
2003, Sept.	9th Session of the UN Working Group on the Draft Declaration.
2004, Sept.	10th Session of the UN Working Group on the Draft Declaration.
2004, Nov.- Dec.	Extended meeting of the 10th Session of the UN Working Group on the Draft Declaration. Final report.
2005, Aug.	Indigenous strategy meeting, Montreal.
2005-6, Dec.-Feb.	Extended meeting of the final session of the UN Working Group on the Draft Declaration. The Chair's paper.
2006	The UN Commission on Human Rights adopts the Declaration.
2006, Sept.	Informal meeting, Pazcuaro, Mexico.
2006, Dec.	The UN General Assembly defers the adoption of the Draft Declaration.
2006, Dec.	Indigenous peoples appoints regional delegates and a global steering group located in New York.
2007, Sept. 13	The UN General Assembly adopts the final text for a Declaration.

IWGIA and the African Commission on Human and Peoples' Rights

In 1994, IWGIA acquired NGO observer status to the African Commission on Human and Peoples' Rights (African Commission). The chance to use this position in a strategic manner came in the wake of a conference on "Indigenous Peoples of Eastern, Central and Southern Africa", organised in Arusha, Tanzania, in January 1999 by IWGIA and Pingo's Forum, an indigenous umbrella organisation based in Arusha. Among the more than 80 participants were representatives from over 30 organisations from eight African countries, observers, NGOs and government representatives from Tanzania. From our perspective, the most important factor was the participation of Nyameko Barney Pityana, a South African member of the African Commission, and Chairperson of the South African Human Rights Commission.

At that time, Barney Pityana was probably the only member of the African Commission interested in indigenous issues – and he was willing to bring the issue to the Commission. Besides his sincere concern for human rights issues, he had gained an overall knowledge of indigenous issues as a refugee in Switzerland and in his work for the World Council of Churches. This was when he also heard about IWGIA. He had a crystal-clear understanding of the controversy that could arise from dealing with indigenous peoples' issues in an African context. Even more important was his perception of the need to focus on indigenous groups separately from other marginalised and vulnerable groups in Africa, coupled with his political understanding of the work of the African Commission. In order to promote the issue in the African Commission, he stressed the essential role of NGOs such as IWGIA (Pityana 1999:49). This was a signal for IWGIA to start becoming active within the African Commission.

The Arusha conference had requested that the African Commission include an agenda item on the rights of indigenous peoples in Africa at all sessions of the Commission, and it recommended that all NGOs concerned about the rights of indigenous peoples in Africa seek observer status with the African Commission. Given these recommendations, Commissioner Pityana raised the issue of the situation of indigenous peoples in Africa during the 26th session of the African Commission, which took place in Kigali, Rwanda. This generated a very tough debate and considerable resistance from some of the other members of the Commission, although there were also a few who saw the need to focus on marginalised groups such as hunter-gatherers and pastoralists (IWGIA 2000).

At the recommendation of Pityana, IWGIA participated in an African Commission session for the first time at its 28th ordinary session in Benin in October 2000. During this session Pityana, the IWGIA representative and two Commissioners who were quite critical of the whole issue met and discussed the way forward. One outcome of this meeting was the proposal to establish a working group consisting of Commissioners, indigenous representatives and independent experts. When the agenda item came up at the open meeting, it was presented by Pityana but IWGIA was the only NGO to address the issue. Pityana had stressed that he needed support from organisations such as IWGIA and, during the closed session of the Commission, he raised the issue of establishing a working group and encouraged IWGIA to investigate the possibility of funding its work (ibid.).

Meeting during the African Commission on Human and People's Rights, Nigeria 2008 – Photo: Marianne Jensen

In the following years, IWGIA worked closely with Pityana, the Commission Chair Rezag Bara and Commission member Chigovera on the indigenous issue. Since October 2000, IWGIA has taken part in all the meetings and worked with indigenous organisations on a model adopted from its work with the United Nations. In the words of an outside observer:

From the outset, IWGIA worked at establishing a network of African-based indigenous groups, underscoring the simultaneous global and local dimensions of the international indigenous rights movement. In so far as it pushed its own agenda, it did so through and with local NGOs. This approach gave it legitimacy derived from being at least partially rooted in the concerns of indigenous Africans at the grassroots level. IWGIA provided financial and technical support to individuals and organizations in African countries to enable them to attend sessions. After regional representation had been assured, and realizing that the acceptance of indigenous peoples' issues depends on the articulation by African voices, IWGIA assisted NGOs working in this field to obtain observer status (Viljoen 2007:410-1).

The need for IWGIA's active involvement in moving the process forward was confirmed by one of the indigenous participants: "This was critical at a number of junctures where all hope for a quick adoption of the resolutions by the Commission was not in sight. The participation and facilitation of IWGIA brought both the moral challenge to the government and encouragement to indigenous peoples' leaders participating and their organisations."[105]

IWGIA's active participation as an independent expert member of the Working Group was an unusual move but nonetheless a deliberate one aimed at making the most of the exceptional opportunity that arose when the African Commission – for the first time ever – took the no less exceptional step to establish a working group that included non-Commission members. Another exception to IWGIA tradition was that, in the years that followed, IWGIA's representative took the floor to give statements at several meetings. IWGIA was urged to do so both by Commissioners and indigenous representatives, as they emphasised the importance of expressing support for indigenous issues.

At the 29th Ordinary Session of the African Commission in Libya in April 2001, five indigenous representatives were allowed to participate and to present a statement, though none of their organizations had observer status. This was rather extraordinary as the African Commission strictly observes the rule that participants from organizations without observer status are not allowed to speak in the sessions. Their participation encouraged the Commissioners to become interested in indigenous issues and, in this way, showed support for establishing a working group on indigenous issues.

The composition of the Working Group was decided upon prior to the 30th Session in The Gambia in October 2001 and consisted of three Commissioners, three indigenous expert members and a representative of IWGIA. The mandate of the working group was 1) to examine the concept of indigenous people and communities in Africa, 2) to study the implications of the African Charter on the Human Rights and well-being of indigenous communities, and 3) to consider appropriate recommendations for the monitoring and protection of the rights of indigenous communities.

The Working Group met for the first time during the 30th Session and decided that it should not start by focusing on defining the term "indigenous" as this could result in deadlock. It was decided that the definition discussion should be integrated into the forthcoming discussion and analysis of concrete issues (ibid.). Although there continued to be strong opposition among some of the Commissioners to applying the term indigenous in an African context, the issue had now been placed on the agenda and was there to stay at all forthcoming meetings.

It was agreed that the first task of the Working Group would be to develop a Conceptual Framework Paper, a draft of which was presented at a roundtable meeting prior to the 32nd ordinary meeting in Pretoria in May 2002. The fact that African indigenous peoples had participated and made statements to the Commission meetings and the discussions on the Working Group progress report revealed an important turnaround in the Commissioners' approach to the issue.

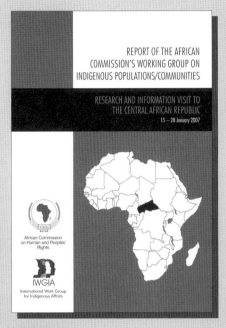
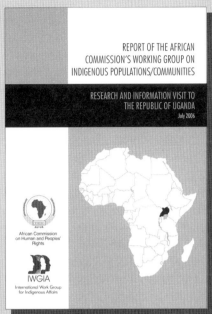
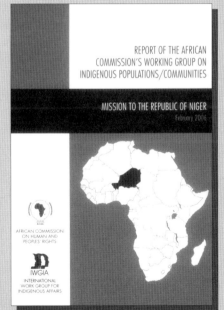
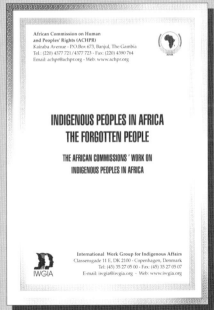

Co-publications of IWGIA and the African Commission on Human and Peoples' Rights

A major step was taken when the first three African NGOs working on indigenous issues were given observer status in May 2003. These organisations were: MPIDO (Mainyoito Pastoralist Integrated Development Organisation) and the NGOs CEMIRIDE (Centre for Minority Rights Development), both from Kenya, and IPACC (Indigenous Peoples of Africa Coordinating Committee), based in South Africa. This improved the status of indigenous issues within the African Commission considerably. From the very first moment of their involvement with the Commission in 2001, African indigenous peoples took a pro-active position towards the governments. The approach was very different to the one taken by indigenous peoples in the UN, where most efforts were made to make public statements on human rights violations. In the African Commission, the indigenous peoples made it their first aim to meet with their governments and lobby them to include indigenous issues in their reports and to establish a dialogue, where this was feasible, while the public statements were most often used to supplement this strategy. To this must be added the fact that the indigenous members in the Working Group and other indigenous representatives soon adopted a strategy of drafting counter-reports to the official government reports examined by the African Commission.

Following a larger consultative meeting in Nairobi in January 2003, the final "Report by the Working Group on Indigenous Populations/Communities" was presented to the African Commission in its spring meeting 2003 and adopted at the 34th session in November 2003. Once the report had been adopted by the General Assembly of States of the African Union, it became a high level and authoritative document, as well as a policy document of the African Commission. The report was published in English and French in 2005.

The resolution adopting the report gave a new mandate to the Working Group that included gathering information, undertaking country visits, formulating recommendations and submitting activity reports at all ordinary sessions of the ACHPR (IWGIA 2004b). Funding was requested from Danida through IWGIA and, when this was granted, IWGIA and the African Commission entered into a formal agreement on the respective responsibilities of the two parties. IWGIA was in charge of the overall funding from Danida, and this funding enabled the African Commission's Working Group to successfully carry out its mandate.

The process towards adopting the report, the establishment of the Working Group and the planning of its future work was a significant achievement not only for indigenous peoples but also for IWGIA. The discussion had moved beyond a discussion of terminology to focus on the real human rights issues as described in the report and elsewhere. It also appeared that the African Commission now recognized that it had an obligation to protect the rights of the most vulnerable groups within African states, such as minorities and indigenous peoples, and that it perceived the indigenous issue to be a genuine human rights issue falling under the mandate of the Commission and the Charter (IWGIA 2004b).

IWGIA's strategy had been vindicated. It was stated that, "Part of IWGIA's (and the Working Group's) success is its combination of solid research with activism. Appropriated by local NGOs at the national level, this report [as mentioned] became a tool for lobbying" (Viljoen 2007:411-2).

IWGIA's pro-active approach to the work of the African Commission and its direct participation in the official Working Group represented a significant change from its traditional policy when dealing with international human rights organisations such as the UN. Given the controversial nature of the issue, which remains the case in an African context, it was both an opportunity and a risk. But the close cooperation with key Commissioners and key indigenous peoples, and the support from people within Danida, for whom the issue of indigenous peoples in Africa was - and still is - quite controversial, ensured its success.

Within IWGIA, the discussions on its connection with the African Commission revolved around two primary issues. One was that this involvement implied a new pro-active and participatory policy, and every step was carefully discussed and coordinated with indigenous organisations. It was also stressed that IWGIA's facilitating role should ensure the prominence of African indigenous organisations rather than IWGIA's own involvement.

The other concern was the controversial and contested character of the indigenous issue in the African reality. The establishment of the Working Group promoted a non-confrontational dialogue, thus initiating a close working relationship between Commissioners, indigenous organisations and IWGIA.

Support was given to indigenous peoples who could produce shadow reports to the Commission and carry out follow-up activities at home, including distributing the African Commission reports, writing newspaper articles, producing radio programmes, etc. The result was a productive symbiosis between projects and human rights efforts on the part of the organisations that received financial support from IWGIA.

When, in 2006, African countries blocked the adoption of the Declaration on the Rights of Indigenous Peoples by the UN General Assembly, the African Commission played an active role in urging the African governments to change their position. This took the form of an Advisory Opinion adopted by the African Commission at is ordinary session in May 2007 (African Commission 2007a), along with further lobbying in New York. Such a step would have been completely out of the question a few years earlier, and bears witness to the results of the process initiated in 2000.

Following the adoption of the Declaration, the African Commission issued a communiqué in which it said:

The UN Declaration on the Rights of Indigenous Peoples is in line with the position and work of the African Commission on indigenous peoples' rights as expressed in the various reports, resolutions and legal opinions on the subject mat-

ter. The African Commission is confident that the Declaration will become a very valuable tool and a point of reference for the African Commission's efforts to ensure the promotion and protection of indigenous peoples' rights on the African continent (African Commission 2007b).

The achievements of the process have been spectacular. The Working Group now organises seminars for governments, civil society and journalists, and has so far carried out country visits to Namibia, Botswana, Niger, Uganda, Burundi, the Republic of Congo, the Central African Republic, Gabon and Libya. Within the Commission, indigenous issues are now always addressed when state reports are examined. The challenge ahead is to get the issue seriously considered by the African Union, the mother body of the Commission.

PART 2

THE PILLARS OF IWGIA

INTRODUCTION

First there was documentation. Then came the close cooperation with international and national indigenous organisations. Once the first indigenous organisations had found a breach in the walls of the United Nations, IWGIA started to be directly involved in human rights activities and, when the political climate made it possible, IWGIA became involved in project activities. IWGIA has always relied on information from anthropologists and others with knowledge of the situation of indigenous peoples and communities. For many years, there was some opposition on the Board to having the organisation directly involved in project activities, which, if nothing else, would require a great deal of travelling. When this attitude changed, networking became an important tool for the organisation in terms of providing new dynamic inputs for IWGIA's other activities.

(right) IWGIA's publications are widely distributed. Tanzania – Photo: Diana Vinding

CHAPTER 6

THE HOLISTIC APPROACH

Towards the end of the 1980s, IWGIA developed a strategy that combined the various activities so that those indigenous people who were supported to attend UN meetings often became project partners and *vice versa*; project partners were urged to write for the publications; networking was used to gain knowledge about project needs and for locating possible candidates for UN meetings and so on. This approach, which was unique among NGOs working with indigenous peoples, provided palpable synergistic benefits; inside the organisation it came to be known as IWGIA's holistic approach.

The philosophy behind the holistic approach is, simply put, that the opportunities and behaviour of indigenous people - just as with all other people – depend on many factors. The effect of IWGIA's holistic approach is that more of these factors are controlled by indigenous peoples themselves. This effect also strengthened IWGIA's own role when dealing with indigenous peoples. The change to a pro-active policy on indigenous issues, which took place during the 1990s, was therefore a logical consequence of the holistic approach.

When formalised in strategies and applications to donors at the end of the 1980s / early 1990s, the holistic approach took its point of departure in the idea of a South-South Communication strategy, which was first developed by IWGIA in 1988 and had, at the time, a primary focus on publications.

One of the positive results from the holistic approach towards indigenous peoples was related to IWGIA's knowledge of the international human rights system and experience with Scandinavian donors, which "opened new spaces for us indigenous peoples on the international level" as stated by an indigenous person from Asia. IWGIA not only introduced partners to the UN but also to governments and EU institutions.

The South-South programme

The South-South programme was the outcome of informal discussions between Board members and the secretariat. It was presented to, and eventually endorsed and funded by, Norad in 1988. A similar programme was funded by Danida, beginning in 1993. This programme presented a sea change in IWGIA's way of thinking and working, probably to a much greater extent than originally envis-

UN Permanent Forum on Indigenous Issues, 5th session May 2006, New York - Photo: Pablo Lasansky

Visiting MPIDO, one of IWGIA's partners in Kenya, 2005 – Photo: Jenneke Arens

aged. Documents from those days show that the basis for the programme were the experiences gained in South America, which, it was felt, could be replicated in other parts of the world. Under the name of the South-South Communication Programme, the aims of the programmes were:

- To support IWGIA's network in rural areas of Third World countries and make contacts with the local indigenous organisations and indigenous communities.
- To promote discussion and dialogue between indigenous peoples and representatives of states and non-indigenous populations, in order to help break down racial, academic and political barriers which prevent the needs and desires of indigenous peoples from being heard.
- To provide indigenous peoples with IWGIA publications free of charge thereby ensuring that no organisation or community was prevented from receiving this information because of economic constraints.
- To use IWGIA's publications as a basis for developing indigenous peoples' capacity to take development into their own hands.
- To provide a service whereby indigenous peoples would have the necessary means at their disposal (information, contacts and dialogue possibilities) to promote their own self-development.

Neither in the first programme funded by Norad nor in the first two phases of the Danida-funded programme were human rights mentioned as an activity in their own right. While the Norad-funded programme targeted indigenous peoples in South and Central America, the Danida-funded programme was aimed at Africa, Asia and the Pacific. For all three regions, the programme included a major conference focusing on the situation and concept of indigenous peoples. Networking was a key component, i.e. visiting indigenous communities and organisations and establishing the possibilities for contacts and networks that could link indigenous peoples from one continent to another. Identifying project partners was another main objective. Although, at that time, human rights activities were not directly integrated into the South-South programme, all activities came to include IWGIA's human rights efforts far more than had ever been the case in the programme implemented in South America.

Seen from an historical perspective, the South-South programme was a building block upon which IWGIA's holistic strategy was constructed. An external evaluation of the programme concluded that "the South-South Communication programme as currently designed and implemented *does provide a strong basis for developing indigenous people's capacity to take development in their own hands*" (Development Associates 1996:37).

The holistic approach, with its strong focus on indigenous peoples and human rights, may have limited IWGIA's capacity to work on other thematic issues such as the environment. But, from the late 1980s onwards, it undoubtedly produced strategic results.

(right) For the pastoralist Maasai in Tanzania rights and access to water is included in titling and demarcation as it appears from this signboard. Photo: Jens Dahl

CHAPTER 7

FROM DOCUMENTATION TO PUBLICATION TO COMMUNICATION

When I laid out all the IWGIA publications on the floor in my home it was "possible to see the spread of the indigenous movement literally moving across the world from the 1960s to the present day" (IWGIA 1989c:35). This statement made by IWGIA at its 20th anniversary was valid in 1988, and remains so 20 years later. The kaleidoscopic view of the evolution of IWGIA's publications mirrors the development of the indigenous movement and is an indicator of the role IWGIA has taken in the development of indigenous issues.

The burning issue for the founders of IWGIA and like-minded NGOs was to make the world aware of and concerned about gross violations of the human rights of indigenous peoples in Central and South America. The aim of our documentation efforts was to raise the awareness of a European and American public. IWGIA's documents were, as already mentioned, written by anthropologists. They all followed the same documentary format and they portrayed indigenous peoples as victims. They were "victims of progress" as so brilliantly reported on in the book of the same name by John Bodley (Bodley 1982). Indigenous peoples did not and should not live in sanctuaries, and the aim of IWGIA was to support initiatives of self-development and self-determination.

The first publications reflected the low or non-existent level of indigenous self-organisation. Those who received the IWGIA documents and newsletters were IWGIA members in Europe and North America, the media, politicians and, importantly, indigenous peoples in this wealthy part of the world. There were probably very few indigenous peoples outside this area who ever saw the publications, let alone who would have been able to read them.

At the beginning of the 1980s, two changes point at important emerging trends. The first was obviously that IWGIA started printing in Spanish, the second was its increasing global orientation, including a growing focus on Asia. Indigenous peoples in Central/South America had started to organise themselves and the publications were being circulated widely in the

Spanish-speaking world. Indigenous peoples in Asia were also starting to organise and were looking to the world for help in coping with multinational mining companies, repressive governments, etc. An indigenous person from Asia once told me that she came in contact with IWGIA in the early 1980s because of her interest in the issues addressed in the document "Is God an American?" (Hvalkof and Aaby 1981).

From the early 1990s on, the issue of indigenous peoples in Africa became a regular theme in the documents as well as in the quarterly journal *Indigenous Affairs*. In the first IWGIA Yearbook (1986), Africa took up a small percentage of the pages; by 2007 this had increased to around 20 per cent. The 1993 IWGIA conference on indigenous peoples in Africa was instrumental in increasing IWGIA's involvement with indigenous peoples in Africa, and one of the first steps taken was to publicise the situation of the continent's indigenous peoples (Veber and Wæhle 1993).

During the 1980s, the indigenous network began to outnumber subscribers, a process that gathered further pace with the adoption of the South-South programme. Indigenous peoples started to write about themselves, in the early years copying the anthropological approach of being victims. The audience was no longer just anthropologists and a Euro-American public but also indigenous peoples. From 1991 on, the journal *Indigenous Affairs* increasingly used and gave preference to articles written by indigenous people.

IS GOD AN AMERICAN

Not all IWGIA publications have been successes. But some of them seem to have been extremely useful.

It was in London in the early 1990s at a meeting on the Chittagong Hill Tracts. During one of the breaks we walked around Hyde Park. I had a discussion with a colleague from London about IWGIA publications, and the document "Is God an American?" was mentioned. I had been published years back in cooperation with Survival International. This was one of the successful IWGIA publications and I regretted that it had been out of print for years. "Oh", my colleague said Arnold, "I have 200 copies at home. I use them to hold up my bed, 50 copies under each of the legs !"

The first *Yearbook* was published in 1986 and the first three volumes were written and compiled by Andrew Gray. From then on until the mid-1990s, the main section with the regional and country overview was written by a group of academics and students working in or closely related to IWGIA, whereas indigenous experts often wrote the section called "Indigenous Rights". It is worth noting that the first indigenous peoples to contribute were those who had worked on indigenous rights at the international level.

From 1994 on, when the *Yearbook* changed its name to *The Indigenous World* we can see an increase in indigenous contributions, also to chapters on regional developments. From 2000, indigenous contributions equalled those of non-indigenous experts. Indigenous peoples were no longer objects but providers of information and analysis. The publication parallels IWGIA's increasing emphasis on the holistic approach.

Most recently, a new development has taken place whereby increasing numbers of publications are produced by indigenous and non-indigenous writers at the specific request of IWGIA. This often takes place in order to follow-up on or support projects that are funded by IWGIA. For example, when IWGIA decides to focus its activities on specific themes, such as political parties, indigenous parliaments, local governments, youth, women etc, this results in the compilation of a Document or a thematic issue of *Indigenous Affairs*, most often written by indigenous persons but initiated by IWGIA and partners who felt that this area needed more attention.

In many places, IWGIA's publications have come to be regarded as a fundamental point of reference on indigenous affairs. Instrumental in this respect has been IWGIA's support for the local publishing of indigenous peoples' own publications such as *Pueblo Indio* in Bolivia, *Nomadic News* in Kenya and *Living Arctic* in Russia. In South and Central America, all IWGIA publications in Spanish are now being produced and distributed there by local partners. While indigenous peoples in South and Central America use Spanish as their *lingua franca*, indigenous peoples in Africa use either English or French, and in Russia Russian; there is no such *lingua franca* in Asia. IWGIA has therefore experimented with publications produced locally by indigenous partners in national or local languages such as Tagalog and Ilokano (Philippines), Hindi (India), Bahasa (Indonesia), Thai and a few others. A recent effort has been the publication of *Indigenous Affairs* in Hindi.

The Internet and new communication channels (fax, mobile phones, videos, iPods) created further opportunities for indigenous peoples to provide information. IWGIA responded by supporting indigenous information centres, first in Peru and Russia. Most projects in South America have a communication component, including support for the production of videos and radio programmes, and these are increasingly diversifying towards different target audiences.

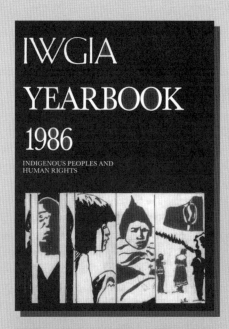
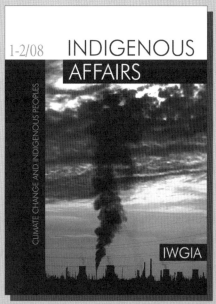
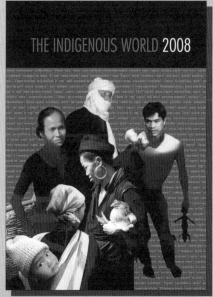
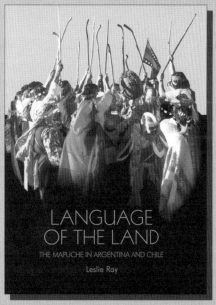

CHAPTER 8

HUMAN RIGHTS

When IWGIA obtained observer status (NGO status) with ECOSOC in 1989, a new era took shape in the organisation's human rights work. An old dream had become a reality, and the activities of the United Nations became the focal point of IWGIA's human rights efforts for decades to come.

IWGIA's human rights strategy, which was developed by IWGIA in the 1980s, had four facets. Firstly, IWGIA has been present since the mid-1980s in virtually all UN meetings dealing with indigenous issues. Where this has not been possible, IWGIA has tried to ally itself with indigenous persons who could report back to their own organisation and to IWGIA. Secondly, IWGIA and the Human Rights Fund for Indigenous Peoples (see below) have funded the participation of indigenous peoples. Thirdly, every year, IWGIA accredited a large number of indigenous persons for the meetings of the Working Group on Indigenous Populations (WGIP) but also meetings of the Sub-Commission and the Commission on Human Rights, as well as later for the Permanent Forum on Indigenous Issues, and the Expert Mechanism on the Rights of Indigenous Peoples. Finally, IWGIA has also made interpretation available at the indigenous caucus meetings and assisted in a number of other practical matters.

IWGIA's participatory strategy at UN meetings has always been to have a strong representation at the WGIP and other key events, and to be present at all other relevant meetings. It was not unusual for 2-3 people to participate in the WGIP, assisted by volunteers from local groups. A similar pattern developed in relation to the Permanent Forum and the Working Group on the Draft Declaration. The result was that IWGIA has probably been the most visible non-indigenous NGO during many of these meetings. Combined with the fact that IWGIA's relationship with many of the indigenous organisations and persons present also included project partnerships and cooperation around publications, this has meant that IWGIA has been a key NGO in all matters relating to the UN and indigenous issues. Indigenous peoples have always shown their appreciation of IWGIA's efforts during these meetings although, as we have already seen, this has by no means always been unproblematic.

From the very first day, it was a firm policy within IWGIA never to speak on behalf of indigenous peoples and to be careful not to compete with indigenous organisations when it came to speaking time. In his presentation to the ILO meeting in 1986, Andrew Gray expressed the situation in the following terms:

> *IWGIA has a policy that we never usually address conferences on indigenous affairs. This is because we are neither indigenous nor experts. Where there are indigenous persons present we would not presume to speak on their behalf. The fact that I am speaking is in itself a comment on the composition of this meeting and the small proportion of indigenous peoples present. I hope you will therefore take great heed of what they say in compensation for their limited representation* (IWGIA 1987c:86).

Over the years, the UN procedures have been liberalised but, even in 1999, Andrew Gray wrote of the Declaration process:

> *Over one hundred indigenous organisations have now been accredited, although a few have been refused, mainly from Africa and Asia. However they can still obtain access to the meeting by working with NGOs who have consultative status [IWGIA] with ECOSOC...Once inside the meeting, indigenous peoples have had to battle for full speaking rights and to be considered as part of the decision-making process* (1999:356).

Towards the end of the century and into the new millennium, IWGIA's human rights strategy came to include a few key regional approaches, firstly in the African Commission on Human and Peoples' Rights (and, to a much lesser extent, the Organisation of American States' human rights mechanisms) and later by supporting national human rights observatories.

From an indigenous point of view, the African Commission is different from the UN in a number of ways. The accreditation procedures are stricter, and all final decisions are taken by the states in closed meetings. The focus of these meetings is on human rights in general, and indigenous issues were not dealt with at all before IWGIA and Commissioner N. Barney Pityana made the first approach to the Commission. The methods adopted by IWGIA in this forum have been the same as in the UN, namely supporting indigenous participation and letting indigenous peoples speak on behalf of IWGIA. The dialogue has been very different, however, due to the controversial position of the discussion in the African context. There are quite simply things that can be said in the UN that would be self-defeating in the African Commission. This has promoted a close strategic cooperation between IWGIA and indigenous peoples and a coordination of their efforts by indigenous organisations to an extent completely unknown in the UN.

In South and Central America, the Inter-American Commission on Human Rights has played an important role in indigenous organisations' strategies. In fact, most of the complaints made against American states come from indigenous organisations, and IWGIA has supported the processes of submitting and monitoring the cases before the Commission.

From a global perspective, new opportunities arose with the appointment of a "Special Rapporteur on the situation of the human rights and fundamental freedoms of indigenous people" (Special Rapporteur) and, from a national perspective, the establishment of human rights observatories may improve the prospects for indigenous peoples in all parts of the world in the long term.

The Human Rights Fund for Indigenous Peoples

The Human Rights Fund (HRF) has been a key component of IWGIA's human rights activities and thus a significant part of IWGIA's holistic strategy. The Fund's significant impact on the participation and role played by indigenous peoples in the UN was highlighted in an evaluation of the Fund conducted in 2006.

> *After more than 20 years of work facilitating the participation of indigenous leaders, the results speak for themselves and the long list of people and organisations who have benefited at some point from the Fund's existence clearly prove the Fund's great task, its enormous contribution to the development of the international indigenous movement. The impact the Fund has had, and continues to have, in the international arena is overwhelming. Without it, many of the most relevant leaders of the international indigenous movement would not have found it so easy to participate in these spaces and, obviously, the indigenous movement would not have had the international strength it has had over the last few decades... It is evident that the Fund is still backing the participation of historical leaders of the indigenous movement who maintain an extremely high level of influence within the indigenous 'caucus' and an extremely high level of political influence at the diplomatic level* (Lopez 2006).

Yet another key factor explaining the success of the Fund is the trust established with indigenous peoples and their organisations. "The margin of freedom of action of indigenous representatives during international events is fundamental and very necessary for building relationships based on equality and trust, and it must continue to be one of the characteristic features of the Human Rights Fund" (Lopez 2006). Mutual respect has grown out of the knowledge and friendship between members of the Fund and those supported and between the indigenous peoples, who come from a wide spectrum of cultural backgrounds.[106]

In the early years, when the Fund only supported indigenous participation in the WGIP,[107] priority was given to broad presentations of violations of indigenous peoples' human rights. A geographical balance was established and critical regions were given priority. Every year the Fund supported people participating for the first time as well as people who had attended in previous years.

Only persons representing indigenous organisations were supported and women were given priority, although they have remained underrepresented. However:

> ... it is important to highlight the Fund's great efforts to identify women leaders of different organisations and peoples who have the capacity to exert influence in the political context. This effort can be appreciated in the fact that some of the most influential women in the indigenous movement are women who have received, and still receive, support from the Fund for the international meetings they attend (ibid).

In quantitative terms, indigenous women made up between 25 and 30 per cent until the turn of the century, when this increased to 47 and 60 per cent in 2006 and 2007 respectively.

Objective criteria were supplemented by subjective criteria, such as knowledge of the person's / organisation's degree of efficiency in the UN meetings and their work on these issues after returning home. During the work of the Working Group on the Draft Declaration, and during the process of establishing the Permanent Forum, it became clear that the Fund had to support a number of key indigenous persons who could make an impact on the processes and who had the backing of the indigenous caucus. This obviously added to the subjective criteria and also to the criticism of the Fund by those not supported, as well as praise for the significant results achieved. Looking back over the Fund's more than 20 years of existence, it has moved from simply supporting grassroots activists to supporting experts and indigenous leaders who have become skilled participants and actors in the UN.

The organisation, its policy and its decisions are independent of indigenous organisations and its activities and funding cannot be appropriated, used or misused by indigenous organisations or individuals. Most indigenous organisations would not wish to be responsible for decisions regarding the funding of individuals and prefer to remain neutral, establish good relationships with the Fund but leave it to the Fund to take decisions. Very few indigenous people have seriously criticized the non-indigenous nature of the Fund and it is generally acknowledged that to take part in the decision-making would also make them ineligible for funding. This is possibly the reason why the Fund has moved away from including indigenous persons in the decision-making, as was the case in the early years: "All decisions taken by the Fund are made by the Board, which consists of members of the organisations involved (...), and several indigenous representatives (currently these are from Chile, West Papua and Bangladesh)" (IWGIA 1987b).[108]

From the earliest days, the Fund organised preparatory meetings for those funded and other interested indigenous persons. These meetings gave the participants a first opportunity to introduce themselves and to be introduced to the practical and political intricacies of the UN system.

The Fund has been at the cutting edge to an extent not possible for the UN Voluntary Fund for Indigenous Peoples and a number of other official support mechanisms. The Fund was able to take the lead in funding indigenous peoples from Africa (for the first time in 1989) and Russia (for the first time in 1990) and also the first participation of indigenous peoples from Taiwan (Taiwan is not a member of the UN). In some of these, as well as other controversial cases, the Fund took the initiative and invited certain persons to participate and give statements to specific meetings.

International, regional and national initiatives: the Special Rapporteur and Human Rights Observatories

In 2001, the UN Commission on Human Rights appointed the first Special Rapporteur, Rodolfo Stavenhagen. IWGIA and Rodolfo Stavenhagen had known each other for many years but his appointment as Special Rapporteur opened new doors for focusing on human rights in selected countries. A way of cooperating was established during the Special Rapporteur's first visit to the Philippines in December 2002,[109] when IWGIA laid the ground work for indigenous organisations from all parts of the country to meet with the Special Rapporteur. Invited by the government and funded by the United Nations, such preparations on the part of indigenous peoples were not possible within the budget of the Special Rapporteur but the approach adopted by the indigenous peoples in the Philippines, in cooperation with IWGIA, gave new opportunities for indigenous voices to be heard.

The model was copied during other, official or unofficial, visits of the Special Rapporteur to countries such as Chile, Colombia, South Africa, Kenya and Bolivia. One outcome of these visits was the establishment of indigenous human rights observatories in Chile and the Philippines, with the support of IWGIA's project programme.

In Chile, the *Observatorio de Derechos de los Pueblos Indígenas* (Indigenous Peoples' Rights Watch) is a non-governmental organisation whose purpose is to promote, defend and document the rights of indigenous peoples in Chile. It was created in September 2004 in the city of Temuco by a group of citizens of different professional and ethnic backgrounds concerned at the lack of legal recognition and respect for indigenous peoples' rights in the country. The work carried out by this pluralistic and multi-disciplinary organization follows the guidelines set out in international conventions, declarations and jurisprudence on human rights and on the rights of indigenous peoples currently in force.

In order to improve indigenous peoples' access to justice, in accordance with the recommendations made by the UN Special Rapporteur following his official mission to the Philippines, the Cordillera Peoples Alliance (CPA) and the National

Rodolfo Stavenhagen during a visit to Bolivia, 2007 - Photo: Wara Vargas

Federation of Indigenous Peoples Organizations in the Philippines (KAMP) decided to set up an indigenous peoples' watchdog, a human rights observatory.

The aim of these initiatives is to increase the capacity of indigenous peoples to monitor, document and report on human rights violations, to give practical and legal aid to victims of human rights abuses and to increase general knowledge and awareness of the human rights situation of indigenous peoples.

The indigenous peoples bring to these human rights observatories their experiences gained in their dealings with ILO Convention No. 169, the Declaration drafting process, and the knowledge gained from the vast amount of statements of human rights violations brought to the WGIP in Geneva. These international experiences have provided indigenous peoples with perspectives on their own situation and insight into the opportunities (and limitations) of human rights mechanisms. With these new perspectives, the human rights observatories aim to transform the local indigenous knowledge of oppression into legal documentation, which is a condition for obtaining access to justice and to putting pressure on the state legal institutions.

CHAPTER 9

PROJECTS AND PARTNERSHIPS

When supporting indigenous projects, IWGIA follows a rights-based approach. This means that IWGIA gives priority to projects dealing with land rights, such as land titling, and empowerment initiatives, such as strengthening an organisation by supporting its activities. It also involves support for a wide variety of initiatives that are aimed at increasing the level of knowledge and awareness among indigenous peoples of their rights through, amongst other things, the dissemination of information. In all this, the general policy is that indigenous peoples themselves must manage and carry out the projects.

The history of IWGIA's involvement in support of indigenous projects has already been described. This narrative also included some of the considerations and discussions that took place within the organisation. These reflections referred mainly to the implications that projects might have for IWGIA's policy towards indigenous peoples and its relationships with the indigenous organisations involved. But many other issues have, over the years, been discussed and considered in relation to IWGIA's project policy, including relations with partners.

Partnership policy and strategy

The concept of partnership does not seem to have been a major issue in the early years of IWGIA's existence. There are at least two simple explanations for this. First and foremost, the main focus was on documentation, primarily provided by anthropologists and observers from outside the indigenous communities. Secondly, given IWGIA's location in Scandinavia, there were few indigenous partners to work with. This changed when IWGIA began working with indigenous organisations. At the time, a large part of IWGIA's efforts were aimed at strengthening the indigenous *movement* and relationships were therefore established with strong indigenous organisations that could promote the rights of indigenous peoples on the national and international stage.

IWGIA's involvement in project work changed this situation. With funding from development agencies, indigenous organisations at all levels were given the opportunity to establish partnerships with NGOs such as IWGIA. For IWGIA, this has posed a number of challenges: indigenous organisations do not constitute a homogeneous category and there were many discussions and many deliberations before a partnership strategy could be developed.

One thing is to have a global perspective, another is to take into consideration the significant regional variations of the ways in which indigenous peoples have organized themselves. Some of these differences are worth noting. In South America and Russia, for instance, the key organisations with which IWGIA has established partnerships are multi-ethnic, often representing hundreds of communities, and their leadership is periodically elected by the people living in these communities. In other regions, such as Africa and Asia (with notable exceptions such as the Philippine Cordilleras), indigenous peoples tend to be represented by indigenous NGOs that often only include people and communities from the same ethnic group.

In principle, IWGIA was committed to giving priority to supporting the weakest indigenous organisations but, in practice, this has often proved difficult and partnerships have been established first and foremost with relatively strong indigenous organisations.

This has been and remains a dilemma for IWGIA. Some of the partnerships established between IWGIA and weak indigenous organisations have led to a great deal of frustration – on both sides. One clear example is IWGIA's partnership with First People of the Kalahari, as described below.

In cases where IWGIA has chosen to work with a relatively strong umbrella organisation that unites a number of weak grassroots or local organisations, the local organisations may feel that they "get too little out of it" or are being patronised. But there have also been cases where the umbrella organisation has been opposed to IWGIA working directly with local or even regional partners because they have been given the responsibility of acting on behalf of their member organisations or, in rare cases, because they want to keep the financial benefits for themselves. There have also been cases where the international link has kept the umbrella organisation alive even when its local legitimacy has long gone.

When it has been impossible or too complex for IWGIA to work directly with a weak organisation, IWGIA has chosen to work through local non-indigenous NGOs and advisors. This was for many years not IWGIA policy, however: the aim was to strengthen the indigenous organisation, and it was feared that when the project contract went through a third partner, the result could well be a strengthening of this partner and not the indigenous organisation in question.

The strategy of working with advisors and local NGOs was first used by IWGIA in South and Central America where, over the last 15 years, emphasis has increasingly been placed on working with local advisors, generally anthropologists or lawyers. One positive outcome of this strategy has been a more systematic follow-up of local processes. Simultaneously, it has also enabled IWGIA to strengthen its combination of support for project activities with systematic dissemination of these experiences through publications.

The same strategy is therefore now used by IWGIA in other parts of the world. In some cases, it has also been adopted because the strong indigenous organisations are often themselves reluctant to work with weak organisations who are unable to manage funding from outside. An important consideration has also been to find support NGOs that can provide crucial technical assistance, for example, in relation to land rights projects in Peru, the Philippines, Laos and India.

The problem of weak organisations remains, however, and is often discussed within IWGIA and in Board meetings.

Another issue is that of the organisation's representativeness. How can we identify the right organisation when there are competing indigenous organisations all claiming to represent the same group or groups? While representativeness has been a serious issue in relation to certain human rights processes, it is interesting to note that, in relation to more traditional projects, this question is of far less significance than most people might think. There are cases when one group, or even one person, makes accusations against another organisation for not being representative but, often, such allegations are a cover for the accuser to obtain access to financial resources or obtain recognition even though unable to organise support at home. Only in a very few cases has IWGIA had to reconsider its support for an organisation on the basis of such claims, and this has created some tensions with that organisation. In most cases, where there were doubts as to representativeness, IWGIA tried not to get involved. Nevertheless, there are some organisations that seem to have been established without the organisation having any real constituency or legitimacy among its own people. Such incidences must not, however, be used to discredit this kind of support in general. It is most significant that donor funding for indigenous organisations in developing countries has often been the last resort for indigenous peoples claiming and fighting for their rights.

Related to this is also the issue of whether an organisation's claim to be indigenous is in line with the reality. If we leave aside cases of fraud, this discussion has mainly taken place between organisations and has never been an important issue for IWGIA.

One of IWGIA's key strategies has been to develop long-term partnerships, often as part of its holistic approach. The challenge for the creation of real partnerships between NGOs such as IWGIA and indigenous organisations is to create bonds of trust. IWGIA and its partners have created a *trust capital* as described by a former Board member.[110] Indigenous peoples have pointed out that this has been most successful when IWGIA has invested time, money and resources in the relationship and when IWGIA has given room for indigenous voices. For IWGIA, in turn, trust is often created when the indigenous organisations make room for *IWGIA's* voice. Mutual trust offers the possibility of going beyond "business-like" relationships that are inevitable when one part has the role of "donor" and the other the role of "beneficiary". Striking the balance between having a "donor role" and being a partner in a political struggle is a constant challenge.

From one of IWGIA's global partnership meetings. Baguio, the Philippines, October 2005
Photo: Anni Hammerlund

Over the last few years, a new generation of indigenous leaders has arisen, usually younger and with more formal education than previous leaders. This is unequivocally a step forward but it is not without problems. Without these young educated people, the indigenous communities would not be able to present their case in an efficient way to the surrounding society.

In the international human rights setting, IWGIA's partnerships have primarily been with such well-educated indigenous people who "often draw their power from the ambiguity expressed by two overlapping cultures, that of their group of origin and that of the dominant society" (Morin and d'Anglure 1997:185). Although "...they today owe their commanding positions much more to classroom instruction than to their knowledge of traditional lore" (ibid.), this does not diminish the legitimacy of well-educated young people but explains positions often taken by them and the opportunities they have for manoeuvring in their local communities. It should also be added that, because of their studies, some of these young leaders have lived outside their communities for several years. This distance sometimes makes it difficult for them to truly understand the problems of the communities they represent.

Project strategy

Since its establishment, IWGIA has broken new ground by focusing on institutional support to indigenous organisations. In 1973 and 1975, small amounts of money were given to the National Indian Brotherhood (Canada), which, at the time, was planning the establishment of the World Council of Indigenous Peoples. Such donations were provided without any conditions attached and can be regarded as the forerunners of institutional support to indigenous organisations, which later became the backbone of IWGIA's strategy for the empowerment of indigenous peoples. Even today, institutional support is a key component of IWGIA's project approach.

For many years, the policy was that IWGIA should support the establishment of indigenous organisations but not maintain them.[111]

This changed over the years, as close cooperation and regular partnerships were established on the basis of a multifaceted relationship, and as it became clear that one has to be realistic when it comes to the possibilities of indigenous peoples' organisations fighting for their rights without support from abroad. Maintaining an office in town, purchasing equipment, paying salaries, travelling back and forth between remote communities, taking part in international meetings etc, requires financial resources that are beyond their capacity. Few governments are willing to provide these resources since they are often the targets of these organisations. Sustainability for these indigenous organisations requires partnerships with other institutions or organisations. It is important, however, not to depend on funding from one partner alone, and IWGIA therefore encourages and supports its partners to diversify their funding base.

The focus of IWGIA's project support has been on empowerment, capacity building and land rights. Support has been given to indigenous organisations, to indigenous participation in national and international human rights endeavours and to a broad range of activities carried out by indigenous organisations. Particular emphasis has been placed on defending indigenous land rights and the titling of their lands and territories, both considered a pre-condition if indigenous peoples are to defend their human rights and control their own future.

All projects have a number of activities and goals. The organisation responsible will carry out activities that are instrumental for reaching these goals. And yet the process is often more important in terms of the capacity building and empowerment of indigenous peoples. What matters is often not what you are doing but that you are organising and doing something. The opportunity for indigenous groups to seek funding from IWGIA and donor agencies has its own impact on indigenous organisations. In the great majority of cases, the effect of such funding has been not only positive but, without it, indigenous organisations would have been unable to continue.

JOSEPH OLE SIMEL, MPIDO

Representing the Maasai organisation, MPIDO in Kenya, Joseph Ole Simel wrote about IWGIA:

"In our view, IWGIA gained trust in relation to us and in relation to the African Commission on Human and Peoples' Rights because it invested seriously at a time when there were no African indigenous capacity and so many other serious matters to take care of. IWGIA's activities were an incentive for us, and we realised that we were not alone. IWGIA's base in Scandinavia is important to us because of the high reputation that these countries have in relation to human rights.

When we think about where we stood a few years ago, we are very proud of the achievements and results of indigenous peoples in the United Nations and the African Commission. Our engagement has enabled many indigenous leaders and organisations to reach countless people through support from partner organisations such as IWGIA.

It has been a privilege to be able to work with IWGIA and to be accorded respect and dignity and for the restoration of our basic human rights. IWGIA is considered an expert organisation on issues of indigenous peoples, and its historical engagement and readiness to support innovate ideas and strategies from indigenous people's communities has inspired many organisations.

The approach of building capacity of local indigenous peoples' organisations is the key demonstration by IWGIA that it supports local peoples to carry out their work themselves. This has given us remarkable results in our dealings with the Kenyan government. We now hear accurate and reliable information about the underlying causes of the problems facing indigenous peoples from the actual people concerned, and the proposed solutions are theirs too. This is because of the capacity developed over a very short period of time due to good relations with IWGIA.

It is unique to see that IWGIA supported our vision and our struggles. This is a critical element of the working relationship or partnership as it allows indigenous peoples' ownership of the process; they become responsible for the success or failure of the process. In this, dialogue, consultation and a continuous flow of information are key characteristics of our experience and relationship with IWGIA. This dialogue and consultation enabled people and organisa-

> tions working for the same goals to know exactly what others think and how they feel, their hopes and dreams.
>
> A key outcome of the engagement of indigenous peoples is the fact that organisations such as MPIDO have been able to build their capacity and engage in a more constructive manner with other key stakeholders. IWGIA's partnership has made it possible for MPIDO to push for institutional participation of indigenous peoples in any process that will affect them directly or indirectly.
>
> The rise of indigenous organisations like MPIDO is now laying the ground for institution-building necessary for political structures that can address the root causes of social injustices, inequalities and marginalisation of indigenous peoples in East Africa and the whole continent".
>
> (April 2008)

It is not possible for IWGIA to support all project proposals it receives although most of them deserve support. Which project to choose is determined by a large number of factors, such as IWGIA's thematic priorities (for example, promoting

Preparing for a meeting. Santa María community, Salta, Argentina 2002 - Photo: Pablo Lasansky

LHAKA HONHAT

The Wichí, Chorote, Chulupí, Toba and Tapiete are hunters, gatherers and fishermen who live on State Plots 55 and 14 in Salta Province, Argentina. About 100 years ago, cattle ranchers from the south settled here. These Criollos practice cattle ranching without enclosures or pastures and, since the indigenous peoples had no titles to their lands, conflicts erupted over land and resources.

As hunters and gatherers, the indigenous peoples need collective title to their lands. In order to negotiate this with authorities, 27 communities have created the organisation Lhaka Honhat, meaning 'our land'.

Family-owned plots of land in the area have been given to the Criollos and to companies but, without collective titles to their lands, indigenous peoples will be left out and the environment further devastated by the roaming cattle. For this reason, IWGIA is supporting the efforts of Lhaka Honhat to get their lands titled, a process that has been brought to the Inter-American Commission on Human Rights.

With the entry onto the scene of cattle ranchers, the land has been severely degraded, with the result that poverty is a serious problem among indigenous peoples as well as Criollos. A solution that respects the needs of both parties must be found and without the indigenous peoples ending up losing their land; collective rights have to be recognised on a par with the family rights of the settlers. In this situation, negotiations between the parties have become complicated by the fact that the indigenous peoples are Anglican Protestants and the Criollos Catholics.

It is difficult for many people to understand why the indigenous peoples should be favoured with so much land, as opposed to some other groups – such as the Criollos – who also live in a very vulnerable situation. This dilemma is not exclusive to this region of Argentina but can also be found in many other areas and, in principle, an attempt is being made to find a solution to the land problem that also includes the non-indigenous population. At the same time, it is necessary to maintain the previous rights of the indigenous people, along with the demand for sufficient land, and for collective ownership by which to develop their traditional economy.

(Sources: Carrasco 2000; 2004; Carrasco and Zimerman 2006; Alejandro Parellada)

indigenous land rights) or empowerment (such as organisational strengthening), regional priorities, priority for women's projects, etc. The need to set priorities is determined by the limited amount of funding available, and IWGIA's knowledge of and contacts in some regions rather than others. Part of the decision-making process also of course includes an evaluation of the technical capacity of the applicant, its organisational strength and legitimacy.

Indigenous organisations that enter into the donor-driven project world are inevitably faced with a number of administrative demands, not least in relation to financial management. This is often a problem for inexperienced indigenous organisations with limited technical capacity. Project administration requires education and language skills that traditional leaders often lack, and which can easily create friction between young educated individuals and the older political leaders. Such problems are further exacerbated when the young educated people are those who gain financially from the projects, monopolise relations with donors and make a career for themselves in the indigenous peoples' movement. Funding from an outside donor such as IWGIA has an impact on local political, social and economic relations. It also has an impact when some individuals are funded to participate in international processes.

Accusations of corruption or mismanagement are sometimes heard. It is no secret that some indigenous organisations have, at some time or another, had problems in coping with the financial conditions stipulated by the donors. It has always been IWGIA's policy, when problems arise, to strengthen the dialogue with the organisation in order to improve the situation and discuss the issues concerned instead of cutting funding as a first step. An example worth mentioning here is that of one of IWGIA's long-term partners in South America got into difficulties at one point due to a lack of financial control mechanisms. There had been a period when the organisation had had a very important political role to play and its efforts, including financial allocations, had been concentrated on this, while little or no consideration was being given to administrative matters. In this case, as with most other organisations, if funds go missing it does not usually mean that a leader has become personally rich but that funds have been diverted to attend to urgent demands that were perhaps strictly speaking not part of the project for which the money was allocated. In other cases, the problem lay with IWGIA, who did not give proper advice to an organisation that had insufficient experience to financially manage a project of this scale.

In some situations, support for indigenous demands may seriously affect other sectors of the society, people who are in a situation that is as disadvantaged as that of the indigenous peoples. One such case is the demand for the restitution of the traditional territories of the indigenous Wichí, Toba and Chorote communities in Salta province, Argentina. Given the several decades-long presence of non-indigenous peasants on lands claimed by indigenous peoples, an integral solution to the system is being sought, maintaining the priority of the indigenous claim but at the same time trying to find a solution for these peasants.

Case studies

As we can see, IWGIA has collaborated with several types of indigenous organisations, has established many partnership relations and has supported a variety of empowerment projects in many different countries. A few case studies are given below to provide an indication of the range of this work and highlight some of the progress made in partnership building between IWGIA and indigenous organisations, as well as some of the problems faced by IWGIA in working with indigenous peoples through project support.

South America was the first region in which IWGIA supported indigenous projects. Projects have been supported primarily in the lowland regions of Peru, Bolivia and Argentina, where IWGIA has established long-term partnerships with local as well as national indigenous organisations. The main emphasis has been on defence of land rights, for example, in the form of demarcation and community titling of indigenous lands and territories. Besides a few major projects that have stretched over several years, IWGIA has funded a large number of smaller projects in South and Central America.

Projects supported in Asia have, on average, been larger than those in South America, lasting several years and involving fewer and stronger partners. Emphasis has been placed on the Philippines, Sabah (Malaysia), North-east India and Thailand, where strong partnerships have been established with key indigenous NGOs. Other smaller projects have been supported in the region, including in Indonesia, Cambodia and Nepal. Thematically, organisational support, community organising (including leadership training) and land rights issues have been prominent.

Indigenous projects in Africa came later, and have been concentrated in Kenya, Tanzania and Botswana along with smaller projects in Rwanda, Burundi and DRC. Defence of indigenous land rights has prevailed although the project portfolio has been quite broad, including amongst other things, information activities and protection of human rights.

Common to all three regions is the fact that the projects are linked to human rights initiatives and, for South America and Africa, to an increasing extent also involving communication and information activities. There are projects supporting women's groups and women's issues in all regions.

Russia is the most recently included region and, as outlined below, the project support structure differs from the three other regions.

IWGIA's project support for indigenous peoples in the Pacific has been limited, apart from institutional support and a partnership established for some years with the Pacific Concerns Resource Centre in Fiji.

Titling of land in Peru and the Philippines

Titling is an extremely complicated process that involves a number of professionals such as surveyors, anthropologists, lawyers, cartographers, etc. But first of all it needs the support of the authorities, and there has to be a firm local organisational background that provides the political and logistical support.

AIDESEP is an umbrella organisation of indigenous communities in the Peruvian Amazon. The IWGIA/AIDESEP land titling project in Peru is probably the largest project ever supported by IWGIA. What lay behind the process leading up to the land titling project was the system of slavery or bonded labour, *enganche*, and other atrocities carried out against indigenous peoples in the Peruvian Amazon with the approval of the authorities. In 1987, the indigenous peoples of Atalaya established a regional organisation, OIRA, and together with AIDESEP they formulated a strategy to deal with these issues (Hierro et al. 1998:10f).

With the new organisational background, AIDESEP was able to sign an agreement with the Ministry of Agriculture for the demarcation and titling of the communities. Without funding, AIDESEP approached IWGIA and a project proposal was accepted and funded by Danida.

Ten years later, more than 200 indigenous communities had had their lands –in total half a million hectares –titled and registered (ibid:198). In the process, more than 100 illegal settlers had been removed with compensation. Even so, in 2008, IWGIA is still involved in improving the demarcation, validating and extending the communities' lands and communal reserves and in other ways providing support to the communities that have received title to lands.

During a second phase of the project, the work was extended to establishing Communal Reserves consisting of common fishing and hunting areas for indigenous communities, as well as Territorial Reserves for peoples in voluntary isolation.

It was IWGIA's opinion that, in order to eradicate debt bondage, servitude and other human rights violations, and in order to guarantee rights to land, indigenous peoples needed control over their own lands and territories. From the early days of the titling process, it was understood that although titling was a condition, strategies also had to be developed to enable the indigenous communities to use their lands in a sustainable manner and for the development of their economy. However, as a human rights organisation, this was not considered to be within the expertise of IWGIA and, although this was discussed with the indigenous partners, it did not play a significant role at that time. During the titling process, much emphasis was placed on administrative, political, legal and financial matters in which cooperation between IWGIA and the partner organisation, AIDESEP, played a major role.

Land titling in the Philippines is as complicated as it is in Peru although the Philippines has a National Commission on Indigenous Peoples (NCIP), and an

The use of modern technology in titling and territorial defence. The Philippines – Photos: Christian Erni

Indigenous Peoples' Rights Act (IPRA). The Philippines can claim to be one of the very few countries with legal protection of the rights of indigenous peoples, including their rights to communal ownership of land, Community Ancestral Domain Title (CADT).

IWGIA's support for titling of indigenous lands is managed through an Ancestral Domain Support Programme, which is set up as a cooperation between Indigenous Peoples' Exchange, an indigenous NGO, and the technical advisory group, AnthroWatch. Titling must go through a long verification and approval process before final approval by the NCIP.

The experiences of the titling process showed that there were various factors beyond the control of the ADSP that determine how quickly the process can be completed. One of

the main factors was the attitude of, and relationship with, the provincial NCIP office since their involvement is mandatory in several stages, such as the survey and validation of proof.

Once the Claim Book (which contains all the proof) and the survey are completed, the role of the IWGIA-funded programme has largely been fulfilled. All it can do then is to continuously follow up on the progress of the application with the NCIP and, if necessary, put pressure on the NCIP national office to place the respective application on the agenda of their en-banc meetings. Good relationships with the Ancestral Domain Office of the NCIP and with some of the Commissioners are very helpful in this respect.

The attitude of the provincial NCIP office and its willingness to cooperate is determined by the extent to which outsiders (above all mining companies and other investors) have an interest in the resources of the area and thus how contested the CADT application is. Experience has unfortunately shown that the NCIP often side with mining and other business interests.

This means that, wherever such interests come into play, the indigenous communities engaged in a CADT application face big challenges with regard to their ability to counter pressure from the NCIP, local government and the company to sign a certificate of Free, Prior and Informed Consent allowing exploration or exploitation in their CADT area. It is not necessarily the CADT itself that is challenged by such outside interests. It is more that CADT applicants or holders are urged to enter into an agreement with companies. As can be expected, communities tend to be divided over such issues, resulting in severe conflicts.

Internal conflicts, either as a result of external interests or existing issues naturally delay the CADT process since the NCIP does not process any applications until conflicts have been resolved. An internal conflict (resulting from competition over leadership and representation) has, for example, delayed the CADT application processing in the community of Aruman (Mindanao) for years.

IWGIA's point of view is that titling of communal lands is necessary for the indigenous communities to remain in control of the lands and to cope with threats from outside. That this is a very thorny problem can be illustrated by the fact that, after eight years of work, five communities have received their titles and the titling and approval of another 14 is in progress.

Titling of communal lands is only the first step for indigenous communities to gain control over their lands. Indigenous communities in Peru and the Philippines that have received their titles are immediately faced with new challenges. Agrobusiness and mining and logging companies strive to get hold of IP lands. Companies with plans for establishing plantations on their lands have approached all five communities under the IWGIA-supported programme and the communities have come under pressure. A similar development is taking place in Peru. Some communities are successful in keeping these forces at bay, others are not.

One reason for indigenous communities to hold title to their lands is to promote economic development. The challenge, however, is for the communities to remain in *control,* to promote self-development. In this respect, the titling processes in Peru and in the Philippines have been successful in terms of empowering and strengthening the organisational capacity of the communities and individuals.

First People of the Kalahari (FPK)

For almost 10 years, from 1993 to 2002, the First People of the Kalahari received more support from IWGIA than any other indigenous organisation in Africa. Besides being the leading partner in southern Africa, it was also one of IWGIA's weakest partners. The discrepancy between the amount of funding (in total more than 10 million DKK) and the capacity of FPK was highlighted in the final evaluation of IWGIA's involvement with FPK (Hitchcock and Enghoff 2004).

First People of the Kalahari was established by the San (formerly known as Bushmen and, in Botswana, as Basarwa) of the Central Kalahari, Botswana in 1992 and formally registered in October 1993.

> *First People of the Kalahari was, in some ways, an outgrowth of efforts on the part of San to have their voices heard and to have themselves identified as a distinct ethnic group which wished to have equal rights with other groups in Botswana. It defined itself from the outset as a San social movement and advocacy organisation with direct links to the grassroots San communities across Botswana* (ibid.).

When the organisation was established, John Hardbattle became its leader. As the son of a San woman and an English police officer, he grew up gaining an indepth knowledge of his mother's culture and language (she lived in a traditional hut on the farm owned by the family) and his father's culture. It was John's

KGEIKANI KWENI

It was in the wake of a "Workshop on Sustainable Rural Development" that a respected San elder, Khomtsha Khomtsha, suggested the creation of an indigenous organisation, Kgeikani Kweni or First People of the Kalahari. This was in 1992, and Roy Sesana and John Hardbattle were also among the San participants, this latter acting as interpreter. This event created substantial concerns on the part of one of the Botswana government ministers, Pelonomi Venson, who asked the San to establish a group to meet with him and other relevant ministers.

The San took it seriously and travelled around to set up a group that represented as many San groups as possible. Logistical problems in getting around the vast region and the fact that the government continuously changed the date for the meeting were obstacles difficult to overcome but, during the travelling, it was probably Khomtsha who suggested that they create an organisation, and a letter on the aims of the organisation was presented to the government, which refused to receive it. The meeting with the government, which took place in the police headquarters, was a catastrophe. The San were severely intimidated but Khomtsa and two other San went further with the idea of creating an organisation. The harsh treatment of the San by the government representatives created quite some concern among foreign delegations and donors in Botswana, and it was clear that they needed support from the outside, including financial support. It was Arthur Krasilnikoff, who had travelled with the San on the tour, who brought the issue to Danida, who referred him to IWGIA.

Kgeikani Kweni was formally incorporated on October 11, 1993.

knowledge of European culture (John had, among other things, been to school in England and done military service in Germany) that made it possible for the organisation to be established. John's links with the San of the Central Kalahari and the traditional leaders of that region made him a legitimate spokesperson and his contacts with people outside Botswana lifted FPK and its issues out of the local setting and into the international arena, where John was able to forge strong alliances. At home, however, the FPK leadership lacked organisational experience and political realism, and this came to be a millstone around the organ-

The Nairobi Prize from IWGIA (Jens Dahl) to First Peoples of the Kalahari (John Hardbattle), October 11, 1993.
Photo: IWGIA archive

isation's neck. When Khomtsa Khomtsa, one of the founders, and John Hardbattle both passed away in 1996, FPK was still extremely weak. Without leaders and faced with an increasing number of challenges in connection with the eviction of San and Bakalagadi from the Central Kalahari Game Reserve, the situation of the organisation went from bad to worse.

It was a Danish writer, Arthur Krasilnikoff, a dedicated supporter of the San and a personal friend of John Hardbattle and other key San people, who instigated IWGIA's contacts with the San of Central Kalahari. He urged IWGIA to raise funds in support of the new organisation, First People of the Kalahari. It was a somewhat symbolic gesture when IWGIA, in October 1993, donated 10,000 DKK to FPK. The donation came from the Danish Nairobi Prize that had been awarded to IWGIA earlier that same year. The first IWGIA/FPK project (1993-6) was funded by Danida (2.3 million DKK) and its aim, initially, was to establish the organisation in the region. The second IWGIA/FPK project (1998-2002) was also funded by Danida (7.8 million DKK), with the objective of establishing and negotiating land claims, including mapping and research in the Central Kalahari Game Reserve, asserting human rights and providing logistical support to the organisation. After 2002, further support was given for the court case claiming the legal rights of the San in the Central Kalahari Game Reserve.[112]

From 1993 onwards, the relationship between IWGIA and FPK was often highly problematic. It would be fair to say that no other project has taken more of

A DONKEY-DRIVEN WHITE ELEPHANT

In February 2002, the government of Botswana (GoB) decided to stop all service deliveries, including water, to the San and Bakhalagadi families living in the Central Kalahari Game Reserve (CKGR) and instead move them to settlements outside the reserve, New !Xade, Kaudwane and Xeri.

A few families, however, decided to remain but, as the dry season approached, they began to experience serious water problems. In July, in the middle of the Danish summer holidays, IWGIA received an urgent funding application from a local NGO in Botswana. They had been approached by one of the remaining CKGR residents who had found out that he could get water to his family from a settlement outside the CKGR but needed means of transportation for doing so. The application to IWGIA therefore concerned the purchase of a donkey cart.

The idea of buying a donkey cart rather appealed to IWGIA because it seemed far more technologically adapted to the San's situation than all the cars (and money for their repairs!) provided throughout the years of our involvement in Botswana. It seemed quite expensive though, given the type of cart you normally see in the countryside, where using bits and pieces - even old car chassis - for carts is more the rule. The explanation was that it was going to be a NEW cart made in Gaborone.

So, after conferring by mail and phone with IWGIA's management (most of them out of office at the time), it was agreed to transfer the necessary amount. A few things had to be clarified first, however: how was the cart going to be delivered to the CKGR – some 600 km from the capital? Who would benefit from the cart – and the water it was going to transport – one family or more? Would the government allow the cart in and out of the CKGR?

All our questions were answered positively: the cart would be transported in a truck owned by a San organisation; several families would benefit; and the GoB seemed willing to allow the traffic.

The money was sent, several months passed but, by mid-October, our enquiry was answered stating that, due to different reasons, the cart was still in Gaborone. More months passed without anything happening until early 2003 when we heard that the donkey cart was now finally in the CKGR. In March, IWGIA received a new urgent request, this time for bridles as apparently no-one had thought about this rather important accessory. We first suggested buying ropes (as this is what most people use for their donkey carts anyway) but that seemed out of the question so IWGIA paid for the bridles. More months went by without any news. In late 2003, we were again in contact with the local NGO and, for the sake of following up on our funding, we asked how things were going with the cart. Not too well, we were told: lions had eaten all the donkeys and the cart had never been used.

Diana Vinding

Photo: Christian Erni

IWGIA's resources (in terms of money, time and psychological energy) than this one. Over 20 supervisory and monitoring visits were undertaken and, at a certain stage of the project, FPK put strong pressure on IWGIA to have an expatriate employed in the office in Ghanzi. This was contrary to IWGIA's policy but, in the end, and realising FPK's weakness, IWGIA gave in to the demand. From this perspective, the results of 10 years of effort were dismal and there was some frustration within IWGIA although there was still also a great deal of sympathy. However, no-one could see the way forward for a partnership supposedly based upon mutual respect and understanding.

In the 50-page long final evaluation report, IWGIA was blamed for not having been realistic in dealing with an organisation as weak as FPK, and FPK was blamed for being unrealistic and inconsistent. The evaluation was probably right on both counts. The report also pointed out the lack of mutual cultural understanding between FPK and IWGIA as a prevalent obstacle to the development of a productive partnership. This may explain the sometimes bizarre situations that ensued.

Seen in retrospect, it seems obvious that IWGIA and FPK failed to discuss what kind of cooperation each was seeking, and IWGIA was unsuccessful in explaining the terms and conditions that prevail when funding is provided by a donor agency, in this case Danida. FPK did not see IWGIA as a human rights organisation and, from their perspective, "IWGIA was seen as a provider of funds and infrastructural support, any other role of IWGIA was understood as unwanted interference in FPK affairs" (Evaluation Report). When IWGIA pressed for activity reports, financial accounts, etc., this was often seen by FPK as external interference in the affairs of an indigenous organisation. In the most extreme case, IWGIA was accused of colonialism and racism. IWGIA, for its part, did not do much to stress the human rights nature of its involvement with FPK, and FPK may have felt that the indigenous card was the only one it could play when under pressure.

IWGIA and FPK never managed to separate indigenous issues from bureaucratic and structural issues. Why were the people employed in the FPK secretariat (at one time 14) unable to understand bureaucratic rules and procedures in matters relating to the IWGIA/FPK project but fully capable of dealing with these issues when it came to their personal contracts, salaries and labour rights? Why did FPK never really attempt to cooperate with the non-indigenous expatriate (it had not been possible to find an indigenous person) they had wanted so badly?

There are no simple answers to these questions. However it seems straightforward to conclude that direct project partnership between a very weak local organisation and a foreign (donor) organisation is impossible or, at least, extremely difficult. The conclusion reached by IWGIA was not, however, to rule out cooperation with the weakest organisations but to try to find alternative ways forward. In the case of FPK, technical assistance from both an expatriate and local individuals and NGOs was tried. In the end, IWGIA recommended that FPK seek funding from other donors. FPK's reaction was that "they felt that IWGIA had 'abandoned them' so that they had to turn to other organisations for support" (ibid.).

However, in one respect, the partnership between IWGIA and FPK was also a success, and should be seen as such. When FPK was founded, it was faced with a number of serious challenges. One of these was the ongoing threat from the Botswana government to evict the indigenous peoples from the Central Kalahari Game Reserve (CKGR). This eventually materialized, first in 1997 and later in 2002. With support from IWGIA, FPK was able to engage in negotiations with the government (these negotiations lasted for several years but eventually failed) and to prepare the documentation and maps that would be needed in order to prove the residence rights of the CKGR people. The struggle for the right of the San to live in CKGR was thus prepared and organised by FPK, a fight that would have been impossible without financial support from outside.

The project partnership between IWGIA and FPK was a new construct in the region. There were, however, other organisations in the area (Botswana and Namibia) representing or working for the San people but FPK often claimed to be the only indigenous peoples' organisation. This fact was important for the partnership with IWGIA but it also restricted cooperation or coordination of human rights efforts with other regional-based organisations.

Asian Indigenous organisations

The Cordillera Peoples' Alliance in the Philippines is the epitome of a strong, robust and resilient indigenous organisation. It grew out of community-based protests against mining and hydro-electric development projects and through internal organisational efforts. It has, over the years, established itself with a mass base and thus has legitimacy in the Cordillera region. These efforts have been further enhanced by support from outside – IWGIA included – and not the other way around. With its more than 30 community branches and a number of other affiliated organisations, CPA has managed to establish a high degree of unity among the indigenous groups in the Cordilleras and to use this strength to cope with external challenges.

As a mass-based organisation, CPA's concerns are focused, first and foremost, on the grass-roots movements and local communities. Increased focus on project support gave rise to internal problems at a certain stage because the political leaders had to set more and more time aside for administration at the cost of political work. CPA may have felt this dilemma more strongly than most other indigenous organisations and IWGIA's priority of project support may have felt like a burden for some time, since there were major developments that CPA had to attend to while also having to implement the project. CPA was also put in a situation of doing more national work together with other IWGIA partners. Despite its strong regional focus, CPA was pushed into a national process without being fully prepared whilst also increasingly relying on project support. This was not all negative, since CPA was able to expand its network at the national level and gained credibility as a key player in the indigenous peoples' movement internationally. The local work of some of its leaders and staff was affected though, in terms of prioritising between a local or national focus. This remains a continuing dilemma. But it must be said that many indigenous peoples' issues are the result of national policies, and these have to be addressed on a national level. Relationships with IWGIA and other donors enabled CPA to become more involved with the international indigenous movement. As a regionally-based umbrella organisation CPA has, in many respects, been an ideal partner for IWGIA. It has used its strength to involve itself in national and international matters and its activities include human rights work, publications, lobbying, organising conferences, leadership development, etc. This fits well with IWGIA's holistic approach and CPA is one of the organisations that has received core funding from IWGIA.

IWGIA's involvement with the peoples in the Cordilleras developed further when the former chair of CPA, Victoria Tauli-Corpuz, established the Tebtebba Foundation in 1996, an indigenous research and educational institution. IWGIA's partnership with CPA and Tebtebba has included a vast number of activities, including capacity building, human rights efforts and projects focused on the role of political parties and local governments, among others.

Since the late 1990s, when IWGIA adopted its pro-active policy in relation to its human rights activities, major initiatives have largely been coordinated with CPA and/or Tebtebba. From IWGIA's side, this partnership has been based on trust and, probably, also on a shared worldview that includes a radical view of the rights of indigenous peoples combined with a vigorous wish to improve their political conditions. On an international level, the partnership with organisations such as Tebtebba and CPA and the establishment of *trust capital* has created legitimacy for IWGIA's efforts to create dialogue and confidence building with governments.

PACOS Trust is a community-based organisation operating in support of indigenous communities in Sabah. It does not have the broad organisational structure of CPA but, through its activities in support of legal rights, land rights and a pioneering programme for training of community organisers, it has established itself with a legitimate platform. Like CPA, PACOS has developed a holistic approach to development and its leaders have been strong allies of IWGIA in international human rights affairs.

The Asia Indigenous Peoples Pact Foundation[113] is an NGO established in 1988 with headquarters in Chiang Mai, Thailand. Its aims include serving as a forum for discussion among indigenous peoples in Asia, establishing research projects and lobbying for and coordinating indigenous activities. Its members are indigenous organisations and movements in 14 Asian countries. AIPP has been a key Asian partner of IWGIA for many years and has developed from being rather weak into a strong regional organisation.

To conclude this section, it may well be that IWGIA's pro-active policy of the late 1990s would have been unthinkable without a partnership with organisations such as CPA and Tebtebba, AIPP and PACOS Trust in Asia, MPIDO in Africa, RAIPON in Russia and the Sámi Council and ICC in the Arctic.

Traditional institutions

While IWGIA's support for and cooperation with CPA, Tebtebba, AIPP and PACOS Trust was a process of entering into partnerships with organisations on their way forward, the Cordillera also provides us with a case in which IWGIA began supporting a traditional institution in crisis. This is illustrative of the general discussion as to the extent to which IWGIA should take initiatives in support of institutions that are strongly rooted in the local culture, with important functions but also under pressure from institutions rooted in the national society. IWGIA has sometimes refused to support institutions aimed at upholding traditional power structures when these were considered to favour old men or hierarchical chiefdoms. In the 1990s, however, IWGIA supported an institution called *bodong* or peace pact, a traditional institution found among some tribes of the Cordillera, used to settle conflicts, prevent and end tribal war. Due to Christianisation, modern education, guerrilla activities and a new government-installed administrative system, the *bodong* institution was under pressure. While the number of conflicts seemed to have been on the increase in the region, the means to deal with these within the indigenous communities was waning. Against this background, IWGIA provided financial support aimed at strengthening the *bodong* system. The idea was to use the *bodong*, which is traditionally a bilateral agreement, and to broaden it into multilateral peace pacts thereby uniting people confronted with mining and hydro-electric development projects, which are often a source of conflict and tribal war in the Cordillera.

A parallel case can be given from Indonesia where IWGIA supported the indigenous AMAN organisation, the basic aim of which was to re-establish and develop the traditional *adat* institution to replace the current village councils. This took place in a situation whereby, in a move towards the democratisation of village governments, there was an "apparent general lack of community interest in establishing *adat*-based government" (IWGIA 2003a). The IWGIA report concludes that: "Establishing a restructured *adat* government on the basis of modernized *adat* principles entails many uncertainties and risks for those who have to bear the consequences. Moreover, traditional *adat* elites who may tend to be sidelined in this reformed order, may find participation in existing *adat* councils more attractive" (ibid.). The report points out the moral force of the *adat* but makes clear that, "establishing fully-fledged *adat* communities in a governmental sense may be an idea whose time has passed in Indonesia" (ibid.).

If any conclusion can be drawn it is that any support for indigenous institutions should relate to indigenous self-development as seen in relation to institutional legitimacy.

Russia

IWGIA became involved with Russia's indigenous peoples as soon as they were allowed to organise themselves. While the first contacts were directly with indigenous representatives, the strength and permanence of this cooperation was achieved by establishing an IWGIA local group in Moscow. All members of the group were distinguished academics, respected and known by indigenous peoples following long working relations. The establishment of a Russia-based IWGIA group was therefore a unique opportunity to create close links with the indigenous organisations.

Apart from some publications such as "Indigenous Peoples of the Soviet North" in 1990, on the founding of the "Organisation of Small Peoples in the Soviet North, Siberia and Far East", and the document "Anxious North" (1996) about indigenous peoples in Soviet and post-Soviet Russia, and support for introducing the indigenous representatives to the international human rights instruments, the first years were primarily investigative. During a networking trip to Siberia and the Russian Far East in 1992, it became clear that indigenous peoples were in deep need of outside funding in order to organise and defend their rights. The Sámi and Inuit in the Nordic countries, Canada and Alaska had at an early stage taken the initiative to cooperate across borders and the Sámi in Russia and the Yupiit in Chukotka were the first indigenous peoples in the former Soviet Union to benefit from contacts with the outside world

For 10 years, IWGIA worked with indigenous peoples in Russia on political and human rights issues. The main collaborating partner was the previously mentioned umbrella organisation, RAIPON (Russian Association of Indigenous Peoples of the North), which represents indigenous peoples in the Russian European North, Siberia and the Far East. An important development took place in 2001 when the Danish Ministry of Foreign Affairs established a programme in support of indigenous peoples' projects in Russia. The same year, IWGIA received funding for a project entitled "Capacity Building and Promotion of Human Rights and Legal Mechanisms Concerning Indigenous Peoples in the Russian Federation", which included three related components. One component focused on federal legislation and included consultation and lobbying work on a weekly basis by experts, the elaboration of written responses to draft laws and raising awareness and providing information on federal legislation by organising regional workshops. The second component was aimed at supporting indigenous representation in federal, regional and local bodies and investigating options for increased indigenous political representation, including the possibilities of establishing an advisory Russian Indigenous Peoples' Parliament. The final component was support for local empowerment projects; this soon developed a special priority for, and focus upon, the establishment of regional information centres. Core support for RAIPON was also included in the programme.

IWGIA's approach to this and to similar EU-supported projects was to establish a strong coordination between RAIPON, IWGIA Moscow and the international secretariat in Copenhagen. This collaboration model was unique in that it was the first time that the design and implementation of a project had been the joint responsibility of IWGIA and an indigenous organisation.

Project screening and discussions on project content were undertaken by an IWGIA-RAIPON steering committee. The only component in which IWGIA was the sole decision maker was a sub-project facility that supported the small projects of regional indigenous organisations. This procedure followed many discussions between IWGIA and RAIPON, as many of the provincial/regional indigenous organisations that submitted proposals to the sub-project facility were members of the RAIPON umbrella organisation. For IWGIA, it was important to be able to make decisions as an external actor, in order to avoid a situation where the applicant and the decision-maker were one and the same. The decision also took into consideration the concerns of some regional organisations, which did not want to see a structure in which the national umbrella organisation alone would decide on the distribution of projects and funding.

The projects and the project procedures enabled the indigenous organisations to develop as a *movement* as they strengthened the link between the secretariat of the umbrella organisation in Moscow and the regional constituents, not least by providing funding for regional empowerment projects. The national organisation developed a different profile, as it was able to establish a network and communicate with regional organisations that finally had the opportunity to develop as organisations. The principal condition for such development is the availability of financial and other resources with which to organise seminars, travel and distribute information and documentation etc.

From a very early stage, it was obvious that problems could arise because of the key position of RAIPON as a national umbrella organisation. The model applied was also challenged in cases where IWGIA wanted to support a regional initiative that was not RAIPON's preferred option. There was no easy solution to this situation given the Russian administrative system, but IWGIA/RAIPON were able to create a system that gave good results in comparison with the resources invested. The procedures have provided IWGIA with invaluable insight into and knowledge of indigenous communities and organisations in Russia.

The first programme funded by the Danish government became the model for IWGIA's Russia activities in the years ahead. While it basically reflected IWGIA's holistic approach, the three-tier programme nevertheless broke new ground. An evaluation of the programme from 2004 (IWGIA 2004a) pointed to some of the advantages and disadvantages attached to the model, and recommended that a clear distinction be made between the political and technical functions of project collaboration.

It should be noted that whereas IWGIA had been a firm supporter of RAIPON's international human rights activities since 1990, and specifically participation in international human rights meetings, the new programme funded by the Danish Foreign Ministry gave IWGIA an opportunity to deal directly with regional indigenous organisations whilst at the same time coordinating these efforts with RAIPON, as the umbrella organisation.

The legal component of the programme involves one or more persons being recruited to follow up parliamentary activities and initiatives as these relate to indigenous issues and peoples. Members of parliament have been lobbied to support the rights of indigenous peoples in the case of new laws and acts being proposed and regional indigenous organisations in all parts of the Russian North, Siberia and the Far East have been made aware of such initiatives and have been mobilised to support the lobbying activities. Seen from a global perspective, this part of the programme has been quite unique and RAIPON has, in a number of instances, been able to make a significant impact on the legal processes and results.

The legal component has been able to draw on the structure, with regional information centres that coordinate their activities with RAIPON, receive information from Moscow and provide the other regions with information about local developments. The establishment of information centres has been made possible by the relatively high level of educational standards, added to the fact that the indigenous organisations have been able to benefit from a firm communist or Russian tradition that has linked even the most remote regions with Moscow in a structural and communicative network.

From an historical perspective, IWGIA's strong association with RAIPON is logical and reflects IWGIA's way of working. Not surprisingly, both the approach and the relationship have been criticised by those who do not consider RAIPON to be representative of all the indigenous peoples of Russia and who have made a number of allegations against RAIPON. The strong centralised structure adopted by RAIPON seems more to reflect a Russian tradition and Russian realities than monopolistic behaviour. The relationship between RAIPON, as the dominant indigenous umbrella organisation in Russia, and foreign partners and donors is not without its pitfalls. Drawing on experiences from others parts of the world, IWGIA has made efforts to reconcile RAIPON's efforts to coordinate indigenous activities with the legitimate wish of local and regional indigenous organisations to implement their own projects. In this respect, the Steering Committee, as a key component in the partnership between IWGIA and RAIPON, has achieved its objectives.

The evaluation from 2004 (IWGIA 2004a) concluded that, in the broadest sense, RAIPON had been successful in its lobbying efforts. RAIPON staff had developed curricula and training materials to improve indigenous peoples' legal understanding and to expand their organisational capacity and that, in spite of the ever-changing political climate in Russia, the various activities, such as addressing parliamentary mechanisms and political participation, had produced output that constituted a sustainable base and a resource for future work.

The overall assessment was that the project component had successfully strengthened the capacity of Russian indigenous organisations to promote indigenous rights in the process of democratisation in the Russian Federation. The project component of the IWGIA-RAIPON cooperation is unique in its focus on legislative and parliamentary mechanisms for indigenous peoples in Russia, and the activities are highly relevant.

When working with indigenous organisations in Russia or elsewhere, it is essential for IWGIA to respect the representative organs of the indigenous peoples and work with the existing structures and organisations. From a global perspective, the presence of an organisation such as RAIPON, with its national networks, election process and regional representation, is unique. Areas of controversy have been discussed between the two organisations in an open atmosphere and out of a true sense of partnership.

Summing up

Being a provider of project support obviously creates a hierarchical relationship between IWGIA and its respective partners. Over the years, however, it has also become clear that it has opened up new opportunities for creating close and lasting relationships between IWGIA and a number of indigenous organisations. The policy change in the 1980s regarding projects was extremely important because it paved the way for the holistic approach that was to become a driving force behind IWGIA's work from the beginning of the 1990s to this day.

Project involvement also gave rise to new relationships between IWGIA and governmental development agencies, initially Norad, Danida, Sida and FINNIDA (the Finnish Department for International Development Cooperation) and, later, the European Commission. IWGIA also managed to link funding from the development agencies to parallel funding from the Nordic Ministries of Foreign Affairs and the fact that IWGIA became a main receiver of funding earmarked for indigenous peoples from Norway and Denmark opened new possibilities of having an impact on policy. While IWGIA became dependent on these agencies for funding not only for projects but also for publications, the development agencies have come to rely on IWGIA and IWGIA's publications for information about indigenous issues.

PART 3

MAJOR ISSUES

Who are the indigenous peoples? How should IWGIA advocate for their rights? How can IWGIA collaborate with other NGOs and what kind of relationship can IWGIA establish with governments? These are some of the key questions that IWGIA has had to deal with since its earliest days.

CHAPTER 10

THE CONCEPT OF INDIGENOUS PEOPLES

Who were the people that came to be known as indigenous and who were the focus of the organisation that called itself the International Work Group for *Indigenous* Affairs?

In the 1970s, the discussions within IWGIA sometimes referred to ILO Convention No. 107 concerning *Indigenous and Other Tribal and Semi-Tribal Populations*, which dated from 1957. This Convention used the word "indigenous" in a narrow sense referring in its Article 1.b) to

> *populations in independent countries which are regarded as indigenous on account of their descent from the populations which inhabited the country, or a geographical region to which the country belongs, at the time of conquest or colonisation and which, irrespective of their legal status, live more in conformity with the social, economic and cultural institutions of that time than with the institutions of the nation to which they belong.*

It is therefore not surprising that Helge Kleivan in 1973 referred to indigenous peoples as those "who were there first" (Kleivan 1973:172), although this did not cover all the peoples IWGIA came to work with.

ILO Convention No. 169, which replaced Convention No. 107 in 1989, has a broader working definition since it was based on the notion of self-identification, and – most important - since it not only referred to conquest or colonisation but also to "present state boundaries". In other words, it took into consideration the fact that groups were marginalized as an effect of the creation of new states, primarily in Africa and Asia. This had hardly been conventional wisdom in the 1950s, 1960s or even in the 1970s and, for IWGIA, it was an important development, as it was in line with its efforts to work with indigenous peoples globally.

The working definitions used by the UN Rapporteur Martínez Cobo[114] in his study from the early 1980s were also much broader and more inclusive in nature and not limited to peoples that had been conquered or colonized, such as the *aboriginal* or *First Nations* peoples living in the Americas, Australia, New Zealand and other settler territories. They included, among others, the Sámi living in the Nordic countries in Europe and indigenous peoples living in Asia. The geographical scope of the concept turned out to be much more than an academic question because, when the first national and international organisations who claimed solidarity with *other* indigenous peoples were established during the 1970s, they generally had a much more limited geographical reference in mind than Martínez Cobo.

In a 1973 article (Kleivan, H 1973), Helge Kleivan tried to introduce the concept of a "Fourth World", undoubtedly inspired by George Manuel; however, the concept was never adopted by indigenous peoples. George Manuel had travelled extensively, including to Tanzania, and although inspired by developments in that country, he clearly saw the difference between the colonialism experienced by people in the "Third World" and that of the indigenous peoples (Manuel and Poslund 1978).

However, from the very first days, the founders of IWGIA were less preoccupied with definitions than with *identifying* the most marginalized, discriminated and oppressed groups. Although IWGIA was established by professional anthropologists, when it came to dealing with indigenous peoples, the approach taken was a pragmatic one, and the strategy adopted was dictated by the urgency of the situation. The anthropologists working with IWGIA have always been experienced in fieldwork, "coming home" with an in-depth knowledge of the conditions in which indigenous peoples live. As Andrew Grey notes: "The term *indigenous* thus is not simply a matter of analysis. It is a matter of life and death for the millions of people covered by the term ..."(Gray 1995:41). The theoretical guidance was, nevertheless, clear.

The relational approach

IWGIA has always worked from a relational rather than an essentialist approach to indigenous peoples and indigenous issues. The Sámi historian Henry Minde (2008) has stressed that the Sámi who became involved in indigenous issues in the early 1970s were under the influence of the relational approach introduced in the study of ethnic groups by the Norwegian anthropologists Fredrik Barth, in general, and Harald Eidheim, specifically in relation to the Sámi. Helge Kleivan was a student of Fredrik Barth and he was without any doubt strongly influenced and impressed by his work. This always impacted on his approach to indigenous peoples in general and the situation of the Greenlanders and the Sámi in particular.[115] For IWGIA, it has always been very important to consider the category of indigenous peoples as being formed on the basis of a discourse on rights and self-determination (Sjørslev 1998:8; Gray 1995).

When IWGIA celebrated its 30th anniversary in 1998, the director of the organisation, Inger Sjørslev, thus wrote:

> *There is fairly general agreement that the indigenous movement has to be understood within a global-local context in which the articulation of culture and 'in-*

digenousness' must be regarded as a reaction to global forces and influences, from hard core economic and political pressures and demands, through the change and dissolution of social structures, to the effect of outside cultural influences and inspirations (Sjørslev 1998:7).

Along the same lines, but taking an African context as their point of departure, Veber and Wæhle had written earlier: "In sum, indigenous identity is highly contextual and constitutes a social fact which may or may not become a platform for social and political activity, or from which to make demands for legislative measures from governments or administrative agencies" (Veber and Wæhle 1993:15).

For IWGIA, it has always been very important to consider the category of indigenous peoples as being formed on the basis of a discourse on rights and self-determination (Sjørslev 1998: 8; Gray 1995).

These positions are important references because they help to explain the close relationship between IWGIA and an organisation such as the World Council of Indigenous Peoples (WCIP), both organisations to a large extent representing relational and global perspectives on indigenous issues.

The first organisations who entered the international scene were primarily from the Americas, Australia and New Zealand. For these organisations, headed by the International Indian Treaty Council (IITC), the Indian Law Resource Centre (originally called the Institute for the Development of Indian Law) and other organisations for whom being indigenous in practice was synonymous with being aboriginal, defining indigenousness may not have posed a great problem (Minde 2008). The definition became an issue, however, when the WCIP was established in 1975 (ibid). Although the founding father of the WCIP, George Manuel, had a global perspective for the new organisation, there were others who were sceptical about including peoples such as the Sámi, and the organisation was never really able to reconcile the discrepancies between indigenous peoples from the different continents. But the global vision of George Manuel may help to explain the close links between WCIP and IWGIA in the 1970s and 1980s.

The IITC was founded as an international organisation in the sense that it claimed to represent sovereign nations – within the United States. Their agreements with the USA were treaties under international law, and this logically brought them into contact with the United Nations and treaty nations from outside the USA. But originally the vision of the IITC was that of a regional, not a global organisation. Thus the Declaration adopted on the founding of the IITC, in 1974, states, that:

We recognize that there is only one colour of Mankind in the world who are not represented in the United Nations. And that is the indigenous Redman of the Western Hemisphere. We recognize this lack of representation in the United Nations comes from the genocidal policies of the colonial power of the United States.[116]

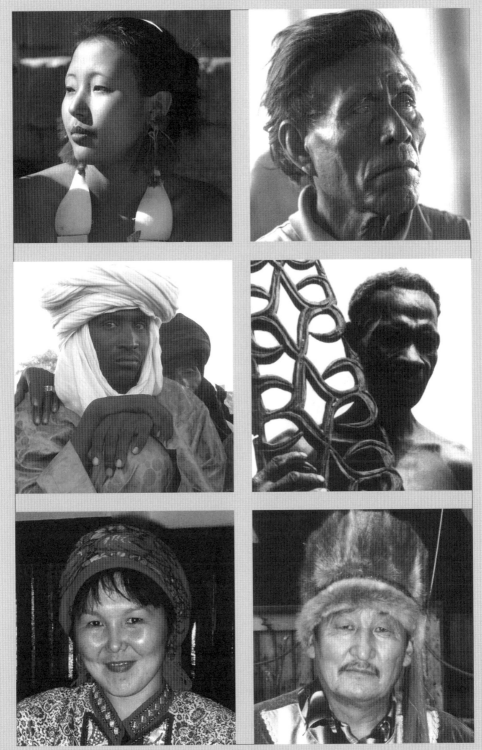

The basic goal of the IITC was legal recognition of their treaties with the United States (Sanders 1989:414), whereas the WCIP was much more global in its scope. But in spite of its name, even the WCIP was organised on the basis of regions that did not include Asia or Africa (the regions were North America, Central America, South America, the Pacific and Northern Europe).

In the long-term, the limited geographical perspective of organisations such as the IITC became very important because these same organisations were also the first to formulate the vision for the work within the United Nations as being primarily standard-setting. The preliminary principles were presented to the Working Group on Indigenous Populations (WGIP) in 1982 by a small group of North American lawyers, and the World Council presented its views in 1985, one year after the WGIP had initiated the drafting process. In these formative years, the drafting was spearheaded, promoted and moved forward by the same people, without whom there probably would have been no Declaration today. However, when indigenous peoples from other continents - from Asia, Africa and Russia - entered the scene, the drafting also needed to include their realities and aspirations, which were often quite different.

For many years, the indigenous caucus managed to reconcile the varied cultural and historical experiences and political backgrounds of indigenous peoples from all parts of the world. Openness, patience and willingness to reach consensus made it possible for the caucus to become a unified body, fighting for a common goal.

Towards the end of the process, however, diverging viewpoints led to tensions and divisions among indigenous peoples. The lines of division changed from time to time but patterns emerged and there were clear differences in the aims that people wanted reflected in a declaration. Moreover, for some it appeared as though the process itself was more important than reaching an agreement on a final text.

As already mentioned, this was one of the reasons that impelled IWGIA to take a pro-active approach to international human rights issues, and new partnerships were created in relation to IWGIA's human rights efforts. IWGIA came to emphasise human rights partnerships with organisations in Asia, Africa, Russia and the Arctic, and with organisations from other regions that realised the need for negotiations around the 1994 Draft Declaration in order to achieve a result.

A global concept

IWGIA has also been an active player in broadening the concept of indigenous peoples, however, since IWGIA's relational approach to who is and who is not indigenous logically led to including work with people from the Pacific, Asia, Russia and Africa. From the 1980s, IWGIA thus facilitated the participation of Asian indigenous peoples in UN meetings. "The initiative for the expansion of the concern with indigenous peoples into Asia was pioneered by the European-based support organizations" (Sanders 1989:416), including IWGIA. IWGIA, on the other hand, was the spearhead in terms of introducing the UN to indigenous persons from Africa and from Russia. When IWGIA supported the first indigenous persons from East Africa to the WGIP, Howard Berman, a legal advisor from North America closely connected to IWGIA, commented: "Who will be the next?" Well, it was the indigenous peoples of Russia!

The policy of promoting the participation in UN meetings of indigenous peoples from regions that had previously had no representation in the UN became a key component of IWGIA's human rights efforts. This proved to be very important because indigenous peoples from these "new" regions later came to play a key role in establishing the Permanent Forum and the adoption of the Declaration.

In the late 1990s, self-organisation among indigenous peoples in Africa was still in its infancy, and an *Indigenous Affairs* editorial from 1999 states

> *Indigenous peoples in Africa face a whole range of problems and suffer from serious human rights abuses. African indigenous peoples are among the poorest and most marginalized populations in Africa. Whether hunter-gatherers or pastoralists, their traditional way of life is often based on extensive land use and their traditional territories are increasingly being encroached upon by states and dominant groups who have an interest in exploiting those areas economically in various ways. African indigenous cultures are threatened by this encroachment, they are looked upon as 'primitive' and 'less developed' and African indigenous peoples experience severe discrimination* (Jensen and Dahl 1999:2).

It was against this backdrop that IWGIA, in partnership with a local organisation (see above), took a pro-active step and convened a meeting in Arusha in January 1999. Peoples in Africa adopted the indigenous agenda as a last resort (Hodgson 2002b) and were, initially, "beneficiaries more than initiators" (Saugestad 2008:171). Supported by IWGIA, donors and indigenous peoples from other parts of the world, indigenous peoples in Africa were, however, soon "adopted" into the international indigenous movement. The experience of suppression and marginalisation that all these African groups came with was transformed into a new language, an "international claim for recognition and rights" (Hodgson 2002a:1040).

The African debate

For IWGIA, the African reality was far from the picture projected by the anthropologist Adam Kuper (2003) and others in their academic dispute against the concept of indigenousness. The discussion, as raised by Kuper, reflects the viewpoint of a large number of anthropologists but, as pointed out by other anthropologists,

THE GRIQUA AND THE REHOBOTH BASTERS

When the Dutch established the Cape Colony in the 17th century, a group of mixed origin began to emerge as descendants of White men and Hottentot or Khoi-San women. They lived on the fringes of the colony in a region south of the Orange River. They were Christians and called themselves Basters.

At one stage, there were two groups of Basters, one of which crossed the Orange River before 1870 and established itself in Rehoboth, at that time South West Africa, today Namibia. The other group remained in South Africa and came to be known as the Griqua.

The Rehoboth Basters developed into a settled community with its own identity. During colonial times, they allied themselves first with the Germans and, after World War I, the South Africans. At independence, the Rehoboth Basters were united but completely isolated, had lost their system of self-government and were trying to be recognised as indigenous by the United Nations.

In South Africa, the Griqua were dispersed and, during the Apartheid regime, grouped as Coloured peoples. As Coloured, the Griqua were discriminated against and were in general not in opposition to the Black majority. When the Apartheid regime was disbanded, the Griqua successfully managed to gain recognition, nationally and internationally, as indigenous.

History made it different for those Basters who moved north and those who remained south of the Orange River. The two groups reacted differently to the colonisers and the Black majorities and, without a relational perspective, we are unable to understand why today the Griqua have received a positive response to their indigenous claim while the Rehoboth Basters have not.

(Sources: Britz, Lang and Limpricht 1999; Kuper 2003)

is based upon a surprisingly low level of knowledge and accuracy,[117] and only tends to increase the gap that has existed between certain parts of the anthropological establishment and IWGIA, since the founding of the organisation.

In his article, Adam Kuper refers to the Boers and the fact that they were rejected by what he calls the "United Nations' indigenous peoples' forum", in contrast to the South African Griqua who have been supported by this same "Indigenous Peoples' Forum". Kuper's writing does not really make much sense, nor does it accord with the reality (Saugestad 2004; Kenrick and Lewis 2004). It is however interesting that he does not mention another issue, which is that the Griqua are accepted as being indigenous by most indigenous peoples participating in international meetings and by organisations like IWGIA, while the Rehoboth Basters from Namibia, to whom they are historically related, are not.

It is interesting for IWGIA because IWGIA has supported the Griqua while similar support would never have been given to the Rehoboth Basters. But it is even more interesting because it reveals – and confirms – the need to take a relational view on being indigenous (beyond the self-definitional issue). In the aftermath that marked the end of the Cold War, numerous new states came into being and, in these new states, new identities had to be negotiated. When the Soviet Union collapsed, there were people whose identity had been suppressed who came forward to claim a "new" identity. Others had been forced to write an ethnic identity in their passports other than their own and yet others had officially chosen the identity that involved the least repression from the authorities. The term "indigenous" evolves in response to developments in state structures and those who identify themselves as such may be known under different terms for example as "tribals", "aboriginal peoples", "adivasis", etc (Gray 1995).

Groups from all continents have tried to use the indigenous UN platform. Some of them have realised that this is not their forum, such as the Tamils from Sri Lanka; others came to the indigenous meetings until they had achieved self-government or independence, such as the East Timorese and the Bougainvilleans. Others try to use any international forum, such as the Dalit from India. Groups like the Rehoboth Basters may feel that they have no other place to go. These cases always give rise to discussions and considerations but there are few cases in which the indigenous course is abused.

It must be borne in mind that, when new groups of indigenous peoples enter the UN, the indigenous movement itself is faced with new challenges, which may cause some tension.

These are the realities that have moulded IWGIA's way of dealing with the issue of definition and the reason why it often distances itself from the academic debate around the issue of indigenousness. IWGIA's point of departure has been from a social, political and cultural position and not from a theoretical discussion. It was the realities and self-representation of indigenous peoples that formed IWGIA's approach to, and analysis of, indigenous issues.

Class versus ethnicity

Another challenge to IWGIA's notion of indigenousness came from the people themselves. In the 1970s and 1980s, primarily in the Americas, indigenous peoples disagreed on the position of the indigenous struggle in relation to the class struggle. Indigenous peoples were oppressed but was indigenousness subordinate to the class struggle or vice versa? It was an issue in the USA when the International Indian Treaty Council was founded and it lay beneath the disagreements between the IITC and the WCIP before and during the 1977 conference in Geneva. In 1980, there were heated debates about this issue[118] during the founding conference of CISA, the South American branch of the WCIP. There were those who advocated that class ideology was a Western concept and as such, to be rejected. Opponents saw the ethnic struggle as part of the class struggle. The issue later came to the fore when Shining Path (*Sendero Luminoso*) implemented a campaign of violence in Peru. The indigenous organisations in general distanced themselves from the armed attacks that were perpetrated against Indian communities.[119]

IWGIA's viewpoint on this has always been that indigenous issues must be analysed in terms of indigenous-state relations. Indigenous peoples have to find their own solutions to their problems and, although there are often overlaps between class relations and ethnic relations, these problems must be resolved within the framework of "self-development with identity", to use a term recently coined by Vicky Tauli-Corpuz from the Philippines.

IWGIA came under some pressure during the conflict in Nicaragua in the early 1980s. It was Helge Kleivan's position that the conflict was nurtured by the violent colonialist attitude of the U.S. and that, in order to find a solution to the unfortunate situation of the Miskitu in Nicaragua, an agreement had to be found with the Sandinistas. This position was upheld by IWGIA as the conflict became more and more blurred and indigenous peoples from the U.S. who had previously been spokespersons for the class struggle now sided with the U.S.-supported right-wing contras.

The issue is of enormous significance to indigenous peoples, and to IWGIA. Indigenous peoples often say, "We know who we are, we don't need anyone to define us", and that a narrow focus on ethnicity limits their capacity to create alliances with other civil society groups, including labour unions, political parties, popular movements, etc. On the other hand, it still seems that those who are willing to accept the relationship between indigenousness and other civil, social, and political groupings have been able to create new platforms and opportunities for themselves.

The Alta case turned environmental and Sámi issues into indigenous issues – Photo: Elisabeth S. Østmo

In the Andes, class issues confronted indigenous issues – Photo:

CHAPTER 11

ADVOCACY, REPRESENTATION OR SELF-DETERMINATION

Another key question is how IWGIA should position itself in relation to indigenous communities and organisations when it comes to promoting their rights.

The political, social, cultural and economic realities of indigenous peoples are diverse and multifaceted. The fact that they are also entangled in larger structural relations increases the complexity of the situation. Working with indigenous rights issues is indeed a minefield as the discussion and promotion of interests, perspectives and rights are closely linked to an asymmetrical power relationship whereby some are marginalized and oppressed.

When IWGIA was founded, very few indigenous groups were able, by their own efforts, to report on their conditions to the outside world, about encroachments upon their lands and violations of their human rights. The question of advocacy (whose interests to support and how) has therefore been a recurrent issue within IWGIA.

Looking back, the organisation has never deviated from stressing that indigenous peoples have the right of self-determination, including the right to present themselves and their case to the outside world. But the mere existence of IWGIA shows that the reality is more complicated.

Like human rights lawyers, the scientists associated with IWGIA have had an idea about what a good society is and have felt a strong desire to address urgent issues such as domination, conflict and structural violence (Henriksen n.d.), not to mention genocide and ethnocide. The practice applied by IWGIA in dealing with indigenous peoples has nevertheless always been to support and enhance the ability and right of indigenous peoples to speak for themselves. As the anthropologist Anthony Cohen is quoted as saying, "I am always a little ambivalent about advocacy. I always want to advocate; but I also always think that they (the people I've studied) could speak better for themselves than I could for them" (Hastrup and Elsass 1990:301).

This fits well with IWGIA's policy and, probably, with the view of most anthropologists and other social scientists. One might have expected therefore that when indigenous peoples were able to organise on the local, national and international scene this would have led to massive support from anthropological academia. But this was not the case, as many anthropologists seem to have a problem with *representativity*. Just like in any other society, indigenous peoples have diverse opinions, and the communities are fragmented into youth/ elders, men/women, educated/non-educated, etc, and hardly any organisation can claim to have equal or full support from all these groups. The argument therefore goes that scientists' support for indigenous peoples implies promoting either the "good" or the "bad", the "traditionalists" or the "modernists" (Hastrup and Elsass 1990:305). So, while anthropologists should report on the context, the requirement is first and foremost "to raise the context awareness of the people themselves so that they may eventually become better equipped to plead their own cause" (ibid:306). The experience learned in IWGIA is, however, that these arguments are a smokescreen covering up the fact that there is a close relationship between theoretical and practical anthropology (Gray 1990:387).

The position between academia and the indigenous reality has always haunted the anthropologists within IWGIA. When Inger Sjørslev, the director in the 1990s, moved back to university work she wrote:

One thing that has struck me in moving back and forth between the world of activism and the academic world is the existence of almost waterproof walls between the two. Not that the indigenous and NGO world does not make use of, and produce, academic knowledge, and not that the academic world – I am talking mainly about anthropologists – does not deal with the indigenous question, but on the whole, they do not seem to interact very much (1998:7).

The need to *analyse* the situation is always there. As Georg Henriksen, for many years the Chair of IWGIA, wrote:

Apart from direct physical abuse, indigenous issues are difficult to report on, because they involve complex inter-relationships between the quality of life of individuals as members of larger groups, and constraints represented by the political, legal, social and cultural structures of the state. The situation of any indigenous peoples therefore demands quite a sophisticated analysis in order to be understood and acknowledged (1998:3).

The right of self-determination has always guided the scientists working with IWGIA, including cases where they have acted as advocates, carried out research, or been middlemen between indigenous groups and those holding power. The many roles of being an anthropologist and the implications, restrictions, possibilities and dangers of each role were often highlighted by Georg Henriksen (Henriksen 1997). A common challenge is when two conflicting groups each seek the support of outsiders, including anthropologists and IWGIA. Georg Henriksen often referred to conflicts between the Innu and the Inuit in Labrador over land claims and mining. In this and similar cases, IWGIA has never tried to protect indigenous peoples from development and has stressed that the right to self-determination includes the right to development. In such situations, IWGIA has instead tried to put forward the facts and the options available.

When supporting indigenous projects there is always a danger of creating clientships, with the indigenous group being the client, a situation that has often been discussed within IWGIA and an issue that Georg Henriksen himself stressed over and over again in his writing (1985) and in Board meetings. In IWGIA's early years, the anthropologists' primary fear was of being (mis)used by governments as middlemen but, later, it became the potential danger of indigenous groups becoming financially dependent on an organisation such as IWGIA. However, the political realities of most indigenous peoples are such that they will only be able to have their rights recognised if they can raise support from "outsiders".

The aim of empowerment, i.e. supporting indigenous peoples to represent themselves, has been a constant factor in IWGIA's dealings with indigenous issues. Within the anthropological discipline, Helge Kleivan can be considered a pioneer in this respect as he realised the key role indigenous peoples' own organisations could play and what the implications were for those dedicated to defending the rights of indigenous peoples. In a letter to Robert Paine in 1983 he wrote:

We must be clear about the great difference between advocacy situations before and after the emergence of indigenous organizations. Many initiatives that could previously be seen as both morally and politically useful to the interests of a client population – and even deemed to be so by the people themselves – cannot be pursued once the clients have their own organization for the defence of their rights.[120]

This also explains why empowerment has been the ideological cornerstone of IWGIA since its foundation. The right of self-determination has remained the guiding principle in everything IWGIA has done, including project activities and partnership building with indigenous organisations.

Even in the early years, IWGIA and other NGOs were already conduits for the spread of information about the fate of indigenous peoples. IWGIA has never represented indigenous peoples and has been careful not to speak on their behalf. Indigenous *issues*, on the other hand, have been promoted in writing, presented to governments and discussed with indigenous peoples and their representatives.

IWGIA is not a missionizing organisation. It does not work with indigenous peoples and organisations without their wishing it. If there is no common understanding of the issues between IWGIA and an indigenous group there can be no cooperation.

It is well-known that indigenous peoples sometimes have a rhetoric in which they distance themselves from all non-indigenous people, institutions, NGOs etc. This upsets and annoys many. Everyone who has worked for an organisation like IWGIA has had such experiences. However, given the historical experience of indigenous peoples, this rhetoric is easy to understand. Generally it is the rhetoric of individuals and has rarely disturbed cooperation between IWGIA and indigenous peoples or their organisations.

The explanation has to do with how one sees the notion of advocacy, as a static or evolving concept. If we take the concept of self-determination seriously, it includes the right to determine one's own future under ever-changing circumstances. IWGIA's cooperation with indigenous organisations has reflected this. The pitfall is to become "disappointed" with the indigenous partners when they adapt to new realities (as referred to earlier), or as a researcher to take refuge in one's own definitional discussions that never leave academia, to which most indigenous peoples have no access.

The principle of non-interference

IWGIA has always claimed to have a neutral position in relation to controversies between indigenous groups – these have been considered as "internal" indigenous affairs. IWGIA has thus done its best to keep out of conflicts such as, for example, that between the Navaho and the Hopi over territories, claimed by both parties, or the dispute between the Iñupiat of the Alaskan North Slope and the Athabascans of the interior concerning oil development. This policy was, and is, well-founded but, in the extreme, it can lead to bizarre situations such as the following.

In the early 1970s, IWGIA published an article on a land rights conflict between indigenous groups in the United States. The article was written by an indigenous person but triggered an angry response[121] from a reader in Denmark who, in a 19-page long critique plus dozens of maps and documentaries, basically accused the author of falsification and of only using material that proved his arguments. No less important, the author was also attacked for only considering the interests of one indigenous group. Six months later, the author came back with a response almost as long as the original critique. Over the next three years, this dispute continued with new letters from the person in Denmark criticising anything IWGIA published about North American Indians. This is not the place to judge the rights and wrongs of this dispute but the outcome was that they each attacked IWGIA for not supporting *his* position. The author's argument was that IWGIA should support the indigenous viewpoint while his opponent criticized IWGIA for (uncritically) publishing that indigenous standpoint.

Everyone who has worked for IWGIA has experienced indigenous peoples trying to involve IWGIA in their own conflicts. In most cases, this has been as part of building up support among friends and partners but it is far more complex when a non-indigenous NGO such as IWGIA is being used as a buffer to avoid open conflicts between two indigenous groups (or viewpoints). It may look like a matter of conflict avoidance but it is also an integral part of building consensus among indigenous groups and individuals by not creating unsolvable splits. For

IWGIA it is a delicate balance between being trusted by both partners and being deemed advocate of only one partner or only one point of view.

A problem that can never be resolved is when IWGIA's cooperation with one indigenous group is taken as being in opposition to other groups. This is a global experience and the following is just one example.

The Naga people declared independence in 1947, the day before India became independent. The letter sent to the United Nations was, however, ignored and later rejected by India. IWGIA has always been a firm supporter of the right of the Naga to determine their own future, including establishing their own state. A document published in 1986 (IWGIA 1986) firmly stressed the Naga peoples' right of self-determination, including their demand for an independent state. It was, however, also pointed out that "the book reflects no particular position within the Naga struggle" (p.1). The situation and the aspirations of the Naga are regularly covered in IWGIA's yearbook *The Indigenous World*. The ethnic situation in North-east India is, however, extremely complicated, and the ambition of the Naga to create their own state is met with resistance by other indigenous peoples and ethnic groups. Some of these see the ambitions of the Naga as a threat to their own rights as indigenous peoples and fear what they consider to be Naga chauvinism. The issue is further complicated by the divide-and-rule policy of the government in Delhi, which is used in combination with military campaigns in its strategy against the Naga resistance movement. IWGIA has often been criticized for its defence of Naga ambitions and has therefore offered to print views other than those of the Naga. As in other cases, project support for one organisation was also met with criticism from those not supported, implying that IWGIA had taken sides with one party in a conflict. Such situations are extremely difficult to handle and, no matter how hard IWGIA tries, it is very difficult to convince everybody of IWGIA's attempt to maintain a neutral position.

For some years, IWGIA had a marginal position in NGO cooperation on environmental processes and initiatives relating to development policies in general. IWGIA's academic background, and the firm support for indigenous peoples' right to self-determination, partly explain why the organisation has made considerable efforts not to take up the categorical positions that characterise many solidarity movements. This is a part of the relational approach to ethnicity adopted by IWGIA, which is very different from the essentialist approach used by many solidarity organisations. While the difference between IWGIA and a number of solidarity organisations and environmental movements is a matter of substance, it is also one of strategy. IWGIA claims the right to have critical positions vis-à-vis indigenous organisations although its policy of non-interference may be mistaken for passivity. This has, in some cases, made it very difficult for the organisation to work with those that unilaterally defend their "objects". The example of IWGIA's differences with the animal rights movements illustrates this.

Zlaqatahyi Project, Argentina 2002 - Photo: IWGIA archive

Visiting a project in the Nenets Autonomous Okrug, Russia, 2004 – Photo: Yasavey

CHAPTER 12

COOPERATION WITH NON-INDIGENOUS NGOS

IWGIA was founded by academics, and its efforts and way of working have always been rooted in an analytical and academic tradition. Although born out of academia, IWGIA's priority has at all times been to work in the political sphere in order to promote the rights of indigenous peoples. The role of academic discussions within IWGIA has been to improve its political work rather than to take part in purely academic discussion. This has been a choice whereby IWGIA has opted to work within the practical realities of the indigenous world without opting out of scientific analysis. In addition to targeted focus on indigenous peoples and indigenous issues, this choice means that IWGIA occupies a unique niche in the NGO world, and this is reflected in its achievements. It also affects IWGIA's relationship and cooperation with other NGOs.

IWGIA is one of the very few non-indigenous international organisations devoted only to indigenous issues. The other major players on the international scene, such as Minority Rights Group (MRG), Cultural Survival, Survival International, Forest Peoples' Programme, Unrepresented Peoples' Organisation (UNPO) and Amnesty International have, or have had, broader objectives. While IWGIA has prioritized the international UN processes and followed a number of them from beginning to end, many of these organisations have therefore only at times and in some settings been active on the international indigenous human rights scene. Very few have maintained a persistent focus on indigenous issues that has enabled them to follow and participate in the, often controversial, Declaration process that lasted for more than 20 years, or in the process leading to the establishment of the Permanent Forum.

For IWGIA, the priority given to international processes has been logical and strategic but it also explains why IWGIA has never developed a broad, formalized long-term cooperation with other NGOs.

What also distinguishes organisations such as IWGIA, Cultural Survival, Survival International and the Minority Rights Group from each other is usually related to audience, publicity, fundraising but also sometimes political approaches. IWGIA's historical relationship with Survival International may give some insight.

In only one case has IWGIA tried to formalise its relationship with another NGO. In the 1970s, IWGIA and Survival International (UK) were in regular contact exchanging information and they were in many respects similar[122], with similar aims and ambitions. It was therefore decided in 1978 that Survival should be represented on IWGIA's Board and vice versa.[123] However, even though the two organisations held a two-day meeting in Helge Kleivan's home north of Copenhagen[124] and produced a joint statement afterwards, nothing formal came out of these efforts.[125] The two organisations did, however, work together on specific issues over the coming years.

Survival International and IWGIA were basically established on the same premise: to disseminate information about the situation of indigenous peoples facing ethnocide. From the start, both organisations were mainly focused on South America. Both organisations tried to raise funds for minor projects in support of local indigenous peoples. In the 1970s, Survival International was far more active in relation to developing projects than IWGIA could claim to be 10 years later.[126]

One important difference was that Survival had a much stronger national base in the UK and their campaigning efforts were far more successful than those of IWGIA. One potential advantage might have been that Survival gave up trying to gain the support of academia at an earlier stage than IWGIA did. But while IWGIA, in the early 1970s, moved towards supporting the organisational efforts of indigenous peoples and, later, to supporting their self-representation in the United Nations, this seems to have been less important for Survival, although its Director wrote in 1977 that, "Although one is a little disheartened by the number of Committees and amount of paper generated by the UN and its fringes, we do, nonetheless, feel it important to ensure that a voice on behalf of the indigenous is heard wherever and whenever possible, and that that voice should be authoritative" (Bentley 1977).

There were other differences between the two organisations, including the fact that IWGIA received support from governments, a step in general rejected by or not available to Survival International (and Cultural Survival in the U.S.). These differences were, however, of no great importance and IWGIA and Survival International coordinated some of their efforts, taking the initiative to co-publish a book on the Summer Institute of Linguistics, a publication entitled "Is God an American" in 1981. At the end of the century, Survival International's campaign against mineral development among the Innu in Canada met with little understanding within IWGIA, who considered this an attack on an indigenous people's right to development. Survival's efforts in defence of the San in the Central Kalahari Game Reserve in Botswana in the late 1990s and early 2000s was seen by IWGIA and its partners as opportunistic and short-sighted. Similarly, its strategy was seen as too confrontational. The director of the organisation, Stephen Corry, has been quoted as saying "The strategy is to mobilise so much outside pressure that the strength of international public opinion leads to the desired changes" (Saugestad 2006:174). Obviously, these remarks should be seen as reflecting differences between a campaigning approach and that of promoting the human and developmental rights of a group, given the political facts and economic realities. But Survival International's campaign against diamonds and tourism – the two major income sources of Botswana and on which most of Botswana's social welfare and modern development are based –backfired locally. At the government level, it was considered inappropriate interference originating from a former colonial power and at the broader public level it was seen by the people in Botswana as an attack on their welfare, creating a general animosity towards the San.

This being said, IWGIA has had very rewarding cooperation with a few issue-focused organisations such as Anti-Slavery International (UK), Forest Peoples Programme (UK) and Chittagong Hill Tracts Solidarity Committee (the Netherlands) as well as with support NGOs such as Amazind (Switzerland), NCIV (originally WIP) in the Netherlands, KWIA (Belgium), *Gesellschaft für Bedrohte Völlker* (Germany), *Fjärde Världen* (Sweden), and Almaciga (Spain), Tapol (UK), Incomindios (Switzerland), the Danish Dalit Solidarity Network, Ibis (Denmark), Nepenthes (Denmark), the Danish Solstice Foundation, the Rainforest Foundation in Norway, and institutions such as Docip, based in Switzerland.

It is important look at a few successful joint efforts between organisations. One example is the Human Rights Fund for Indigenous Peoples, a coalition between IWGIA, NCIV, Anti-Slavery International and KWIA. Working within a context that has, from the start, been goal-oriented, limited in scope and with clear and focused aims, it is fair to say that this coalition has been extremely successful. The cooperation between these organisations was replicated when the European Alliance with Indigenous Peoples (EAIP) was established.

Another successful coalition was the Chittagong Hill Tracts Commission (see above). If we analyse the reasons for these successes, three important points are worthy of note. Firstly, there needs to be a clear agreement on aims and strategies. Secondly, there must be a good personal chemistry between the representatives of the respective organisations and, thirdly, there should not be any competition for resources. There have been cases where two organisations had problems working together but the chemistry between the representatives was good. Competition is always a factor; without an open attitude this can spoil any kind of cooperation. There are obviously cases where cooperation between EU-based NGOs has been hampered because all are dependent upon the same EU funds.

For IWGIA, another example of focused and constructive collaboration with NGOs takes place within the African Commission on Human and Peoples' Rights. In its advocacy for indigenous peoples' rights, IWGIA has collaborated with indigenous organisations and a number of European NGOs, including the Forest Peoples Programme (FPP), Minority Rights Group (MRG), Anti-Slavery International, INTERRIGHTS and Amnesty International, all of which are based in the UK. An especially close collaboration has developed with FPP in terms of coordinating support for the participation of indigenous peoples' representatives

THE EUROPEAN ALLIANCE WITH INDIGENOUS PEOPLES

At the end of the 1980s IWGIA became interested in receiving support from the European Union. One of our partners, Anti-Slavery International (ASI) had contacts in the European Commission and had also received some funding for specific activities. In the first instance there was a need for obtaining support for the Human Rights Fund for Indigenous Peoples of which Anti-Slavery was a member. Approaching the EU Commission and keeping in touch with them was no easy task because it was important regularly to go to Brussels. Travelling to Brussels from Copenhagen those days was very expensive, and the partners in the HRFIP discussed the possibility of establishing a more permanent structure for funding of activities relating to indigenous peoples. The idea of creating such an alliance was discussed with the Sámi Council who had experiences with EU funding, but as an indigenous organisation they choose not to become a member of the alliance.

There were many organisations interested in such an alliance but practical reasons and the administrative demands of the EU Commission determined the result that was a small alliance with well-established NGOs. The European Alliance with Indigenous Peoples had its Founding General Assembly on 4 December, 1991. The founding members were besides IWGIA Anti-Slavery International, KWIA, WIP and 12th October Manifest from the Netherlands. The wish to include the German-based Gesellschaft für Bedrohter Völker never became a reality.

An office was established in Brussels and a highly qualified person employed. For some years the EAIP succeeded to raise funds for the HRFIP and it also managed to make important contacts to members of the European Parliament and to bureaucrats within the Commission. A newsletter was produced. However, in order to raise funding for its own work and keeping an office in Brussels the EAIP needed to have its own projects, a situation in which the Alliance competed with its funding member organisation. In the end this did not work and the Alliance was finally dissolved .

and developing shadow reports. IWGIA also cooperates with FPP on a concrete forest project in Africa.

IWGIA's publications have been a way of cooperating with other NGOs, academic NGOs and institutions. Co-publishing has been a result of jointly organised seminars or the start of further collaboration. IWGIA has co-published with the Forest Peoples Programme (FPP), Survival International, Anti-Slavery International, the Anthropology Resource Centre, and with a number of organisations in the Americas and Asia. IWGIA has supported the work of the FPP and others in the Inter-American Human Rights systems and international meetings have been coordinated or organised with many of these NGOs: IWGIA had a fruitful and active cooperation with MRG in Finland for years and worked productively with Amnesty Canada and Human Rights and Democracy (Canada) in support of indigenous peoples in the final deliberations on the adoption of the Declaration. Individuals from most of these organisations have contributed to IWGIA's publications.

Being based in Denmark, IWGIA has also worked with many Danish organisations on a case-by-case basis. However, IWGIA has always been somewhat marginalised in the Danish NGO world. This is, to some extent, because it is an international organisation with international legitimacy whereas most other NGOs position themselves on a national Danish platform.

We can conclude that IWGIA has a vast and expanding network and has arrangements for cooperation with other NGOs in Denmark, Europe and in other parts of the world. This includes non-indigenous local NGOs that work in support of indigenous organisations in Asia, Africa and the Americas. The key observation is that these alliances have been overwhelmingly symbiotic and often strategic to IWGIA's work.

Without these many-stranded relationships and issue-based cooperation, IWGIA would not have been able to achieve what it has. This is arguably further substantiated by the fact that IWGIA and the other like-minded NGOs each have their own geographical, cultural and political base and tradition. By working together, they are able to supplement each others' resources and efforts. These are exactly the same reasons that explain why such organisations, whilst having different approaches and strategies in relation to certain issues, are able to cooperate on other specific issues.

Temporary camps of indigenous in isolation along the Las Piedras river, Peru – Photo: Anders Krogh (2004)

Machigenka family contacted a few years ago in the Peruvian Amazon – Photo: IWGIA archive

CHAPTER 13

IWGIA AND GOVERNMENTS

A number of issues relating to IWGIA and governments have been reported in earlier chapters and will therefore not be summarised here. However, the following three issues could be said to illustrate an aspect of IWGIA's development over 40 years.

Government responsibility

In the early years following its establishment, IWGIA made great efforts to document and report on the precarious situation of the Indians in the Amazon, Paraguay and Brazil. "Genocide" was sometimes used to denote the decimation of Indian groups by ranchers, miners, loggers, the military and even missionaries. IWGIA blamed the governments and appealed to their sense of responsibility. In March 1970, Danish television broadcast a documentary from Brazil that included comments by David Maybury-Lewis, a highly respected anthropologist. His statements had probably been heard in many other countries. Maybury-Lewis did not deny the reports of killings of Indians in Brazil but he defended the Brazilian government by saying that the atrocities were not planned or instigated by the authorities. The only conclusion had to be that the reports being put forward by IWGIA and others, including Lars Persson, were exaggerated and therefore untrustworthy.

IWGIA reacted strongly[127] to the broadcast and stressed that the relevant government had tolerated the killings and other atrocities. An anthropologist with in-depth knowledge of the region commented in a newspaper that part of the story was that Maybury-Lewis depended on the goodwill of the authorities for his large research project in the country.[128]

Sometimes history repeats itself. Some years later, when IWGIA published Mark Münzel's reports on the Aché in Paraguay (Münzel 1973; 1974), the U.S. Embassy (USAID office) in Asunción funded Maybury-Lewis and a team of researchers to investigate the situation of the indigenous peoples in the country (Maybury-Lewis and Howe 1980:4ff). The report concentrated on Münzel's allegations and the following "international outcry" (ibid. 35). Their conclusion was that there had been killings, and atrocities had taken place, but that these were neither carried out by the government nor were they planned as part of government policy. This turned into a discussion on the definition of the term "genocide", which had the effect of concealing the discussion about responsibility. The conclusion to be drawn was that Mark Münzel's report was untrustworthy and the government thus avoided responsibility. The internal report, including the attacks on Mark Münzel, was released by the U.S. Embassy[129] and published by Cultural Survival in 1980.[130]

These examples are given in order to focus on what IWGIA and other human rights defenders were up against when trying to raise public and professional awareness of the atrocities that were taking place in Latin America in the 1960s and 1970s. We must also remember that there were very few indigenous organisations in the region at that time. Moreover this was a time when governments in general considered the plight of indigenous people to be an internal matter. IWGIA's approach was not confrontational but focused heavily on the governments' responsibilities; these efforts were often obstructed by governments and ignored by the press and the research community. IWGIA held governments responsible for their indigenous peoples not only in Brazil, Paraguay and Canada but also in Norway, Denmark and Sweden.

Collaborating with governments

From an historical perspective it is possible to see changes and developments in IWGIA's interaction with governments.

IWGIA's physical location in Denmark and psychological location in Scandinavia can be seen to have had a significant impact on how the organisation has cooperated with governments.

The liberal, political and cultural traditions of governmental support to NGOs in Scandinavia are very different from the situation in countries such as the UK, Germany, France and the U.S. Without support from the Scandinavian governments, IWGIA would not have been able to develop as an international organisation, publishing in non-Scandinavian languages and often working in countries that are of minor significance to Scandinavian development aid. This fact has obviously characterised its working relationships with governments and it also explains why cooperation with other non-indigenous NGOs has more often been symbiotic than competitive.

It is noteworthy that IWGIA has become increasingly dependent on funding from the Nordic governments and the EU. The combination of core funding and earmarked funding has made it possible for IWGIA to take initiatives that were not necessarily in line with the contemporary policy of governments and donor agencies. When this author joined IWGIA in the 1980s, we met annually with representatives of the Danish Ministry of Foreign Affairs. I recall the meetings as being very cordial, with an exchange of points of view and information, and although we always agreed to disagree on a number of issues, it did not affect our funding. One major reason for this was that IWGIA provided information to a government that was sincerely concerned about the fate of indigenous peoples.

In the early years, IWGIA criticised governments for their irresponsible policy towards indigenous peoples and made strenuous efforts to get the Nordic governments and donors to put pressure on countries in South and Central America, Asia and Africa, where atrocities were taking place against indigenous peoples. Today, IWGIA still puts considerable efforts into making an impact on donor policies towards indigenous peoples through its publications and documentation but direct criticism of governments is now most often dealt with by local indigenous partners, albeit with support from IWGIA. At the same time it has also been a high priority for IWGIA to support indigenous peoples who may have the opportunity of establishing relationships of respect with their *own* governments. This has resulted in concrete initiatives in, for example, Russia and through land-titling projects in Peru and in the Philippines.

It has not been possible for IWGIA to have such close relationships with other countries' governments as it has with the Nordic ones. However, looking back over IWGIA's work with donor policies, the establishment of the Permanent Forum, the Declaration process, etc., the conclusion is that it *has* been and *is* possible to establish a constructive dialogue with governments. This has not always been the case but the global concern surrounding human rights and the emergence of strong indigenous organisations in an increasing number of countries has paved the way for dialogue instead of confrontation. This has involved a change in IWGIA's policy towards many governments.

Indigenous peoples' participation in national institutions

In the 1990s, as indigenous organisations grew stronger so did their opportunities to deal with authorities and governmental institutions. IWGIA took this challenge of focusing on institutions that were sometimes ignored in the struggle of the indigenous movement to focus on the highly politicised issue of *rights*. These studies were funded by the EU and Nordic governments.

Urged on by indigenous organisations in South and Central America, IWGIA decided to analyse the indigenous experience of joining or allying with political parties and participating in elections. Although indigenous peoples have very diverse experiences of these institutions they are still all a "part" of political systems that are not their own (Wessendorf 2001:10). A key question was whether opportunities were being utilized to the fullest. Regional meetings organised by indigenous partners were convened in Mexico, Norway, Malaysia, Fiji and Canada and Kenya. The visible result was the book "Challenging Politics" published

Workshop "challenging politics" in Malaysia, 2000 - Photo: PACOS

as an IWGIA Document, and focusing, amongst other themes, on conditions that favour or disadvantage indigenous peoples' political participation.

Using a similar approach, IWGIA took up the issue of local governments. The focus was whether indigenous peoples were able to promote their position within, or with the support of, local and regional governments. The conditions varied enormously from continent to continent so there was a strong regional emphasis, albeit with the aim of reaching some global conclusions.

IWGIA has also compared the experiences indigenous peoples have had with self-government institutions, primarily in the Arctic. The Greenlanders opted for a public government, the Sámi in Scandinavia for an ethnic government and the indigenous in Alaska agreed to the establishment of corporate structures. In Canada we find a combination of these. With this variety of models, indigenous peoples from around the world can look to the Arctic for inspiration.

No unanimous conclusions emerged from these processes other than the fact that the right of indigenous peoples to determine their own future, including the choice of institutional affiliation, was underscored once more. Hopefully, this has opened the eyes of some to the opportunity for improving living conditions without having to frame this as a human rights issue.

PART 4

IWGIA:
HISTORY AND FUTURE

CHAPTER 14

AN ORGANISATION OF PROFESSIONALS

IWGIA was founded by professionals, mainly anthropologists, and has always been led, managed and controlled by professionals. IWGIA never was and never developed into a grass-roots organisation, and did not aspire to doing so. In this respect, IWGIA differs from most other similar NGOs that were established and run by grassroots volunteers but which, as they developed, became bodies managed by a permanently employed staff.

The growth of an organisation

For approximately 15 years, the organisation developed under the direction and leadership of Helge Kleivan. No decision was taken without Helge Kleivan's acceptance and, for years, the Board only convened when he called it. It was under his dedicated and charismatic leadership that the organisation developed its well-established relationship between professional documentation, analysis and active and personal engagement.

A few years after its founding, IWGIA was in a situation of stalemate. Governments were unresponsive and meetings with politicians led to nothing; the organisation *de facto* had no structure; there was no office; it all relied on the individual efforts of a few people. In late 1970, Helge Kleivan got Peter Aaby, a student of anthropology, involved in the organisation, a secretariat and an office were established on the premises of the University of Copenhagen, and a network of members was set up. Documents were published and funded by membership fees and continuity was established, even though the documents were only published and distributed when there was enough money. The conditions were rather basic and a lot of work had to be done during the evenings and weekend. Helge Kleivan's archive reveals, and his wife, Inge Kleivan, confirms, that many letters were written and phone calls made at night. It is a matter of record that the physical, political and financial conditions of those years were tough.

Helge Kleivan and those who worked with him in the beginning did so on a voluntary basis. They had university backgrounds and they wanted to use their professional knowledge to work for the benefit of indigenous peoples. They were joined by others who had a human rights, teaching or journalistic background. In the late 1970s, when their efforts were gradually being recognised by indigenous

WORLD FAMOUS – BUT NOT HERE

"Frederiksholms Kanal 4. Into the yard. Descending the dilapidated backstairs in a dilapidated building. On fifth floor a small cardboard sign announces that this is where IWGIA resides. The door conceals a few ascetic rooms where 2-3 persons work energetically while the coffee pot boils over. This is the international headquarters of the world organisation that is feared by the Brazilian government and that the continued existence of the Indians most of all depends upon."

This was from an article in the Danish newspaper, Aktuelt March 25, 1972. A picture reveals the famous poster of Geronimo hanging on the wall. This was way before computers. Faxes were unknown. The people there worked on a voluntary basis. There was a duplicator to print the documents. The archive reveals that, when IWGIA wanted an article or a comment to be printed in a newspaper, the letter included stamps for a reply!

What a difference to the 15 rooms at IWGIA's offices today, with 12-15 salaried staff, computers, indigenous art on the walls and with a fancy bell at the entrance door that keeps out any uninvited guest. One can but note the symbolism: that although standards have changed, IWGIA's office has remained in a backyard.

In the middle of the night of November 12, 1968, Helge Kleivan wrote to Lars Persson telling him that that Saturday afternoon he had finally managed to find a duplicator and to produce Newsletter No.2 (3 pages) with the help of some students.

The similarity between 1972 and 2008 is that, although IWGIA is now internationally known, it is basically still unknown in Denmark. Newspapers stated this in 1972 but, in this respect, very little has changed since. The University of Copenhagen hosted IWGIA from its beginning in 1968 until 1999 when the secretariat moved to its own premises.

peoples and governments, IWGIA was able to employ its first salaried staff members. This was a first step towards streamlining the organisation's structure.

The annual budget increased significantly in the 1980s and 1990s; the staff increased, as did the number and size of projects. The documents developed into professionally produced books and a quarterly magazine. This development demanded structural changes, including changes in the decision-making structure and, obviously, it fostered internal tensions and conflicts. But this was to be expected, given the growth from a small working group led and headed by one man to a professional organisation. What is important from a long-term perspective is that the ideological foundation created and defended by Helge Kleivan and the other founders was transferred to the newcomers. Those values have endured to this day.

Professionalisation

In the initial phase, IWGIA's contacts were primarily with individuals, both indigenous and non-indigenous. Helge Kleivan had an enormous network of personal contacts with which he maintained an impressive correspondence (this was before the advent of e-mail). Many of these contacts were sadly lost when Helge Kleivan died in 1983. Later, specifically after the introduction of project work, the network became increasingly dominated by organisations, first and foremost indigenous organisations.

The introduction of e-mails improved the communication and networking enormously, and it is hard to see how the international achievements of indigenous peoples would have happened without. But lost were also the long handwritten or typewritten letters that people who wanted to get in touch with IWGIA took time to write. These were not circular letters to 'whom it may concern' but written with elaborated introductions to make a sincere impact upon the receiver in IWGIA, knowing that it could take weeks or months to have an answer.

As the organisation grew so did the bureaucracy: budgets, accounts, auditing and reporting to donors took more and more time and effort. In the beginning, these activities were taken care of by the same people who made the policy decisions. When the first staff were employed, everyone received the same salary and there remained an air of internal solidarity. Before this, back in 1975, the seven volunteers shared a "salary" of 1,000 DKK (approx. US$150) a month – when there was money. This equal salary policy also included the conscientious objectors and long-term unemployed who were recruited in the 1980s and 1990s (paid by the government and municipal authorities). Staff usually worked as volunteers in the organisation before becoming more permanently employed. For a number of years, the organisation was directed by three, and later two, co-directors. With regard to day-to-day matters, the weekly staff meeting was the highest decision-making body in the secretariat. This system could no longer be maintained as the budget increased and more external staff were recruited; the Board of the organisation, which in practical terms did not exist until the late 1970s, became the cornerstone of the institution. In the 1980s and 1990s, the or-

Helge Kleivan, Geronimo and Peter Aaby in Frederiksholms Kanal 4, 1972 – Photo: Aktuelt

From IWGIA's premises in 2007 – Photo: IWGIA archive

ganisation was unable to sustain its level of activity without volunteers – by the turn of the century the organisation could no longer rely solely on volunteers!

The annual budget increased to the point where it was no longer possible to go around "with IWGIA's money in one pocket and one's own in the other". Demands for administrative procedures, auditing etc, could no longer be dealt with so informally. The streamlining of the organisation and the administrative procedures can be seen in the increasing amounts of planning documents, mission statements, 4-year plans, and in regional and thematic strategy papers. These have often proved useful for the organisation but have also often been produced to meet demands from donors.

Expansion in the number of people employed and increased professionalisation was followed by specialisation. Andrew Gray is remembered as having been of the opinion that IWGIA should never develop into an organisation with specialised desk officers. Nevertheless, this is exactly what did happen – as was the case with so many other NGOs. At the turn of the century, IWGIA had 5-6 desk coordinators, each responsible for a region or a thematic issue. It has, however, remained a key principle that all coordinators should take on responsibilities that relate not only to their own region but also to publishing, human rights activities etc.

After 40 years, IWGIA is still an international organisation with its secretariat in Copenhagen. While other NGOs, primarily development NGOs, have established regional offices in developing countries, IWGIA has unerringly focused on an international and human rights-based approach to indigenous issues. As part of IWGIA's general strategy, efforts have been made to link local indigenous organisations with the international indigenous community in order to give priority to issues and activities in which IWGIA has developed experience and expertise. In recent years, IWGIA has *shared* certain activities when local capacity has been created. There are many examples of this, such as the production of Spanish publications in South America, the establishment of information centres in Russia and South America, and the agreement on cooperation with the African Commission on Human and Peoples' Rights, to name but three. Priority is determined by IWGIA's holistic approach; the promotion of empowerment is thus favoured rather than developing proficiency in the management of a big project portfolio, supervised by a local IWGIA office.

For many years, IWGIA had no by-laws or statutes. The first statutes were legally drafted in the 1990s.[131] In the 1980s and 1990s, there were, in the opinion of some, an endless number of discussions and Board meetings about statutes, internal rules for local groups etc. In hindsight these discussions sometimes look hilarious, with extended discussions on minor details, but they illustrated problems associated with combining the voluntary work being done in the secretariat and in the local groups with the work of those who were employed in the international secretariat.

Meeting in Fiolstræde 10 in 1982 – Photo: Espen Waehle

IWGIA board meeting in Sweden in 2006 – Photo: Anni Hammerlund

Helge Kleivan and Lars Persson made up the first IWGIA Board. During the 1970s and up until 1978 when an international board was appointed, all decisions on a practical level were taken by Helge Kleivan. The new Board was composed of persons recruited by Helge Kleivan and it continued to be self-recruiting. From 1989 and during the 1990s, the directors, the administrator and representatives of the national groups were included on the Board.

A membership organisation

In 2000, IWGIA became a membership organisation. This came about as a result of both internal and external pressure. The large Board with self-recruited members, representatives from the local groups and the secretariat staff no longer met the more professional requirements of a politically and financially responsible organisation. Self-recruitment of the Board had become out of touch with the general political developments in society. The decision to turn IWGIA into a membership-based organisation gave further impetus to streamlining, and meeting the institutional demands of a professional organisation.

IWGIA never aimed to have as many members as possible. It was unrealistic to achieve a membership base that could match those of campaigning organisations. IWGIA gave priority to establishing a smaller, more active working group that would serve IWGIA's purpose rather than the other way around. IWGIA's Board obviously intended to have a membership larger than the current 250 people, and it is worth remembering that IWGIA had 1,000 members in the early 1970s. But it illustrates the tendency to create *networks*, which in IWGIA's case includes indigenous persons, organisations and institutions.

IWGIA is based upon anthropological knowledge, and most people recruited to the Board and the secretariat have an anthropological background. In the 1980s, when indigenous participants came to Geneva to take part in human rights discussions, more focus was placed on legal issues. The biodiversity processes in the 1990s increased the need for biological knowledge. To cope with these trends and to involve more people in IWGIA's work, an advisory board was established. This was discussed for the first time in 1983 but was only established 10 years later.

IWGIA's international platform and partnership with international indigenous organisations opened up contacts with new groups of researchers. From the mid-1980s on, when the UN bodies dealing with indigenous peoples became a cornerstone of IWGIA's human rights efforts, issues of "indigenous rights", "self-determination", "free, prior and informed consent", "inherent rights" etc, became the focus of discussions within the organisation.

The fact that peoples from all parts of the globe had found a new platform and had become united around the common identity of being indigenous only sporadically entered academic anthropological discussions. Simple observation

IWGIA Forum 2008, Indigenous Peoples and Climate Change – Photo: Espen Wæhle

tells us that only a few anthropologists ever took part in the UN meetings in Geneva; it was lawyers with expertise in international law that headed the analytical discussions, which also involved IWGIA.

An important change took place in this respect when the anthropologists started flying to indigenous meetings in Geneva *after* the adoption of the Draft Declaration on the Rights of Indigenous Peoples and they started flying into New York *after* the establishment of the Permanent Forum. For IWGIA, which was born out of anthropology, this opened up new possibilities for linking international discussions with the implementation of international human rights in national and local contexts. Africa demonstrated that change was underway. IWGIA *did* discuss the issue of indigenous peoples in Africa and *did* manage to advance a pioneering discussion in the African Commission on Human and Peoples' Rights. For a long time these discussions were only occasionally carried into the academic sphere (by IWGIA or others), but they were taken up by national initiatives in several African countries.

Development of a corporate spirit

While IWGIA may have missed opportunities to give priority to, or may not have had the courage to, make its presence felt in important academic discussions, it *did* develop a strong corporate spirit in dialogue with indigenous peoples. It is probably fair to call this spirit unique. No other organisation enabled the individual representatives to act so constructively, quickly and efficiently in a given situation. Directors and regional co-ordinators were able to act on trust and take policy decisions without first having to go through the bureaucratic decision-making procedure. Unique because controversial issues could be taken up with indigenous peoples themselves – often the self same issues that IWGIA was discussing internally but did not take up in academic fora.

The corporate spirit was based on internal solidarity, trust and intimate personal knowledge of the people involved. Over the years, personal relationships developed between Board members and the secretariat staff and between staff members. Staff members and Board members often remained in IWGIA for many years, promoting loyalty and team building. It is well known that NGOs (as many other institutions) can build up a wall of internal solidarity that protects them from external criticism. In IWGIA's case the corporate spirit was used to build partnerships with indigenous peoples and organisations.

Partners, indigenous as well as non-indigenous, quite often commented upon this spirit. A German partner expressed it thus:

In IWGIA I came across an organisation of 'relaxed professionalism', which is so unusual outside Scandinavia. If problems were there, they were there to be solved, whereas we start complaining about the complexity of work and life in general and then start work, yet so often in an isolated context. Einzelkaempfer we say. With us, team work is so often individual work in a team with the object to qualify oneself against the others.[132]

NGOs are often characterised by their engaged and dedicated membership. Like many other organisations, IWGIA was established by a few concerned and engaged persons who devoted a significant part of their lives to the organisation and to its aims. Even when an organisation such as IWGIA expands and grows into a professional institution, those employed are expected to be driven by commitment and not salaries. Such expectations come from within, from the Board and the membership, and externally from donors and "customers". IWGIA has been no different to similar NGOs in this respect, and although working for IWGIA may be life absorbing, leaving scant surplus to incorporate new persons, it also promotes solidarity and loyalty.

Experience tells us that the transitional phase from the voluntary to the professional is critical. Many organisations cannot manage to reconcile the internal demands of growth while holding onto the integrity and dedication that are typical of voluntary organisations.

Many organisations do not survive the crises; they either split, in other ways disintegrate or change their character completely. IWGIA's history has been dif-

Les Malezer and Lola García-Alix - UN Permanent Forum on Indigenous Issues, 2006, New York
Photo: Christian Erni

Sille Stidsen and Jens Dahl - Launch of The Indigenous World 2006,
UN Permanent Forum on Indigenous Issues, 2006, New York – Photo: Pablo Lasansky

THE NAME IWGIA

One of IWGIA's main handicaps is its name: it defies pronunciation. In some languages it sounds quite hilarious. Only indigenous peoples seem to be comfortable with it.

A change of name has been a recurrent theme for the organisation's Board. In the early 1990s it was therefore renamed 'Indigenous Affairs' and new letterheads and stamps were produced. The problem was, however, that nobody noticed the change, and even those who used any opportunity to criticize IWGIA for its name continued to use 'IWGIA'. Board members seem to have forgotten and, had it not been for the statutes, IWGIA would technically no longer exist.

The good side of the story about this impossible name is that people recognise it whenever they see it in print. It is also a good entry point for socialising:

We were three IWGIA people sitting around a table at Moscow's Sheremetievo airport waiting for the check-in to open. We were discussing IWGIA matters and, after a while, a man from a neighbouring table came over, opening the conversation with, "I hear you also work for IKEA!"

ferent. Not that IWGIA's history has been without crisis but because continuity has prevailed without the organisation's integrity or aims being seriously endangered.

During the expansion from a small working group, run by a few volunteers, to a body with 10-15 employees, IWGIA lost good people who had worked hard for the organisation. It is all the more surprising to note that the organisation was able to continue in spite of the premature departure of some key individuals. The first was Helge Kleivan who succumbed to cancer in his late 50s. In 1995, the Russian Board member and driving force behind IWGIA's Russian engagement, Alexander Pika, died in a boating accident. A few years later, Andrew Gray, Board member and former director, disappeared in a plane crash. In 2007, the long serving Chair of the Board, Georg Henriksen, died prematurely of cancer. Each of these individuals had a strong effect on the organisation and played a significant role. This is not to diminish the work of others but it serves to illustrate the fact that the spirit, knowledge and engagement of those involved in IWGIA are shared by the organisation and serve to promote continuity.

It is difficult to pinpoint the character of this spirit and what nurtures it. One element is a collegiate spirit, characterised by common dedication and concern rather than competition; this fosters the friendship shared by Board members, those employed in the international secretariat and members of the national and local groups.

There have been different points of view, within the Board, within the international secretariat and between the two bodies. Despite diverging opinions, discussions have always aimed at creating consensus – a process that has been enormously effective and has been helped along by socialising and the sharing of food and drink. Of special importance is the close relationship with indigenous peoples but also the continuous flow of information about the violations of their human rights. This has promoted political and professional discussions that deter IWGIA from being turned into a bureaucratic institution.

CHAPTER 15

FUTURE CHALLENGES

The challenges facing IWGIA are linked to its historical development, including its achievements. They are also related to developments in the indigenous communities and the indigenous movement.

From opposition to policy making

In 40 years, IWGIA has developed from being in opposition to being a part of policy making. Documenting human rights violations and outright atrocities will always be part of IWGIA's work but new opportunities, mechanisms and institutions have made it possible for IWGIA to play a pro-active role to an extent only dreamt of in 1968.

This takes place through projects, cooperation with governments, and through a pro-active policy in relation to UN activities. IWGIA has always been fairly critical of private corporate companies and international agencies such as the World Bank, UNDP and others. But, a few years ago, IWGIA entered into an agreement with the Danish Industrial Fund for Developing Countries (IFU), which gave IWGIA an advisory role in relation to a logging project in the Republic of Congo. This small example reflects a trend by which indigenous peoples are becoming more directly involved in private corporate companies and governmental agencies. This is again a result of indigenous organisations' efforts to be involved in all matters that relate to them.

With the establishment of the Permanent Forum and the adoption of the Declaration, indigenous peoples have attained considerable institutional and legal status. The way forward will be to look at *implementation* from a broad perspective. The Millennium Development Goals, World Bank policies, UNDP policies, the biodiversity processes etc, are all objectives of indigenous endeavour in respect to implementation. IWGIA will most likely have to develop new strategies in relation to multilateral institutions and its involvement in these processes at the international as well as at the local level.

IWGIA's impact

40 years of effort – *what* has come of it and *why*? This book has hopefully documented a number of results so only a few overall comments are needed to address this final question. IWGIA has consistently insisted on indigenous peoples' right to self-determination, right to development and right to an identity. This

> **EXCERPT FROM A STATEMENT MADE BY PROF. ERICA-IRENE A. DAES ON THE OCCASION OF THE 40TH ANNIVERSARY OF IWGIA**
>
> One of my first visits in my capacity as Chairperson –Rapporteur of the United Nations Working Group on Indigenous Populations (WGIP) was to an organization which was already well-known globally, the International Work Group for Indigenous Affairs in Copenhagen, in 1986. I was impressed by the constructive work and the enthusiasm, dynamism and determination of Andrew Gray and the other members of the staff in promoting the role and implementing the objectives of IWGIA. Although the relevant financial resources of IWGIA are limited, they have succeeded in publishing a number of reports and newsletters concerning indigenous peoples living in different corners of the globe.
>
> IWGIA is organizing important seminars, workshops and conferences in which crucial and timely subjects concerning indigenous rights, and human rights in general, are debated. Its constructive role in the elaboration and adoption of the UN Declaration on the Rights of Indigenous Peoples was of decisive importance.
>
> IWGIA has succeeded, through its countless country reports, publications, reviews and papers, in warning the world's public opinion about the suffering and problems of indigenous peoples and in contributing highly to the protection of their human rights and fundamental freedoms. It should be noted that the most remarkable books published by IWGIA are considered reference books, which provide, inter alia, useful information and data on indigenous issues.
>
> I would like once again to congratulate the administration of IWGIA - its Board of Directors, the director, the secretariat, the contributors, etc. and wish them every success in implementing fully the noble goals of IWGIA.

has guided IWGIA in relation to third parties, to conservation efforts and other political interests. This is fundamental to IWGIA's support of the titling of the lands and territories of indigenous communities. The aim has primarily been to support the indigenous peoples' opportunities to control their own future and to create a dialogue on the specific strategies open to indigenous peoples to use their lands and resources in a sustainable manner.

IWGIA has been able to make a difference because of its holistic perspective combined with a massive presence in key activities, both locally and internationally. But more important maybe is the fact that IWGIA has cooperated with those indigenous peoples and organisations that needed partners when new paths and strategies were being considered. The type of long-term partnerships adopted by IWGIA with other organisations has combined institutional cooperation with personal ties. This has created a relationship of trust and ensured that the professional attitude favoured by most donor agencies is in harmony with the dedication needed to work in true partnership with indigenous peoples. This will no doubt remain a major challenge in the future. One of the benefits of partnership has been that IWGIA has been able to maintain its own position, and to have an open dialogue with indigenous organisations.

A new development has recently taken place whereby indigenous and other peoples, at the specific request of IWGIA, are producing an increasing numbers of publications. This often takes place as a follow-up to, or in support of, projects that are funded in other ways by IWGIA. It reflects the fact that IWGIA has become an active partner of indigenous organisations in this as in other respects.

Networks and regional focus

For some years now there has been a change in IWGIA's international human rights activities from primarily focusing on global processes to opening up regional perspectives and focus-based networks. This was the case when IWGIA facilitated discussions on the role of political parties, local government, indigenous youth and people in voluntary isolation etc, a process that still has a long way to go. The WCIP did not survive as a global interest organisation and most continental organisations are unable to organise a large number of indigenous peoples. The adoption of the Declaration and the ensuing efforts towards implementation will probably add to these decentralising trends.

There will be indigenous peoples who feel that they have gained knowledge from the UN human rights processes but who, due to the controversial nature of promoting the indigenous angle, will choose other ways. Hodgson (2008) writes about how some Maasai in Tanzania have decided to give priority to pastoral issues and, instead of focusing on indigenous rights, now focus on livelihood issues. There, most probably, lies a challenge to IWGIA to adopt a flexible strategy that will be needed when international processes are challenged by local realities.

I would like to finish this history of IWGIA with an issue that everyone in the organisation has been confronted with: why does IWGIA have no indigenous Board members? People often ask about indigenous members of IWGIA and indigenous members of the IWGIA Board. Governments specifically have questioned the legitimacy of IWGIA with reference to the lack of indigenous members on the Board.

The fact is that this has never been an issue and IWGIA does not have a policy on the matter. There are indigenous members of IWGIA and, for some years, there was once an indigenous Board member. This was not a result of his being indigenous but, amongst other reasons, because of his in-depth knowledge of indigenous and environmental issues, and his insight into animal rights organisations.

The key point is that indigenous individuals who fight for the general good of indigenous peoples will probably prefer to remain active in their own organisations and work with organisations such as IWGIA from that platform. And this will most probably remain the case in the future.

Jorge Agurto, Servindi - UN Permanent Forum on Indigenous Issues, 5th session May 2006, New York - Photo: Pablo Lasansky

NOTES

1. Cited in Native Power (eds) J. Brøsted et al., 11.
2. Karsten Soltau pers. communication.
3. See f. ex. Venne 1998 and Barsh 1994.
4. See f. ex. Hodgson 2002a; 2002b.
5. René Fuerst, pers. communication.
6. Personal communication with Milton R. Freeman, Cyril Belshaw and Georg Henriksen.
7. Referred to in the Norwegian newspaper *Verdens Gang* August 31, 1968.
8. Kaleb Hindar in *Verdens Gang*, September 4 with response from Helge Kleivan September 23.
9. Established as the "Primitive Peoples Fund" in the summer of 1969. The name changed to Survival International in 1971.
10. Østergaard 1969. While nothing seems to have come of the meeting with Poul Hartling, his social democratic successor K.B. Andersen had, at least, a much more positive attitude.
11. Translated from IWGIA's notes of the discussion that took place on February 13, 1972.
12. Un-numbered Newsletter, August 1971.
13. Peter Aaby, pers. communication.
14. The first local group was established in Lund, Sweden, in 1971, followed by groups in Geneva, Oslo, Copenhagen, Aarhus, Gothenburg, Zürich, Basel, Moscow, Tromsø, Madrid and Paris.
15. In 1971 the individual members paid $3, in 1973 $5 and in 1975 $6. In November 1970 small grants were given by Amnesty International in Denmark, Norway and the Faroe Islands. In 1972, another grant (10,000 DKK) was donated by the Columbus Foundation.
16. According to a secretariat meeting of 27 September 1971. IWGIA archive.
17. *Verdens Gang*, August 22, 1972
18. Among these were a group around the Amazind Bulletin in Switzerland founded by René Fuerst, *Indígena* (later to be followed by the Anthropology Resource Center) headed by Shelton Davis in the US, Cultural Survival in the US and Survival International in the UK.
19. Personal letter from Helge Kleivan, dated February 28, 1974. Helge Kleivan's archive.
20. Peter Aaby, pers. communication.
21. Mark Münzel, pers. communication.
22. 11 anthropologists participating in a "Symposium on Inter-Ethnic Conflict in South America" in Barbados in January 1971 had analysed the critical situation of the Indians and urged religious missions, social scientists and states to take action as formulated in a statement that came to be known as the Declaration of Barbados (published as IWGIA Document no.1).
23. Interview, May 2008.
24. Cited from a letter to the Swedish Minister of Foreign Affairs July 22, 1969.
25. Newsletter no. 3 from May 1969
26. Helge Kleivan in an obituary for Lars Persson in IWGIA Newsletter 27, 1981.
27. IWGIA Newsletter 18
28. IWGIA Newsletter 18
29. It seems as if IWGIA's role in the planning of the World Conference of Aboriginal Peoples and the close cooperation in this respect with National Indian Brotherhood must have played a role when contact was made with IWGIA to co-facilitate the Arctic Peoples' Conference.
30. A compiled report of the conference is given in Inge Kleivan, 1992.
31. IWGIA Newsletter no. 11, 1974.
32. Information June 17, 1972. See also Sanders 1983:15.
33. The correspondence between IWGIA and the National Indian Brotherhood reveals that the NIB planned to have a NIB executive council meeting with 20 participants in Copenhagen. This was criticized by IWGIA, which also suggested a planning meeting be postponed to 1974.

34 Ha-Shilth-Sa vol.2,no.8, Dec. 4, 1975. Port Alberny
35 National Indian Brotherhood 1974. IWGIA was invited to the meeting but found it more appropriate to use the money for other purposes. Letter from Helge Kleivan to George Manuel, March 8, 1974. Helge Kleivan's archive.
36 IWGIA Newsletter no. 12, 1975. The participants came from New Zealand, Australia, Greenland, Scandinavia, USA, Canada, Colombia and Guyana.
37 This ad-hoc Committee was set up by the Chair of the Association of Greenlanders in Denmark.
38 There was a rather heated dispute between Robert Petersen and the Chairman of the Greenland Provincial Council, Lars Chemnitz, as referred to in the Greenlandic newspaper *Atuagagdliutit/Grønlandsposten* no. 29, July 24, and no. 31, August 7, 1975. After the meeting in Port Alberny, the cautious position of the Provincial Council was also criticized by one of the Greenlandic participants, Aqqaluk Lynge (Lynge 1975).
39 Ha-Shilth-Sa vol.2, no.8, Dec.4 1975. Port Alberny
40 Australia, New Zealand, US, Canada, Denmark (Greenland), Norway, Sweden, Finland, Mexico, Nicaragua, Panama, Venezuela, Colombia, Ecuador, Peru, Paraguay, Bolivia and Argentina.
41 When the NIB discussed the proposal for such a conference for the first time there was very little reference to indigenous peoples in Asia and no mention of indigenous peoples in Africa or the Pacific Islands, except for New Zealand, Australia and Hawai'i (National Indian Brotherhood 1972). In 1982 the indigenous peoples of the Philippine Cordillera used IWGIA to explore the possibility of being associated with WCIP. Given the similar colonial background of the Philippines and South and Central America (including the Spanish-American War), the indigenous peoples of the Cordilleras were in a favourable position for creating such a linkage (Joji Cariño and Geoff Nettleton, pers. communication).
42 IWGIA Newsletter 18, August 1977.
43 Ziegler, Volkmar and Peirrette Birraux. 1986 *Indian Summer in Geneva*. Video. Geneva: Docip.
44 According to information given to Helge Kleivan (letter from Helge Kleivan dated 28 February 1974). Helge Kleivan's archive.
45 Personal information from Nilo Cayuqeo. See also Akwesasne Notes vol. 9, no.5, 1977.
46 Editorial ("How it is with us") in Akwesasne Notes p. 25, vol. 9, no. 5 1977.
47 Correspondence from Helge Kleivan. Helge Kleivan's archive.
48 Small amounts were raised in Norway, and the Swedish Sida contributed its first support in 1973.
49 Politiken, July 30, 1972.
50 Helge was himself from northern Norway and his wife, Inge Kleivan, recalls the enormous amount of time he spent on the issue, including several trips to Norway. Inge Kleivan, pers. communication.
51 Cited from IWGIA Newsletter, December 1978.
52 Diana Vinding personal communication.
53 NKr 210,000 in 1978.
54 Nilo Cayuqueo, pers. communication.
55 Letter from Helge Kleivan to a Norwegian anthropologist. Helge Kleivan's archive.
56 Confidential note from Helge Kleivan, April 22, 1982. The first suggestion was to establish a documentation centre in Nicaragua. Helge Kleivan's archive
57 The members of the Commission were Theo van Boven (Chair), José Carlos Morales (WCIP), Bernardo Jaen (CORPI), Juana Vazques (CORPI), Reiulf Steen (MP, Norway), Mark Münzel (IWGIA Board member) and Harald Eidheim (anthropologist, Norway)
58 Letter from the Minister to IWGIA, dated June 14, 1982. Helge Kleivan's archive.
59 Press release: Statement about Nicaragua. March 26, 1984.
60 See also Brysk 2000:112ff.
61 Letter from Helge Kleivan, Nov. 29, 1982. Helge Kleivan's archive.
62 Mark Münzel, pers. correspondence.
63 When the WCIP had a dialogue with the Nicaraguan government on a peaceful solution to the conflict that respected the rights of the indigenous peoples, the President of the WCIP, Clem Cartier, visited the Coastal region under the protection of the armed guerrilla (IWGIA: Yearbook 1987).

64 "Draft Declarations of Principles for the Defence of the Indigenous Nations and Peoples of the Western Hemisphere".
65 From "Report on the 1985 Session of the U.N: Working Group on Indigenous Populations, July 29- August 2, and on the Indigenous Peoples' Pre-Working Group Meeting, July 22- July 26, 1985, by Indian Law Resource Center.
66 The persons were: Ron Andrade, Howard Berman, Clem Cartier, John Clinebell, Jeanette Hantke, Leroy Little Bear, Sharon O'Brien, Douglas Sanders, David Weissbrodt, Armstrong Wiggins, Curtis Berkey, Joseph Ryan, Steven Tullberg, and Robert T. Coulter. (Memorandum from Indian Law Resource Center, July 13, 1982).
67 Diana Vinding, pers. communication.
68 This ambition was first launched in 1973 (Newsletter no.8).
69 The first sketch was developed in 1981.
70 The Commission was re-established and its membership renewed at a meeting in Copenhagen, May 31-June 1, 2008.
71 Finn Lynge was a Board member of IWGIA from 1992-1995.
72 Helge Kleivan's archive.
73 Only ICC did not respond.
74 www.cpaphils.org.
75 Information from Joji Cariño and Geoff Nettleton.
76 Members of the group were the anthropologists Alexander Pika, Igor Krupnik, Olga Murasjko, Vladimir Lebedev, Elena Oborotova, the geographer Boris Prokhorov, the demographers Dmitry Bogoyavlenskiy and Tatyana Terent'eva and biologists Lyudmila Bogoslovskaya and Irina Pokrovskaya.
77 Information from Olga Murasjko.
78 Cultural Survival took up the issue of indigenous peoples in Russia in 1992 and has since published regularly on that region.
79 At that meeting IWGIA informed the organisers that it might be more correct to invite an organisation such as the Sámi Council instead of an academic institution like the Nordic Sámi Institute, but obviously to no effect.
80 In 1992, a meeting of San had been organised in Namibia.
81 The indigenous caucus is an informal meeting that is convened before and during meetings. Although it has no formal status it is considered as a legitimate indigenous forum by indigenous peoples as well as governments.
82 Information given by Julian Burger.
83 In 1984, the first year, five indigenous persons were supported but, a few years later, this had increased, varying from 30 in 1987 to only 6 in 1988 and then increasing to more than 50 each year since the turn of the century,
84 Internal IWGIA note from Espen Wæhle, 26 September 1982
85 It is, among other places, referred to in the IWGIA Board meeting of November 1986 and an internal Norad note from January 16, 1987.
86 IWGIA Annual Report 1989.
87 Minutes from IWGIA Board meeting, April 20-22, 1990 and an internal Norad note from August 17, 1987.
88 In 1989-90 Norad went through a phase of restructuring that included its indigenous programme, and IWGIA's funding from Norad came under threat. IWGIA was asked to take over the programme for an intermediary period, and Norad expressed a wish to extend its cooperation with IWGIA to direct funding for its indigenous programme. This instigated a long discussion within the organisation about the role of development projects. It was discussed in meetings with Norad in June 1989 and again in 1990 but nothing materialised, mainly because of a reluctance on the part of IWGIA to be directly responsible for the handling of projects. The fears expressed by IWGIA were firstly that it could be difficult to achieve a balance between the different indigenous organisations and could create conflicts that would jeopardize IWGIA's traditional neutral position vis-à-vis indigenous organisations. At one stage it was suggested that IWGIA establish a subsidiary NGO called the Foundation for Indigenous Peoples (Bylaws for the Foundation for Indigenous Peoples were drafted but never adopted by the Board) in order to separate the role of

decision-making (who to receive and who not) from IWGIA's human rights and publication activities. Norad may have lost patience with IWGIA and the year-long debate ended when Norad gave the programme to the Norwegian research institution, Fafo, in 1991. Negotiations between IWGIA and Fafo on a possible continuation of the consultancy agreement came to nothing although IWGIA was represented on the committee advising on the selection of projects and policies.

89 In May 1985, the issue was again discussed at an IWGIA Board meeting and it was stressed that it "is a recognised change of policy from a few years ago but [one member] felt that the change was necessary provided it did not interfere with IWGIA's main publication work" (from the minutes).

90 Commission Working Document on support for indigenous peoples in the development cooperation of the community and the Member states, Brussels 11.05.1998, SEC (1998) 773 Final.

91 Cited from "Strategy for Danish Support to Indigenous Peoples".

92 It was an article by Ward Churchill in a North American Document (Doc. 68) that gave rise to a comment at a Board meeting. The document was generally controversial and gave rise to quite some correspondence between IWGIA's Chair, the editors and the author.

93 IWGIA 1997a.

94 See IWGIA 1998a and 1998b.

95 Among the participants at this meeting were: Aqqaluk Lynge, Suhas Chakma, Alberto Saldamando, Bot Epstein, John Henriksen, Vicky Tauli-Corpuz, Juan León, Marcial Arias. Ambassador Tyge Lehmann and Anders Ørnemark from the Danish Ministry of Foreign Affairs were asked to address the meeting. Jens Dahl and Lola García-Alix participated from IWGIA.

96 The document entitled "Recommendations of the Indigenous Caucus on the establishment of the Permanent Forum for Indigenous Peoples in the United Nations system, Geneva, 12-13 February 2000" became an official conference paper, E/CN.4/AC.47/2000/CRP.1.

97 A revised version entitled "The Permanent Forum on Indigenous *Issues*" (García-Alix 2003) was published following the establishment of the Forum and reflecting the final name that was adopted.

98 IWGIA "Report of the International Conference on the Permanent Forum for Indigenous Peoples, Iyara Hotel, Chiangmai, Thailand, January 28-31, 2000.

99 Joseph ole Simmel and Joan Carling pers. communication.

100 The participants in this meeting were: Tove Søvndahl Pedersen, Juan Leon, Tarcila Rivera, Bob Epstein, Vicky Tauli-Corpuz, Wilton Littlechild, Tonia Fishner, Ratnaker Bhengra, Carol Kalafatic, Taki Anaru, Michael Todyshev, Alona Yefimenko, Alberto Saldamando, Cecil le Fleur, Marcial Arias, Hjalmar Dahl, Aqqaluk Lynge, Lucy Mulenkey, John Henriksen, Niels Ole Gaup and Marcus Terena. Mick Dodson, Naomi Kipuri and Suhas Chakma were not able to attend. Jens Dahl and Lola García-Alix participated from IWGIA. Ambassador Tyge Lehman from the Danish Ministry of Foreign Affairs was invited to address the meeting.

101 The representatives of indigenous organisations were Suhas Chakma, Hjalmar Dahl, Tonya Fichner, Vanesa Jimenez, Paul Joffe, Johnson ole Kaunga, Willie Littlechild, Devashish Roy, Dalee Sambo, Michael Todyshev, Mathias Åhrén, Jocelyn Therese and Romeo Saganash. The other participants were Paul Joffe, Miriam Anne Frank, Maivan Lâm, and Kim Gotschalk. Lola García-Alix, Andrea Müehlebach and Jens Dahl participated from IWGIA.

102 "Conclusions and Recommendations of the Indigenous Peoples' Meeting on the United Nations Declaration on the Rights of Indigenous Peoples". Copenhagen, Denmark, 3-5 May, 2003.

103 For an in-depth report of this meeting see Åhrén 2007.

104 For an in-depth treatment of this process, see Åhrén 2007.

105 Joseph ole Simmel, pers. Communication.

106 To increase such mutual understanding, the Fund for many years organised a picnic in the mountains of Geneva which took place during the weekend on those years when the WGIP met for two weeks.

107 An early exception was made in 1987 when the Fund planned to bring people from the Chittagong Hill Tracts to the Commission on Human Rights (Minutes from the Human Rights Fund meeting in Amsterdam 12 October 1986).

108 At the Human Rights Fund meeting in October 1986 there were also representatives of indigenous peoples from Australia (NAILS) and Chittagong Hill Tracts (Minutes from the meeting).
109 For a report from this visit, see IWGIA 2003b: 431-9.
110 Dan Rosengren, pers. communication.
111 IWGIA Board meeting, January 1982.
112 There is a rich literature on this very important court case. This includes Hitchcock and Vinding 2001; Vinding 2003, and developments are referred to every year in The Indigenous World, published by IWGIA.
113 www.aippfoundation.org
114 Special Rapporteur of the UN Sub-Commission on Prevention of Discrimination and Protection of Minorities. After many years of work he published a report, Study of the Problem of Discrimination against Indigenous Populations. It is generally recognised that the report should be credited to Augusto Williamson Diaz, human rights lawyer from Guatemala.
115 See also Saugestad 2001.
116 Reprinted in Akwesasne Notes vol.6, 3. 1974.
117 Current Anthropology vol.45, no.2, 2004 printed a number of reactions to Kuper's earlier article.
118 Various documents in Helge Kleivan's archive. Nilo Cariqueo pers. communication.
119 See IWGIA Newsletter 31/32, 1982, and 33, 1983
120 Printed in Robert Paine 1985:150-1.
121 The correspondence is in the IWGIA archive.
122 Survival International was originally established as the Primitive Peoples' Fund. "The idea of the Primitive Peoples Fund was first mooted by Nicholas Guppy and Francis Huxley in a letter to the London Sunday Time of 9th March, 1969. Two weeks later a foundation committee was formed to set up a charitable trust and prepare for a national campaign"(From an undated Draft of Proposed letter to Lars Persson, Chair of IWGIA (IWGIA archive)). In the letter the people behind the Primitive Peoples' Fund urged IWGIA to cooperate in view of the similarity of the goals of the two organisations. (The Primitive Peoples Fund became Survival International in 1971 with Robin Hanbury-Tenison as Chairman). The establishment of the Primitive Peoples' Fund followed an article in the Sunday Times Magazine by Nicholas Guppy who reported on his travels to British Guyana (Bentley 1979).
123 Survival International Review Summer 1978 (vol.3,3); IWGIA Newsletter Dec. 1978; Survival International Review Spring 1979.
124 Interview with Karsten Soltau and correspondence in Helge Kleivan's archive.
125 The organisations were mutually sceptical about having a person from the other organisation as a full Board member.
126 Survival International's approach to projects, the first established in 1974: ".. we do not theoretically instigate projects (...). Rather, through field trips and correspondence, we learn that some action is taking place with a specific group of tribal people. That action whatever it may be, might be directed by the people themselves or by some non-tribal individual or entity (usually an anthropologist, but it might be a missionary or even a government body). Most of our projects are actually found during the course of field trips by a member of our executive or by someone closely allied with us. The next step is to visit the location of the action and spend some days or weeks making as thorough an investigation as possible" (Corry 1979).
127 Correspondence between IWGIA, other anthropologists and Peter Dalhoff, who compiled the documentary for Danish television. Helge Kleivan's archive.
128 Niels Fock in the newspaper *Politiken* March 17, 1970.
129 Münzel 1974:8.
130 A review of the Aché case will be published by IWGIA in the autumn of 2008.
131 There were statutes from August 1968, amended in 1978, 1981, 1985, 1994, 1997, 2000, 2002 and 2004.
132 Personal communication.

Board and partnership meeting in Kenya, 2005 – Photo: Espen Wæhle

Board and partnership meeting in Peru, 2007 – Photo: Espen Wæhle

ACRONYMS

When choosing between small and capital letters in the acronyms the latest available official spelling has been used.

ACHPR	African Commission on Human and Peoples' Rights
AFN	Assembly of First Nations, Canada
AIDESEP	Asociación Interétnica de Desarollo de la Selva Peruana, Peru
AIM	American Indian Movement, USA
AIPP	Asia Indigenous Peoples Pact
AITPN	Asian Indigenous and Tribal Peoples Network, Delhi
AMAN	Indigenous Peoples of the Archipelago, Indonesia
CADT	Community Ancestral Domain Title, Philippines
CCPY	Comissão Pró Yanomami, Brazil
CEMIRIDE	Centre for Minority Rights Development, Kenya
CHR	UN Commission on Human Rights
CISA	Consejo Indio de Sud America
COICA	La Coordinadora de las Organizaciones Indígenas de la Cuenca Amazónica
CORPI	(Regional Organisation of Indigenous Peoples in Centralm America)
CPA	Cordillera Peoples' Alliance, the Philippines
DANIDA	Danish International Development Agency
EAIP	European Alliance with Indigenous Peoples
ECOSOC	United Nations' Economic and Social Council

FINNIDA	Finnish Department for International Development Cooperation
FPK	First People of the Kalahari, Botswana
FPP	Forest Peoples' Programme, UK
HRF	Human Rights Fund for Indigenous Peoples
ICC	Inuit Circumpolar Conference (Council)
IITC	International Indian Treaty Council
ILO	International Labour Organisation
ILRC	Indian Law Resource Center, USA
IPACC	Indigenous Peoples of Africa Coordinating Committee
IPRA	Indigenous Peoples' Rights Act, Philippines
ISI	Indigenous Survival International
ITC	Inuit Tapirissat of Canada (Inuit Tapiriit Kanatami, ITK)
IUAES	International Union of Anthropological and Ethnological Sciences
JSS	Jana Samhati Samiti (People's United Party), Bangladesh
KAMP	National Federation of Indigenous Peoples Organizations in the Philippines
KWIA	Flemish Support Group for Indigenous Peoples, Belgium
MITKA	Movimiento Indio Túpac Katari, Bolivia
MPIDO	Mainyoito Pastoralist Integrated Development Organisation, Kenya
NCIP	National Commission on Indigenous Peoples, Philippines
NCIV	Netherlands Centre for Indigenous Peoples (originally WIP)
NIB	National Indian Brotherhood, Canada

NORAD	Norwegian Agency for Development Cooperation
OCCHTC	Organizing committee Chittagong Hill Tracts Campaign
OIRA	Organización Indígena Regional de Atalaya, Peru
PACOS	Partner of Community Organizations, Sabah, Malaysia
PFII	(UN) Permanent Forum on Indigenous Issues
RAIPON	Association of Indigenous Peoples of the Russian North, Siberia and the Far East
SIDA	Swedish International Development Cooperation Agency
TEBTEBBA	Indigenous Peoples' International Centre for Policy Research and Education, the Philippines
WCIP	World Council of Indigenous Peoples
WGIP	(UN) Working Group on Indigenous Populations
WIP	See NCIV
WSPA	World Society for the Protection of Animals

BOARD MEMBERS OF IWGIA

1968 –   Lars Persson (fmd) and Helge Kleivan (ad-hoc board)

1978 – 80 Mark Münzel, Bent Østergård (fmd), and Henning Siverts

1980 – 81 Mark Münzel (fmd), Bent Østergård, Henning Siverts, Helge Kleivan and Espen Wæhle

1981 – 82 Mark Münzel (fmd), Bent Østergård, Henning Siverts, Espen Wæhle, Helge Kleivan, and Georg Henriksen

1982 – 83 Mark Münzel, René Fuerst, Espen Wæhle, Tove Skotvedt and Georg Henriksen (fmd),

1983 – 85 Mark Münzel, Espen Wæhle, Georg Henriksen (fmd), René Fuerst, and Aud Talle

1985 – 87 Mark Münzel, Espen Wæhle, Georg Henriksen, René Fuerst (fmd), and Aud Talle

1986 – 87 Espen Wæhle, Georg Henriksen, René Fuerst (fmd), and Aud Talle

1987 – 89 Espen Wæhle, Georg Henriksen, René Fuerst (fmd), Aud Talle, and Jens Dahl

1989 – 92 Espen Wæhle, Georg Henriksen, René Fuerst (Aud Talle, Jens Dahl, Andrew Gray, Teresa Aparicio, Karen B. Andersen + representatives of local groups

1992 – 93 René Fuerst, Georg Henriksen, Espen Wæhle, Aud Talle, Andrew Gray, Kaj Århem, Finn Lynge, Teresa Aparicio, Karen B. Andersen, Jens Dahl and representatives of national groups.

1993 – 94 René Fuerst, Georg Henriksen, Espen Wæhle, Aud Talle, Andrew Gray, Kaj Århem, Finn Lynge, Karen B. Andersen, Jens Dahl and representatives of national groups.

1994 – 95 René Fuerst , Georg Henriksen, Espen Wæhle, Andrew Gray, Finn Lynge, Dan Rosengren, Inger Sjørslev, Karen B. Andersen, Jens Dahl and representatives of national groups.

1995 – 97 René Fuerst , Georg Henriksen, Espen Wæhle, Andrew Gray, Dan Rosengren, Inger Sjørslev, Karen B. Andersen, Jens Dahl and representatives of national groups.

1997 – 98 Georg Henriksen, Espen Wæhle, Andrew Gray, Dan Rosengren, Jens Dahl, Lola García-Alix, Alejandro Parellada and representatives of national groups.

1998 Georg Henriksen, Espen Wæhle, Andrew Gray, Dan Rosengren, Birgitte Feiring, Lola García-Alix, Alejandro Parellada and representatives of national groups.

1999 Georg Henriksen, Espen Wæhle, Andrew Gray, Dan Rosengren, Birgitte Feiring, Christian Erni, Annette Kjærgård, and representatives of national groups.

2000 Georg Henriksen, Espen Wæhle, Birgitte Feiring, Olga Murashko, Søren Hvalkof, Andrea Mühlebach, and Diana Vinding.

2001 – 03 Georg Henriksen, Espen Wæhle, Birgitte Feiring, Søren Hvalkof, Andrea Mühlebach, Diana Vinding, and Jenneke Arens.

2003 – 05 Georg Henriksen, Espen Wæhle, Søren Hvalkof, Andrea Mühlebach, Jenneke Arens, Mark Nuttall, and Marianne Wiben Jensen.

2005 – 06 Georg Henriksen, Espen Wæhle, Søren Hvalkof, Jenneke Arens, Mark Nuttall, María Teresa Quispe, and Marianne Wiben Jensen.

2006 – 07 Espen Wæhle, Diana Vinding, Jenneke Arens, Mark Nuttall, María Teresa Quispe, Robert Hichcock, and Lola García-Alix/ Christian Erni.

2007 – Espen Wæhle, Diana Vinding, Mark Nuttall, María Teresa Quispe, Robert Hichcock, Thomas Skielboe, and Kathrin Wessendorf.

CHAIRPERSONS (PRESIDENTS) OF IWGIA'S BOARD

1968 – 1971	Lars Persson
1971 – 1979	Helge Kleivan
1979 – 1981	Bent Østergård
1981 – 1982	Mark Münzel
1982 – 1985	Georg Henriksen
1985 – 1993	René Fuerst
1993 – 2005	Georg Henriksen
2005 –	Espen Wæhle

IWGIA'S DIRECTORS

1968 – 1971	Lars Persson, Helge Kleivan
1971 – 1981	Helge Kleivan
1981 – 1983	Collective leadership of Jørgen Brøchner Jørgensen, Diana Vinding/Elisabeth Nonell/Fiona Wilson and Teresa Aparicio
1983 – 1987	Andrew Gray, Teresa Aparicio and Jørgen Brøchner Jørgensen
1987 – 1989	Andrew Gray and Teresa Aparicio
1989 – 1994	Teresa Aparicio and Jens Dahl
1994 – 1998	Inger Sjørslev
1998 – 2006	Jens Dahl
2006 –	Lola García-Alix

REFERENCES

African Commission on Human and Peoples' Rights. 2005: *Report of the African Commission's Working Group of Experts on Indigenous Populations/Communities.* Banjul/Copenhagen: ACHPR/IWGIA.
African Commission on Human and Peoples' Rights. 2007a: *Advisory Opinion of the AfricanCommission on Human and Peoples' Rights on the United Nations Declaration on the Rights of Indigenous Peoples.* Banjul: African Union.
African Commission on Human and Peoples' Rights. 2007b: *Communiqué on the UN Declaration on the Rights of Indigenous Peoples.* Banjul 27. Nov.: African Union.
AITPN. 1999: The possible positions of the indigenous peoples. *Mimeo.* Delhi: AITPN.
Aktuelt **Newspaper.** Copenhagen.
Akwesasne Notes. Newspaper., N.Y.: Mohawk Nation
Atuagagdliutit/Grønlandsposten. Newspaper. Godthåb/Nuuk.
Barsh, Russel Lawrence. 1994: Indigenous Peoples in the 1990s: From Object to Subject of International Law. *Harvard Human Rights Journal* 7: 33-86.
Bentley, Barbara. 1977: Directors report. *Survival International Review* 2,3: 3.
Bentley, Barbara. 1979: The Story of Survival International 1969-1979. *Survival International Review* 4,1: 4-7.
Berger, Thomas R. 1977: *Northern Frontier – Northern Homeland. The Report of the Mackenzie Valley Pipeline Inquiry, vol.1-2.* Ottawa: Indian Affairs and Northern Development.
Berman, Howard. 1989: The International Labour Organization and Indigenous Peoples: Revision of ILO Convention 107 at the 75th session of the I.L.O. Conference, 1988. *International Commission of Jurists Review* 48.
Bodley, John H. 1982: *Victims of Progress.* 2nd edition. Menlo Park: The Benjamin/Cummings Publishing Co.
Britz, Rudolf G., H. Lang and C. Limpricht. 1999: *A Concise History of the Rehoboth Basters until 1990.* Windhoek: Klaus Hess Publishers.
Brysk, Alison. 2000: *From Tribal Village to Global Village.* Stanford: Stanford University Press.
Burger, Julian. 1987: *Report from the Frontier. The State of the World's Indigenous Peoples.* London: Zed Books.
Cameron, Greg. 2001: Taking Stock of Pastoralist NGOs in Tanzania. *Review of African Political Economy* 28: 55-72.
Carrasco, Morita. 2000: An overview of the Hunter-Gatherers of the Gran Chaco. *IndigenousAffairs* 2: 72-76.
Carrasco, Morita. 2004: *Pertenecer a la tierra/Belonging to the land.* IWGIA: Copenhagen.
Carrasco, Morita and Silvina Zimerman. 2006: El caso Lhaka Honhat. *Informe IWGIA 1.* IWGIA, Copenhagen.
Chittagong Hill Tracts Commission. 1991: *'Life is not ours'. Land and human rights in the Chittagong Hill Tracts, Bangladesh.* Copenhagen, IWGIA.
Coates, Ken. 2004: *A Global History of Indigenous Peoples. Struggle and Survival.* New York: Polgrave MacMillan.
Cohen, Fay. 1993: UNWGIP: Indigenous Participation. Report on a Study of Indigenous Experience and the role of the Human Rights Fund for Indigenous Peoples. *IWGIA Newsletter* 1: 49-53.
Corry, Stephen: 1979: Survival International Projects. *Survival International Review* 4,1: 9.
Coulter, Robert T. 1977: The Continual Denial of Our Existence. *Akwesasne Notes* 9,3: 16-17.
Danish Ministry of Foreign Affairs. 1994: *Strategy for Danish Support to Indigenous Peoples.* Copenhagen: Ministry of Foreign Affairs.

Development Associates. 1996: IWGIA's South-South Communication Programme, Phases 1& 2 (January 1993-November 1995) covering Asia and Africa. *Evaluation Report.* Copenhagen, IWGIA.

Dunbar-Ortiz, Roxanne. 2006: The First Decade of Indigenous Peoples at the United Nations. *Peace & Change* 31,1: 58-74.

Feiring, Birgitte. 1997/8: Towards a European Policy on Indigenous Peoples and Development Co-operation. *The Indigenous World*: 379-387. Copenhagen, IWGIA.

Frühling, Pierre, Miguel Gonzales and Hans Petter Buvollen.2007: *Etnicidad y Nación. El Desarrollo de la Autonomía de la Costa Atlántica de Nicaragua (1987-2007).* Guatemala: F&G Editores.

García-Alix, Lola. 1999a: *The Permanent Forum for Indigenous Peoples. The Struggle for a New Partnership.* Copenhagen, IWGIA.

García-Alix, Lola. 1999b: The Ad hoc Working Group on the Establishment of a Permanent Forum for Indigenous Peoples in the UN system. *The Indigenous World* 1998-99: 373-388.

García-Alix, Lola. 2003: *The Permanent Forum on Indigenous Issues.* Copenhagen, IWGIA.

Gray, Andrew. 1990: On Anthropological Advocacy. Current Anthropology 13,4: 387-390.

Gray, Andrew. 1995: The Indigenous Movement in Asia. In *Indigenous Peoples of Asia* (eds) R.H. Barnes, A. Gray and B. Kingsbury, 35-58.

Gray, Andrew. 1999: The UN Declaration on the Rights of Indigenous Peoples is still Intact. In *The Indigenous World* 1998-99: 355-72. Copenhagen, IWGIA.

Gurr, Ted Robert. 2000: *Peoples versus States. Minorities at Risk in the New Century.* Washington D.C.: United States Institute of Peace Press.

Ha-Shilth-Sa. Newspaper. Port Alberny

Hastrup, Kirsten and Peter Elsass. 1990: Anthropological Advocacy. A Contradiction in Terms? *Current Anthropology* 13,3: 301-11.

Helge Kleivan's archive. Journal 07270. Copenhagen: The Danish National Archive.

Henriksen, Georg. 1985: Anthropologists as Advocates – Promoters of Pluralism or Makers of Clients? In *Advocacy and Anthropology* (ed) Robert Paine, 119-29. St. Johns: Memorial University.

Henriksen, Georg. 1997: Noen refleksjoner over sosialantropologisk advokatur med særlig referanse til urfolk. *Norsk Antropologisk Tidsskrift* 8(2): 120-31.

Henriksen, Georg. 1998: Editorial. *Indigenous Affairs* 3: 2-5.

Henriksen, Georg. n.d: Consultancy and advocacy as radical anthropology. *Mimeo.*

Hitchcock, Robert and Diana Vinding. 2003: A chronology of major events relating to the Central Kalahari Game Reserve II: An update. *Botswana Notes and Records* 33, 2001: 61-72.

Hitchcock, Robert and Martin Enghoff. 2004: Capacity-Building of First People of the Kalahari, Botswana. An Evaluation of IWGIA's Involvement. *Report.* Copenhagen, IWGIA.

Hierro, Pedro García, Søren Hvalkof and Andrew Gray. 1998: *Liberation through land rights in the Peruvian Amazon.* Copenhagen, IWGIA.

Hodgson, Dorothy L. 2002a: Introduction: Comparative Perspectives on the Indigenous Rights Movement in Africa and the Americas. *American Anthropologist* 104(4): 1037-49.

Hodgson, Dorothy L. 2002b: Precarious Alliances: The Cultural Politics and Structural Predicamentsof the Indigenous Rights Movement in Tanzania. *American Anthropologist* 104(4): 1086-97.

Hodgson, Dorothy L. 2008: Cosmopolitics, Neoliberalism, and the State: The Indigenous Rights Movement in Africa. In *Anthropology and the New Cosmopolitanism: Rooted, Feminist and Vernacular Perspectives* (ed) Pnina Werbner, in press. London: Berg.

Hvalkof, Søren and Peter Aaby (eds). 1981: *Is God an American? An anthropological Perspective on the Missionary Work of the Summer Institute of Linguistics.* Copenhagen/London: IWGIA/Survival International.

Houtman, Gustaaf. 1985: Survival International: going public on Amazonian Indians. *Anthropology Today* 1,5: 2-4.

ILO. 1957: *Convention 107 concerning the Protection and Integration of Indigenous and Other Tribal and Semi-Tribal Populations in Independent Countries.* Geneva: ILO.

ILO. 1989: *Convention 169 Concerning Indigenous and Tribal Peoples in Independent Countries.* Geneva: ILO.

Information **Newspaper.** Copenhagen.

IWGIA. 1986: *The Naga Nation and its Struggle against Genocide*. Document no.56. Copenhagen, IWGIA.
IWGIA. 1987a: Evaluation to NORAD on indigenous project-co-ordination in the Cordillera region (Philippines). *Mimeo*. Copenhagen, IWGIA.
IWGIA. 1987b: Human Rights Fund for Indigenous Peoples. *Report*. IWGIA, Copenhagen.
IWGIA. 1987c: *Yearbook 1986*. Copenhagen, IWGIA.
IWGIA. 1987d: *Self-determination and Indigenous Peoples. Sámi Rights and Northern Perspectives*. Copenhagen, IWGIA.
IWGIA. 1988: *Yearbook 1987*. Copenhagen, IWGIA.
IWGIA. 1989a: *Indigenous Self-development in the Americas. Proceedings of the IWGIA Symposium at the Congress of Americanists, Amsterdam 1988*. Copenhagen, IWGIA.
IWGIA. 1989b: Report of Andrew's IWGIA Trip to the USA, January, 1989. *Mimeo*. Copenhagen, IWGIA.
IWGIA. 1989c: *Yearbook 1988*. Copenhagen, IWGIA.
IWGIA. 1994: *The International Work Group for Indigenous Affairs and Indigenous Peoples. Strategy paper*. Copenhagen, IWGIA.
IWGIA. 1997a: 1st International Indigenous Conference on the Establishment of a Permanent Forum for Indigenous Peoples in the United Nations. *Report*. Copenhagen, IWGIA.
IWGIA. 1998a: 2nd International Indigenous Conference on the Establishment of a Forum for Indigenous Peoples in the United Nations. *Report*. Copenhagen, IWGIA.
IWGIA. 1998b: First Asian Indigenous Peoples Workshop on a Permanent Forum for Indigenous Peoples Within the United Nations. *Report*. Copenhagen, IWGIA.
IWGIA. 2000: The 28th Ordinary session of the African Commission on Human & Peoples' Rights. *Report*. Copenhagen, IWGIA.
IWGIA. 2001: The First Meeting of the Working Group on Indigenous Peoples/Communities in Africa, and the 30th Ordinary Session of the African Commission on Human andPeoples'Rights, Banjul, The Gambia 13-27 October. *Report*. Copenhagen, IWGIA.
IWGIA. 2002: Roundtable Meeting of the Working Group on Indigenous People and Communities in Africa (under the African Commission) and the 31st Ordinary Session of the African Commission on Human and Peoples Rights, Pretoria, South Africa 2-16 May, 2002. *Report*. Copenhagen, IWGIA.
IWGIA. 2003a: Report on the interim evaluation of Aliansi Masyarakat Adat Nusantara project: "Strengthening Customary Law and Revitalizing Indigenous Institutions in Indonesia. *Report*. Copenhagen, IWGIA.
IWGIA. 2003b: The Special Rapporteur Visits the Philippines. *The Indigenous World* 2002-3: 431-9.
IWGIA 2004a: Capacity building and promotion of rights of indigenous peoples. IWGIA – RAIPON, 2002-4. *Mimeo*. Copenhagen, IWGIA.
IWGIA. 2004b: The 35th Ordinary Session of the African Commission on Human and Peoples' Rights, Banjul, the Gambia 21st May to 4th June. *Report*. Copenhagen, IWGIA.
Jensen, Marianne and Jens Dahl. 1999: Editorial. *Indigenous Affairs* 2: 2-3.
Kenrick, Justin and Jerome Lewis. 2004: Indigenous peoples' rights and the politics of the term 'indigenous'. *Anthropology Today* 20(2): 4-9.
Kleivan, H. 1973: Den fjerde verden. *Tidsskriftet Grønland* 5/6: 172-80.
    1976: Indledning: Storsamfundet og de indfødte folk. In *Vort Land, Vort Liv* (eds) Helge Kleivan og Karen Nørregaard. København: Institut for Eskimologi.
    1982: Terrorisme, økonomi og indianere. *Politikens kronik*. February 25.
Kleivan, I. 1992: The Arctic Peoples' Conference in Copenhagen, November 22-25, 1973. *Études/Inuit/Studies* 16(1-2): 227-36.
Kuper, Adam. 2003: The Return of the Native. *Current Anthropology* 44,3: 389-402.
López, Mikel Berraondo. 2006: Evaluation Report of the Human Rights Fund for Indigenous Peoples. *Report*. Copenhagen, IWGIA.
Lynge, Aqqaluk. 1975: Europa er død – den Fjerde Verden leve! *Tidsskriftet Grønland* 10: 289-295.
Manuel, George and Michael Posluns. 1978: *Den Fjerde Verden*. København: Informations Forlag.
Mey, Wolfgang, ed. 1984: *Genocide in the Chittagong Hill Tracts, Bangladesh*. Copenhagen: IWGIA.

Maybury-Lewis, David and James Howe. 1980: *The Indian Peoples of Paraguay. Their Plight and their Prospects.* Special Report. Cambridge, Mass.: Cultural Survival.

Minde, Henry. 2005: The Alta case: From the local to the global and back again. In *Discourses and Silences. Indigenous Peoples, Risks and Resistance* (eds) Garth Cant, Anake Goodall and Justine Inns, 13-34. Christchurch: University of Canterbury.

2007. En erklæring I emning: Urfolk og De forente nasjoner fra 1960-tallet til 1985. *Mimeo.*

2008: The Destination and the Journey: Indigenous Peoples and the United Nations from the 1960s through 1985. In *Self-Determination, Knowledge, Indigeneity* (ed) Henry Minde. Delft: Eburon.

Ministry of Foreign Affairs. 1994: *Strategy for Danish Support to Indigenous Peoples.* Copenhagen: Ministry of Foreign Affairs.

Morin, Francoise and Bernard Saladain d'Anglure. 1997: Ethnicity as a Political Tool for Indigenous Peoples. In *The Politics of Ethnic Consciousness* (eds) Cora Govers and Hans Vermeulen, 157-193. New York: St. Martin's Press.

Münzel, Mark. 1973: *The Aché Indians: Genocide in Paraguay.* Copenhagen, IWGIA.

Münzel, Mark. 1974: *The Aché: Genocide Continues in Paraguay.* Copenhagen, IWGIA.

National Indian Brotherhood. 1972: International Aboriginal Peoples' Conference. Oct. 13. Ottawa.

1974: *Report of the Preparatory Meeting of the International Conference of Indigenous People held in Georgetown, Guyana April 8-11, 1974.* Ottawa: National Indian Brotherhood. *New Statesmen.* Newspaper. London.

Niezen, Ronald. 2003: *The Origins of Indigenism. Human Rights and the Politics of Identity.* Berkeley: University of California Press.

OCCHTC 1986: The Charge of Genocide. Human Rights in the Chittagong Hill Tracts of Bangladesh. *Report*. Amsterdam: OCCHTC.

Paine, Robert (ed). 1985a: *Advocacy and Anthropology.* St. Johns: Memorial University.

Paine, Robert. 1985b: Ethnodrama and the 'Fourth World': The Saami Action Group in Norway, 1979-81. In *Indigenous Peoples and the Nation-State: 'Fourth World' Politics in Canada, Australia and Norway* (ed) Noel Dyck, 190- 235. St. John's: Memorial University.

Pityana, Nyameko Barney. 1999: The African Commission on Human and Peoples' Rights and the Issue of Indigenous Peoples. *Indigenous Affairs* 2: 44-9.

Politiken **Newspaper.** Copenhagen.

Ramos, Alcida R. 1994: The Hyperreal Indian. *Critique of Anthropology* 14,2: 153-72.

Rossel, Pierre (ed). 1988: *Tourism: Manufacturing the Exotic.* Copenhagen, IWGIA.

Sanders, Douglas E. 1977: *The Formation of the World Council of Indigenous Peoples.* Copenhagen, IWGIA.

1983: The Re-Emergence of Indigenous Questions in International Law. *Canadian Human Rights Yearbook*: 3-30.

Sanders, Douglas E. 1985: Mosquitia and Nicaragua: An Incomplete Revolution In *Native Power* (eds) Brøsted et.al, 77-103. Oslo: Universitetsforlaget.

Sanders, Douglas E. 1989: The UN Working Group on Indigenous Populations. *Human Rights Quarterly* 11: 406-33.

Saugestad, Sidsel. 2001: Contested images: 'first peoples' or 'marginalized minorities' in Africa. In *Africa's Indigenous Peoples: 'First Peoples' or Marginalized Minorities'?* (eds) Alan Barnard and Justin Kenrick, 299-322. Edinburgh: Univ. of Edinburgh.

Saugestad, Sidsel. 2004: Comments on Kuper's 'Return of the Native'. *Current Anthropology* 45(2): 263-4.

Saugestad, Sidsel. 2006: San Development and Challenges in Development Cooperation. In *Updating the San: Image and Reality of an African People in the 21st Century* (eds) Hichcock, Robert K., K. Ikeya, M. Biesele and R.B. Lee, 171-180. Osaka: National Museum of Ethnology.

Saugestad, Sidsel. 2008: Beyond the 'Columbus Context': New Challenges as the Indigenous Discourse is Applied to Africa. In *Indigenous Peoples: Self-determination, Knowledge, Indigeneity* (ed) Henry Minde, 157-76. Eburon: Delft.

Sjørslev, Inger. 1998: Activism and Research – after 30 years, what do we need to know? *Indigenous Affairs* 3: 6-10.

Stern, Pamela. 2006: Land Claims, Development, and the Pipeline to Citizenship. In *Critical Inuit Studies* (eds) Pamela Stern and Lisa Stevenson, 105-18. Lincoln: University of Nebraska Press.
Sverre, Knut. 1985: Indigenous Populations and Human Rights: The International Problem from a Nordic Point of View. In *Native Power* (eds) Jens Brøsted et al, 188-95. Oslo: Universitetsforlaget.
Veber, Hanne and Espen Wæhle. 1993: "...Never Drink from the Same Cup". An Introduction. In *"Never Drink from the Same Cup"* (eds) Hanne Veber et al, 9-19. Copenhagen: IWGIA.
Venne, Sharon Helen: 1998. *Our Elders Understand Our Rights. Evolving International Law Regarding Indigenous Rights.* Penticton, British Columbia: Theytus Books Ltd. *Verdens Gang.* Norwegian newspaper. Oslo.
Viljoen, Frans. 2007: *International Human Rights Law in Africa.* Oxford: Oxford University Press.
Vinding, Diana. 2003: Struggling for the Right to Return: The Residents of the Central Kalahari Game Reserve vs. The Government of Botswana. *Indigenous Affairs* 4: 20-4.
Wessendorf, Kathrin. 2001: Introduction. In *Challenging Politics: Indigenous Peoples' Experiences with Political Parties and Elections* (ed) Kathrin Wessendorf, 10-18. Copenhagen: IWGIA.
World Council of Churches. 1971: *Declaration of Barbados.* Copenhagen, IWGIA
Wright, Robin M. 1988: Anthropological Presuppositions of Indigenous Advocacy. *Annual Review of Anthropology* 17: 365-90.
Ziegler, Volkmar and Peirrette Birraux. 1986: *Indian Summer in Geneva.* Video. Geneva: Docip.
Østergaard, Bent. 1969: Indianere udrydder man da. Ekstra Bladet December 15, 1969.
Århem, Kaj. 1985: *The Maasai and the State. The impact of rural development policies on a pastoral people in Tanzania.* Copenhagen, IWGIA.
Åhrén, Mattias. 2007: The UN Declaration on the Rights of Indigenous Peoples – How was it adopted and why is it significant. *Gáldu Cála* 4: 84-129.